SOFTWARE TEST

BCS, THE CHARTERED INSTITUTE FOR IT

BCS, The Chartered Institute for IT champions the global IT profession and the interests of individuals engaged in that profession for the benefit of all. We promote wider social and economic progress through the advancement of information technology, science and practice. We bring together industry, academics, practitioners and government to share knowledge, promote new thinking, inform the design of new curricula, shape public policy and inform the public.

Our vision is to be a world-class organisation for IT. Our 70,000 strong membership includes practitioners, businesses, academics and students in the UK and internationally. We deliver a range of professional development tools for practitioners and employees. A leading IT qualification body, we offer a range of widely recognised qualifications.

Further Information
BCS, The Chartered Institute for IT,
First Floor, Block D,
North Star House, North Star Avenue,
Swindon, SN2 1FA, United Kingdom.
T +44 (0) 1793 417 424
F +44 (0) 1793 417 444
www.bcs.org/contact

http://shop.bcs.org/

SOFTWARE TESTING
An ISTQB–BCS Certified Tester
Foundation guide
Third edition

**Brian Hambling (editor), Peter Morgan, Angelina
Samaroo, Geoff Thompson and Peter Williams**

bcs

The
Chartered
Institute
for IT

Reprinted January 2017

Published by BCS Learning & Development Ltd, a wholly owned subsidiary of BCS, The Chartered Institute for IT, First Floor, Block D, North Star House, North Star Avenue, Swindon, SN2 1FA, UK.
www.bcs.org

Paperback ISBN: 978-1-78017-299-6
PDF ISBN: 978-1-78017-300-9
ePUB ISBN: 978-1-78017-301-6
Kindle ISBN: 978-1-78017-302-3

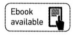

British Cataloguing in Publication Data.
A CIP catalogue record for this book is available at the British Library.

BCS books are available at special quantity discounts to use as premiums and sale promotions, or for use in corporate training programmes. Please visit our Contact us page at www.bcs.org/contact

Typeset by Lapiz Digital Services, Chennai, India.
Printed by Hobbs the Printers Ltd, Totton, Hampshire SO40 3WX

CONTENTS

FIGURES AND TABLES

AUTHORS

Brian Hambling has experienced software development from a developer's, project manager's and quality manager's perspective in a career spanning over 35 years. He has worked in areas as diverse as real-time avionics, legacy systems maintenance and ebusiness strategies. He contributed to the development of software quality standards while at the Ministry of Defence and later became the head of systems and software engineering at The University of Greenwich. He was technical director of ImagoQA and general manager of Microgen IQA, a specialist company providing consultancy in software testing and quality assurance primarily to the financial services sector. He is now concentrating on writing.

Peter Morgan was a freelance testing practitioner, now mainly retired. He worked as a hands-on tester for a number of years, often on large projects. He has worked in many business sectors in the UK, and has been involved with the examination side of testing since taking the Foundation Certificate in 2001. Peter still writes exam questions and regularly reviews course submissions of testing courses on behalf of the UKTB, looking for syllabus compliance and to see that potential students are well prepared for their own exams.

Angelina Samaroo has a degree in Aeronautical Engineering from Queen Mary University of London. She is a Chartered Engineer and Fellow of the Institution of Engineering and Technology (IET). She spent 10 years working on the mission software for the Tornado ADV fighter jet. During this time she took an interest in the career development of new engineers and led the company graduate development scheme. She then joined a small consultancy in software testing, specialising in providing training to test professionals worldwide. She now works for Pinta Education Limited and provides training in software testing, business analysis and programming.

Geoff Thompson is the Consultancy Director for Experimentus Ltd, a leading software quality management consultancy based in the UK. He has a real passion for quality and software testing and over the last 25 years has an excellent track record in test management and process improvement.

In 1997, he started working with BCS/ISEB developing the original Software Testing Foundation syllabus and exams; he then managed the development of the original Software Testing Practitioner syllabus and exam in 2002. Geoff initiated the International Software Testing Qualification Board (ISTQB) and is its UK representative. He chairs the UK Testing Board.

He is a founding member of the TMMi Foundation and chairman of the TMMi Foundation management executive (see www.tmmifoundation.org.uk)

He is also the vice-chairman and treasurer of the BCS specialist group in software testing (SIGiST).

In 2008, Geoff was awarded the European Testing Excellence Award.

He is a popular speaker, and has recently delivered keynote presentations in India and Australia, as well as being a regular speaker at EuroSTAR, for which he was the programme chair in 2011.

Peter Williams previously worked in methods and systems improvement before moving into systems development and subsequently software testing. He has been a self-employed contract test manager or consultant in both financial services and the public sector. He has evaluated test processes and subsequently implemented improvements, at various organisations, including test management and execution tools as appropriate. He has an MSc in computing from the Open University and was chairman of the Examinations Panel for the ISEB Foundation Certificate in Software Testing.

ABBREVIATIONS

AUT	Application Under Test
BACS	Bankers Automated Clearing Services
CFG	Control Flow Graph
CMMI	Capability Maturity Model Integration
COTS	Commercial Off-The-Shelf
CTFL	Certified Tester Foundation Level
DOS	Denial of Service
DSDM	Dynamic Systems Development Methodology
FTP	Fundamental Test Process
GUI	Graphical User Interface
ISEB	Information Systems Examination Board
ISTQB	International Software Testing Qualifications Board
MISRA	Motor Industry Software Reliability Association
RAD	Rapid Application Development
RUP	Rational Unified Process
SDLC	Software Development Life Cycle
SIGiST	Specialist Interest Group in Software Testing
SQL	Structured Query Language
ST	State Table
TPI	Test Process Improvement
UML	Unified Modeling Language
XML	Extensible Markup Language

PREFACE

When I started work on the first edition of this book in 2006, I little thought that I would be drafting a preface to a third edition in 2015. My fellow authors and I have been amazed at the continuing success of this simple guide to understanding the ISTQB Foundation Certificate in Software Testing and passing the exam, yet feedback from readers who have passed the exam by using this book as their sole preparation has been steadily amassing.

In this third edition, we have tried to provide some new material and even better exam preparation resources. Many of the exercises, examples and sample questions have been updated to reflect the way the exam has evolved over the years, and for this edition we have put together a complete mock examination. This gives commentary to explain the correct answer and why each of the distracters is incorrect. Moreover, as a mock exam, the candidates can time themselves to check they are prepared for the real thing. We think that this is a major improvement on previous editions and we hope you will find it really useful.

INTRODUCTION

NATURE AND PURPOSE OF THE BOOK

The Foundation Certificate in Software Testing was introduced as part of the BCS Professional Certification portfolio (formerly ISEB) in 1998; since then over 300,000 Foundation Certificates have been awarded. An intermediate level certificate was introduced in 2007 as a step towards the more advanced Practitioner certificates. (Visit www.bcs.org/certifications for more information.)

The International Software Testing Qualifications Board (ISTQB) (www.istqb.org) was set up in 2001 to offer a similar certification scheme to as many countries as wished to join this international testing community. The UK was a founding member of ISTQB and, in 2005, adopted the ISTQB Foundation Certificate syllabus as the basis of examinations for the Foundation Certificate in the UK. The Foundation Certificate is now an entry qualification for the ISTQB Advanced Certificate. The Certified Tester Foundation Level (CTFL) syllabus has been updated and released in a 2010 version, and this book relates to the 2010 version of the syllabus.

This book has been written specifically to help potential candidates for the ISTQB–BCS CTFL examination. The book is therefore structured to support learning of the key ideas in the syllabus quickly and efficiently for those who do not plan to attend a course, and to support structured revision for anyone preparing for the exam.

In this introductory chapter we will explain the nature and purpose of the Foundation Level and provide an insight into the way the syllabus is structured and the way the book is structured to support learning in the various syllabus areas. Finally we offer guidance on the best way to use this book, either as a learning resource or as a revision resource.

PURPOSE OF FOUNDATION

The CTFL Certificate is the first level of a hierarchy of ISTQB–BCS certificates in software testing, and leads naturally into the next level, known as the Intermediate Certificate in Software Testing, which in turn leads on to the ISTQB Advanced Level, followed by the various ISTQB Expert Level examinations.

The Foundation Level provides a very broad introduction to the whole discipline of software testing. As a result coverage of topics is variable, with some only briefly mentioned and others studied in some detail. The arrangement of the syllabus and the required levels of understanding are explained in the next section.

1

The authors of the syllabus have aimed it at people with various levels of experience in testing, including those with no experience at all. This makes the certificate accessible to those who are or who aim to be specialist testers, but also to those who require a more general understanding of testing, such as project managers and software development managers. One specific aim of this qualification is to prepare certificate holders for the next level of certification, but the Foundation Level has sufficient breadth and depth of coverage to stand alone.

THE CERTIFIED TESTER FOUNDATION LEVEL SYLLABUS

Syllabus content and structure

The syllabus is broken down into six main sections, each of which has associated with it a minimum contact time that must be included within any accredited training course:

1. Fundamentals of testing (155 minutes).
2. Testing throughout the software life cycle (115 minutes).
3. Static techniques (60 minutes).
4. Test design techniques (285 minutes).
5. Test management (170 minutes).
6. Tool support for testing (80 minutes).

The relative timings are a reliable guide to the amount of time that should be spent studying each section of the syllabus.

Each section of the syllabus also includes a list of learning objectives that provides candidates with a guide to what they should know when they have completed their study of a section and a guide to what can be expected to be asked in an examination. The learning objectives can be used to check that learning or revision is adequate for each topic. In the book, which is structured around the syllabus sections, we have presented the learning objectives for each section at the beginning of the relevant chapter, and the summary at the end of each chapter confirms how those learning objectives have been addressed.

Finally, each topic in the syllabus has associated with it a level of understanding, represented by the legend K1, K2, K3 or K4:

- Level of understanding K1 is associated with recall, so that a topic labelled K1 contains information that a candidate should be able to remember but not necessarily use or explain.

- Level of understanding K2 is associated with the ability to explain a topic or to classify information or make comparisons.

- Level of understanding K3 is associated with the ability to apply a topic in a practical setting.

- Level of understanding K4 is associated with the ability to analyse a situation or a set of information to determine what action to take.

The level of understanding influences the level and type of questions that can be expected to be asked about that topic in the examination. More detail about the question style and about the examination is given in **Chapter 7**. Example questions, written to the level and in the formats used in the examination, are included within each chapter to provide generous examination practice.

Syllabus updates and changes

The syllabus was last updated in 2011 and the book is in line with the changes and additions introduced in that version of the syllabus. Since then an extension to the Foundation syllabus has been introduced to cover a significant aspect of software testing that has grown in prominence in recent years. The Foundation Level Extension – Agile Tester is a complete new syllabus with its own separate examination and that syllabus is not addressed in this book.

Throughout this book you will find references to different testing standards that form reference points for parts of the ISTQB Software Testing Foundation syllabus. In 2013, ISO replaced the following standards with ISO/IEC/IEEE 29119 *Software Testing*:

- IEEE 829 *Test documentation*
- IEEE 1008 *Unit testing*
- BS 7925-1 *Vocabulary of terms in software testing*
- BS 7925-2 *Software component testing standard*

At the time of going to press, ISTQB were reviewing the new standard to understand which elements need to be included within all of its syllabuses, so we have not included any detailed references within this book. However, because this is the first international testing standard to cover all elements of the test discipline, it is important that the reader is aware of its existence and, at a high level, what it covers.

ISO/IEC/IEEE 29119 *Software testing* is an internationally agreed set of standards for software testing that can be used within any software development life cycle or organisation. There are currently five standards within ISO/IEC/IEEE 29119:

- ISO/IEC 29119-1: *Concepts & definitions* (published September 2013) facilitates understanding and use of all other standards and the vocabulary used within the 29119 series.
- ISO/IEC 29119-2: *Test processes* (published September 2013) defines a generic process model for software testing that can be used within any software development life cycle.
- ISO/IEC 29119-3: *Test documentation* (published September 2013) defines templates for test documentation that cover the entire software testing life cycle.
- ISO/IEC 29119-4: *Test techniques* (anticipating publication in 2015) defines software test design techniques (also known as test case design techniques or test methods).
- ISO/IEC 29119-5: *Keyword driven testing* (anticipating publication in 2015) defines an international standard for supporting keyword-driven testing.

- ISO/IEC 33063 *Process assessment model* (anticipated publication date not known) is an additional standard being worked on alongside ISO/IEC/IEEE 29119. The purpose of 33063 is to define a process assessment model for software testing for use in performing a conformant assessment in accordance with the requirements of ISO/IEC 33002 (*Process assessment – Requirements for performing process assessments*).

RELATIONSHIP OF THE BOOK TO THE SYLLABUS

The book is structured into chapters that mirror the sections of the syllabus so that you can work your way through the whole syllabus or select topics that are of particular interest or concern. The structure enables you to go straight to the place you need, with confidence either that what you need to know will be covered there and nowhere else, or that relevant cross references will be provided.

Each chapter of the book incorporates the learning objectives from the syllabus and identifies the required level of understanding for each topic. Each chapter also includes examples of typical examination questions to enable you to assess your current knowledge of a topic before you read the chapter, and further questions at the end of each chapter to provide practice in answering typical examination questions. Topics requiring K3 level of understanding are presented with worked examples as a model for the level of application expected from real examination questions. Answers are provided for all questions, and the rationale for the correct answer is discussed for all practice questions.

A final chapter explains the Foundation Level examination strategy and provides guidance on how to prepare for the examination and how to manage the examination experience to maximise your own performance.

HOW TO GET THE BEST OUT OF THIS BOOK

This book is designed for use by different groups of people. If you are using the book as an alternative to attending an accredited course you will probably find the first method of using the book described below to be of greatest value. If you are using the book as a revision aid you may find the second approach more appropriate. In either case you would be well advised to acquire a copy of the syllabus (available from www.istqb.org) and a copy of the sample examination paper (available from BCS) as reference documents, though neither is essential and the book stands alone as a learning and revision aid.

Using the book as a learning aid

For those of you using the book as an alternative to attending an accredited course the first step is to familiarise yourself with the syllabus structure and content by skim reading the opening sections of each chapter where the learning objectives are identified for each topic. You may then find it helpful to turn to **Chapter 7** and become familiar with the structure of the examination and the types and levels of questions that you can expect in the examination. From here you can then work through each of the six main chapters in any sequence before returning to **Chapter 7** to remind yourself of the main elements of the examination.

For each chapter begin by attempting the self-assessment questions at the beginning to get initial confirmation of your level of confidence in the topics covered by that chapter. This may help you to prioritise how you spend your time. Work first through the chapters where your knowledge is weakest, attempting all the exercises and following through all the worked examples. Read carefully through the chapters where your knowledge is less weak but still not good enough to pass the exam. You can be more selective with exercises and examples here, but make sure you attempt the practice questions at the end of the chapters. For the areas where you feel strong you can use the chapter for revision, but remember to attempt the practice questions to confirm positively your initial assessment of your level of knowledge. Each chapter contains a summary section that reiterates the learning objectives, so reading the first and last sections of a chapter will help you to understand how your current level of knowledge relates to the level required to pass the examination. The best confirmation of this is to attempt questions at the appropriate K level for each topic; these are provided in the book.

Using the book as a revision aid

If you are using this book for final revision, perhaps after completing an accredited course, you might like to begin by using a selection of the example questions at the end of each chapter as a 'mock examination'. **Appendix A1** contains a complete mock exam, with all the answers in **Appendix A2**, which will provide some experience of answering typical questions under the same time pressures that you will experience in the real examination, and this will provide you with a fairly reliable guide to your current state of readiness to take the real examination. You can also discover which areas most need revision from your performance in the mock exam, and this will guide you as you plan your revision. There is a complete question-by-question commentary on the mock exam in **Appendix A3** so that you can identify why you got any questions wrong.

Revise first where you feel weakest. You can use the opening sections of each chapter, containing the learning objectives and the self-assessment questions, together with the summary at the end of each chapter to refine further your awareness of your own weaknesses. From here you can target your studies very accurately. Remember that every K3 or K4 topic will have at least one worked example and some exercises to help you build your confidence before tackling questions at the level set in the real examination.

You can get final confirmation of your readiness to sit the real examination by taking the sample examination paper available from BCS.

1 THE FUNDAMENTALS OF TESTING

Peter Morgan

BACKGROUND

If you were buying a new car, you would not expect to take delivery from the showroom with a scratch down the side of the vehicle. The car should have five wheels, a steering wheel, an engine and all the other essential components, and it should come with appropriate documentation, with all pre-sales checks completed and passed satisfactorily. The car you receive should be the car described in the sales literature; it should have the correct engine size, the correct colour scheme, and whatever extras you have ordered, and performance in areas such as fuel consumption and maximum speed should match published figures. In short, a level of expectation is set by brochures, by your experience of sitting in the driving seat, and probably by a test drive. If your expectations are not met you will feel justifiably aggrieved.

This kind of expectation seems not to apply to new software installations; examples of software being delivered not working as expected, or not working at all, are common. Why is this? There is no single cause that can be rectified to solve the problem, but one important contributing factor is the inadequacy of the testing to which software applications are exposed.

Software testing is neither complex nor difficult to implement, yet it is a discipline that is seldom applied with anything approaching the necessary rigour to provide confidence in delivered software. Software testing is costly in human effort or in the technology that can multiply the effect of human effort, yet is seldom implemented at a level that will provide any assurance that software will operate effectively, efficiently or even correctly.

This book explores the fundamentals of this important but neglected discipline to provide a basis on which a practical and cost-effective software testing regime can be constructed.

INTRODUCTION

In this opening chapter we have three very important objectives to achieve. First, we will introduce you to the fundamental ideas that underpin the discipline of software testing, and this will involve the use and explanation of some new terminology. Secondly, we will establish the structure that we have used throughout the book to help you to use the book as a learning and revision aid. Thirdly, we will use this chapter to point forward to the content of later chapters.

The key ideas of software testing are applicable irrespective of the software involved and any particular development methodology (waterfall, Agile etc.). Software development methodologies are discussed in detail in **Chapter 2**.

We begin by defining what we expect you to get from reading this chapter. The learning objectives below are based on those defined in the Software Foundation Certificate syllabus, so you need to ensure that you have achieved all of these objectives before attempting the examination.

Learning objectives

The learning objectives for this chapter are listed below. You can confirm that you have achieved these by using the self-assessment questions at the start of the chapter, the 'Check of understanding' boxes distributed throughout the text, and the example examination questions provided at the end of the chapter. The chapter summary will remind you of the key ideas.

The sections are allocated a K number to represent the level of understanding required for that section; where an individual topic has a lower K number than the section as a whole, this is indicated for that topic; for an explanation of the K numbers see the **Introduction**.

Why is testing necessary? (K2)

- Describe, with examples, the way in which a defect in software can cause harm to a person, to the environment or to a company.
- Distinguish between the root cause of a defect and its effects.
- Give reasons why testing is necessary by giving examples.
- Describe why testing is part of quality assurance and give examples of how testing contributes to higher quality.
- Recall the terms error, defect, fault, failure and the corresponding terms mistake and bug, using examples.

What is testing? (K2)

- Recall the common objectives of testing. (K1)
- Provide examples for the objectives of testing in different phases of the software life cycle.
- Differentiate testing from debugging.

General testing principles (K2)

- Explain the seven principles in testing.

Fundamental test process (K1)

- Recall the five fundamental test activities and respective tasks from planning to closure.

The psychology of testing (K2)

- Recall the psychological factors that influence the success of testing. (K1)

- Contrast the mindset of a tester and of a developer.

Self-assessment questions

The following questions have been designed to enable you to check your current level of understanding for the topics in this chapter. The answers are given at the end of the chapter.

Question SA1 (K1)
A non-functional requirement concerning performance is missing from the system documentation. How should this be described?

    a.   It is a mistake.

    b.   It is a failure.

    c.   It is a fault.

    d.   It is an error.

Question SA2 (K1)
Which of the following gives MOST independence in testing?

    a.   Testing performed by the person who wrote the code.

    b.   Testing performed by an external consultancy.

    c.   Testing performed by another member of the same Agile team.

    d.   Testing performed by a separate department.

Question SA3 (K1)
Running the same set of tests will not continue to find new defects. Which of the seven testing principles does this illustrate?

    a.   Defect clustering.

    b.   Testing shows the presence of bugs.

    c.   Absence of errors fallacy.

    d.   The pesticide paradox.

WHY SOFTWARE FAILS

Examples of software failure are depressingly common. Here are some you may recognise:

- After successful test flights and air worthiness accreditation, problems arose in the manufacture of the Airbus A380 aircraft. Assembly of the large subparts into the completed aircraft revealed enormous cabling and wiring problems. The wiring of large subparts could not be joined together. It has been estimated that the direct or indirect costs of rectification was $6.1 billion. (Note: this problem was quickly fixed and the aircraft entered into service within 18 months of the cabling difficulties being identified.)

- When the UK Government introduced online filing of tax returns, a user could sometimes see the amount that a previous user earned. This was regardless of the physical location of the two applicants.

- In November 2005, information on the UK's top 10 wanted criminals was displayed on a website. The publication of this information was described in newspapers and on morning radio and television and, as a result, many people attempted to access the site. The performance of the website proved inadequate under this load and the website had to be taken offline. The publicity created performance peaks beyond the capacity of the website.

- A new smartphone mapping application (app) was introduced in September 2012. Among many other problems, a museum was incorrectly located in the middle of a river, and Sweden's second city, Gothenburg, seemed to have disappeared from at least one map.

- A small, one-line, change in the billing system of an electrical provider blacked out the whole of a major US city.

What is it about these examples that make them so startling? Is it a sense that something fairly obvious was missed? Is it the feeling that, expensive and important as they were, the systems were allowed to enter service before they were ready? Do you think these systems were adequately tested? Obviously they were not, but in this book we want to explore why this was the case and why these kinds of failure continue to plague us.

To understand what is going on we need to start at the beginning, with the people who design systems. Do they make mistakes? Of course they do. People make mistakes because they are fallible, but there are also many pressures that make mistakes more likely. Pressures such as deadlines, complexity of systems and organisations, and changing technology all bear down on designers of systems and increase the likelihood of errors in specifications, in designs and in software code. These errors are where major system failures usually begin. If a document with an error in it is used to specify a component the component will be faulty and will probably exhibit incorrect behaviour. If this faulty component is built into a system the system may fail. While failure is not always guaranteed, it is likely that errors in specifications will lead to faulty components and faulty components will cause system failure.

An error (or mistake) leads to a defect, which can cause an observed failure (Figure 1.1).

Figure 1.1 Effect of an error

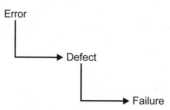

There are other reasons why systems fail. Environmental conditions such as the presence of radiation, magnetism, electronic fields or pollution can affect the operation of hardware and firmware and lead to system failure.

If we want to avoid failure we must either avoid errors and faults or find them and rectify them. Testing can contribute to both avoidance and rectification, as we will see when we have looked at the testing process in a little more detail. One thing is clear: if we wish to influence errors with testing we need to begin testing as soon as we begin making errors – right at the beginning of the development process – and we need to continue testing until we are confident that there will be no serious system failures – right at the end of the development process.

Before we move on, let us just remind ourselves of the importance of what we are considering. Incorrect software can harm:

- people (e.g. by causing an aircraft crash in which people die, or by causing a hospital life support system to fail);
- companies (e.g. by causing incorrect billing, which results in the company losing money);
- the environment (e.g. by releasing chemicals or radiation into the atmosphere).

Software failures can sometimes cause all three of these at once. The scenario of a train carrying nuclear waste being involved in a crash has been explored to help build public confidence in the safety of transporting nuclear waste by train. A failure of the train's on-board systems or of the signalling system that controls the train's movements could lead to catastrophic results. This may not be likely (we hope it is not) but it is a possibility that could be linked with software failure. Software failures, then, can lead to:

- loss of money;
- loss of time;
- loss of business reputation;
- injury;
- death.

KEEPING SOFTWARE UNDER CONTROL

With all of the examples we have seen so far, what common themes can we identify? There may be several themes that we could draw out of the examples, but one theme is clear: either insufficient testing or the wrong type of testing was done. More and better software testing seems a reasonable aim, but that aim is not quite as simple to achieve as we might expect.

Exhaustive testing of complex systems is not possible

The launch of the smartphone app occurred at the same time as a new phone hardware platform – the new app was only available on the new hardware for what many would recognise as the market leader at that time. The product launch received extensive world-wide coverage, with the mapping app given a prominent place in launch publicity. In a matter of hours there were tens of thousands of users, and numbers quickly escalated, with many people wanting to see their location in the new app and see how this compared with (for example) Google Maps. Each phone user was an expert in his/her location – after all they lived there, and 'test cases' were generated showing that problems existed.

If every possible test had been run, problems would have been detected and rectified prior to the product launch. However, if every test had been run, the testing would still be running now, and the product launch would never have taken place; this illustrates one of the general principles of software testing, which are explained below. With large and complex systems it will never be possible to test everything exhaustively; in fact it is impossible to test even moderately complex systems exhaustively.

For the mapping app, it would be unhelpful to say that not enough testing was done; for this particular project, and for many others of similar complexity, that would certainly always be the case. Here the problem was that the right sort of testing was not done because the problems had not been detected.

Testing and risk

Risk is inherent in all software development. The system may not work or the project to build it may not be completed on time, for example. These uncertainties become more significant as the system complexity and the implications of failure increase. Intuitively, we would expect to test an automatic flight control system more than we would test a video game system. Why? Because the risk is greater. There is a greater probability of failure in the more complex system and the impact of failure is also greater. What we test, and how much we test it, must be related in some way to the risk. Greater risk implies more and better testing.

There is much more on risk and risk management in **Chapter 5**.

Testing and quality

Quality is notoriously hard to define. If a system meets its users' requirements that con-
stitutes a good starting point. In the examples we looked at earlier the online tax returns
system had an obvious functional weakness in allowing one user to view another user's
details. While the user community for such a system is potentially large and disparate,
it is hard to imagine any user that would find that situation anything other than unacceptable. In the top 10 criminals example the problem was slightly different. There was
no failure of functionality in this case; the system was simply swamped by requests for
access. This is an example of a non-functional failure, in that the system was not able
to deliver its services to its users because it was not designed to handle the peak load
that materialised after radio and TV coverage.

The Airbus A380 aircraft problems is an interesting story, because although completed
subparts could not be brought together to build an entire aircraft, each of the subparts
was 'correctly manufactured'. Aircraft are increasingly sophisticated, and the A380
aircraft has approximately 530 km of cables, 100,000 wires and 40,300 connectors.
Software is used both to design the aircraft and in the manufacture. However, the large
subparts were made in two different counties, with different versions of the software
in each manufacturing base. So when Airbus was bringing together two halves of the
aircraft, the different software meant that the wiring on one did not match the wiring in
the other. The cables could not meet up without being changed. Testing may have taken
place, but it did not test something as straightforward as the versions of the design
software, and whether they were compatible (which in this case they were plainly not).
Each large subpart was built according to its own version of the CATIA (Computer Aided
Three-Dimensional Interactive Application) software. The result did not give an aircraft
that could fly.

Of course the software development process, like any other, must balance compet-
ing demands for resources. If we need to deliver a system faster (i.e. in less time), for
example, it will usually cost more. The items at the corners (or vertices) of the triangle
of resources in Figure 1.2 are time, money and quality. These three affect one another,
and also influence the features that are or are not included in the delivered software.

Figure 1.2 Resources triangle

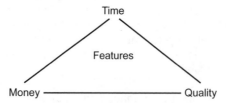

One role for testing is to ensure that key functional and non-functional requirements
are examined before the system enters service and any defects are reported to the
development team for rectification. Testing cannot directly remove defects, nor can it
directly enhance quality. By reporting defects it makes their removal possible and so

contributes to the enhanced quality of the system. In addition, the systematic coverage of a software product in testing allows at least some aspects of the quality of the software to be measured. Testing is one component in the overall quality assurance activity that seeks to ensure that systems enter service without defects that can lead to serious failures.

Deciding when 'enough is enough'

How much testing is enough, and how do we decide when to stop testing?

We have so far decided that we cannot test everything, even if we would wish to. We also know that every system is subject to risk of one kind or another and that there is a level of quality that is acceptable for a given system. These are the factors we will use to decide how much testing to do.

The most important aspect of achieving an acceptable result from a finite and limited amount of testing is prioritisation. Do the most important tests first so that at any time you can be certain that the tests that have been done are more important than the ones still to be done. Even if the testing activity is cut in half it will still be true that the most important testing has been done. The most important tests will be those that test the most important aspects of the system: they will test the most important functions as defined by the users or sponsors of the system, and the most important non-functional behaviour, and they will address the most significant risks.

The next most important aspect is setting criteria that will give you an objective test of whether it is safe to stop testing, so that time and all the other pressures do not confuse the outcome. These criteria, usually known as completion criteria, set the standards for the testing activity by defining areas such as how much of the software is to be tested (this is covered in more detail in **Chapter 4**) and what levels of defects can be tolerated in a delivered product (which is covered in more detail in **Chapter 5**).

Priorities and completion criteria provide a basis for planning (which will be covered in **Chapter 2** and **Chapter 5**) but the triangle of resources in Figure 1.2 still applies. In the end, the desired level of quality and risk may have to be compromised, but our approach ensures that we can still determine how much testing is required to achieve the agreed levels and we can still be certain that any reduction in the time or effort available for testing will not affect the balance – the most important tests will still be those that have already been done whenever we stop.

CHECK OF UNDERSTANDING

1. Describe the interaction between errors, defects and failures.
2. Software failures can cause losses. Give three consequences of software failures.
3. What are the vertices of the 'triangle of resources'?

WHAT TESTING IS AND WHAT TESTING DOES

So far we have worked with an intuitive idea of what testing is. We have recognised that it is an activity used to reduce risk and improve quality by finding defects, which is all true. However, we need to understand a little more about how software testing works in practice before we can think about how to implement effective testing.

Testing and debugging

Testing and debugging are different kinds of activity, both of which are very important. Debugging is the process that developers go through to identify the cause of bugs or defects in code and undertake corrections. Ideally some check of the correction is made, but this may not extend to checking that other areas of the system have not been inadvertently affected by the correction. Testing, on the other hand, is a systematic exploration of a component or system with the main aim of finding and reporting defects. Testing does not include correction of defects – these are passed on to the developer to correct. Testing does, however, ensure that changes and corrections are checked for their effect on other parts of the component or system.

Effective debugging is essential before testing begins to raise the level of quality of the component or system to a level that is worth testing, that is a level that is sufficiently robust to enable rigorous testing to be performed. Debugging does not give confidence that the component or system meets its requirements completely. Testing makes a rigorous examination of the behaviour of a component or system and reports all defects found for the development team to correct. Testing then repeats enough tests to ensure that defect corrections have been effective. So both are needed to achieve a quality result.

Static testing and dynamic testing

Static testing is the term used for testing where the code is not exercised. This may sound strange, but remember that failures often begin with a human error, namely a mistake in a document such as a specification. We need to test these because errors are much cheaper to fix than defects or failures (as you will see). That is why testing should start as early as possible, another basic principle explained in more detail later in this chapter. Static testing involves techniques such as reviews, which can be effective in preventing defects, for example by removing ambiguities and errors from specification documents; this is a topic in its own right and is covered in detail in **Chapter 3**. Dynamic testing is the kind that exercises the program under test with some test data, so we speak of test execution in this context. The discipline of software testing encompasses both static and dynamic testing.

Testing as a process

We have already seen that there is much more to testing than test execution. Before test execution there is some preparatory work to do to design the tests and set them up; after test execution there is some work needed to record the results and check whether the tests are complete. Even more important than this is deciding what we are trying to achieve with the testing and setting clear objectives for each test. A test designed to give confidence that a program functions according to its specification, for example, will be quite different from one designed to find as many defects as possible. We define a test process to ensure that we do not miss critical steps and that we do things in the right order. We will return to this important topic later, where we explain the fundamental test process in detail.

Testing as a set of techniques

The final challenge is to ensure that the testing we do is effective testing. It might seem paradoxical, but a good test is one that finds a defect if there is one present. A test that finds no defect has consumed resources but added no value; a test that finds a defect has created an opportunity to improve the quality of the product. How do we design tests that find defects? We actually do two things to maximise the effectiveness of the tests. First we use well-proven test design techniques, and a selection of the most important of these is explained in detail in **Chapter 4**. The techniques are all based on certain testing principles that have been discovered and documented over the years, and these principles are the second mechanism we use to ensure that tests are effective. Even when we cannot apply rigorous test design for some reason (such as time pressures) we can still apply the general principles to guide our testing. We turn to these next.

CHECK OF UNDERSTANDING

1. Describe static testing and dynamic testing.
2. What is debugging?
3. What other elements apart from 'test execution' are included in 'testing'?

GENERAL TESTING PRINCIPLES

Testing is a very complex activity, and the software problems described earlier highlight that it can be difficult to do well. We now describe some general testing principles that help testers, principles that have been developed over the years from a variety of sources. These are not all obvious, but their purpose is to guide testers, and prevent the types of problems described previously. Testers use these principles with the test techniques described in **Chapter 4**.

Testing shows the presence of bugs

Running a test through a software system can only show that one or more defects exist. Testing cannot show that the software is error free. Consider whether the top 10 wanted criminals website was error free. There were no functional defects, yet the website failed. In this case the problem was non-functional and the absence of defects was not adequate as a criterion for release of the website into operation.

In **Chapter 2**, we will discuss retesting, when a previously failed test is rerun, to show that under the same conditions, the reported problem no longer exists. In this type of situation, testing can show that one particular problem no longer exists.

Although there may be other objectives, usually the main purpose of testing is to find defects. Therefore tests should be designed to find as many defects as possible.

Exhaustive testing is impossible

If testing finds problems, then surely you would expect more testing to find additional problems, until eventually we would have found them all. We discussed exhaustive testing earlier
when looking at the smartphone mapping app, and concluded that for large complex systems, exhaustive testing is not possible. However, could it be possible to test small pieces
of software exhaustively, and only incorporate exhaustively tested code into large systems?

> **Exhaustive testing – a test approach in which all possible data combinations
> are used. This includes implicit data combinations present in the state of the
> software/data at the start of testing.**

Consider a small piece of software where one can enter a password, specified to contain
up to three characters, with no consecutive repeating entries. Using only western alphabetic capital letters and completing all three characters, there are 26 × 26 × 26 input
permutations (not all of which will be valid). However, with a standard keyboard, there
are not 26 × 26 × 26 permutations, but a much higher number, 256 × 256 × 256, or 2^{24}.
Even then, the number of possibilities is higher. What happens if three characters are
entered, and the 'delete last character' right arrow key removes the last two? Are special key combinations accepted, or do they cause system actions (Ctrl + P, for example)?
What about entering a character, and waiting 20 minutes before entering the other two
characters? It may be the same combination of keystrokes, but the circumstances are
different. We can also include the situation where the 20-minute break occurs over the
change-of-day interval. It is not possible to say whether there are any defects until all
possible input combinations have been tried.

Even in this small example, there are many, many possible data combinations to
attempt. The number of possible combinations using a smartphone might be significantly less, but it is still large enough to be impractical to use all of them.

Unless the application under test (AUT) has an extremely simple logical structure and
limited input, it is not possible to test all possible combinations of data input and circumstances. For this reason, risk and priorities are used to concentrate on the most
important aspects to test. Both 'risk' and 'priorities' are covered later in more detail.
Their use is important to ensure that the most important parts are tested.

Early testing

When discussing why software fails, we briefly mentioned the idea of early testing. This
principle is important because, as a proposed deployment date approaches, time pressure can increase dramatically. There is a real danger that testing will be squeezed, and
this is bad news if the only testing we are doing is after all the development has been
completed. The earlier the testing activity is started, the longer the elapsed time available. Testers do not have to wait until software is available to test.

Work-products are created throughout the software development life cycle (SDLC). As
soon as these are ready, we can test them. In **Chapter 2**, we will see that requirement
documents are the basis for acceptance testing, so the creation of acceptance tests can

begin as soon as requirement documents are available. As we create these tests, it will highlight the contents of the requirements. Are individual requirements testable? Can we find ambiguous or missing requirements?

Many problems in software systems can be traced back to missing or incorrect require-ments. We will look at this in more detail when we discuss reviews in **Chapter 3**. The use of reviews can break the 'error–defect–failure' cycle. In early testing we are trying to find errors and defects before they are passed to the next stage of the development process. Early testing techniques are attempting to show that what is produced as a system specification, for example, accurately reflects that which is in the requirement documents. Ed Kit discusses identifying and eliminating errors at the part of the SDLC in which they are introduced.[1] If an error/defect is introduced in the coding activity, it is preferable to detect and correct it at this stage. If a problem is not corrected at the stage in which it is introduced, this leads to what Kit calls 'errors of migration'. The result is rework. We need to rework not just the part where the mistake was made, but each sub-sequent part where the error has been replicated. A defect found at acceptance testing where the original mistake was in the requirements will require several work-products to be reworked, and subsequently to be retested.

Studies have been done on the cost impacts of errors at the different development stages. While it is difficult to put figures on the relative costs of finding defects at differ-ent levels in the SDLC, Table 1.1 does concentrate the mind!

Table 1.1 Comparative cost to correct errors

Stage error is found	Comparative cost
Requirements	$1
Coding	$10
Program testing	$100
System testing	$1,000
User acceptance testing	$10,000
Live running	$100,000

This is known as the cost escalation model.

What is undoubtedly true is that the graph of the relative cost of early and late identification/ correction of defects rises very steeply (Figure 1.3).

The earlier a problem (defect) is found, the less it costs to fix.

[1] Kit, E. (1995) *Software Testing in the Real World*. Addison-Wesley, Reading, MA.

Figure 1.3 Effect of identification time on cost of errors

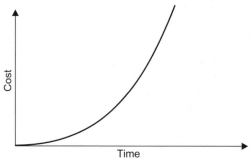

The objectives of various stages of testing can be different. For example, in the review processes, we may focus on whether the documents are consistent and no errors have been introduced when the documents were produced. Other stages of testing can have other objectives. The important point is that testing has defined objectives.

One of the drivers behind the push to Agile development methodologies is to enable testing to be incorporated throughout the software build process. This is nothing more than the 'early testing' principle.

Defect clustering

Problems do occur in software. It is a fact. Once testing has identified (most of) the defects in a particular application, it is at first surprising that the spread of defects is not uniform. In a large application, it is often a small number of modules that exhibit the majority of the problems. This can be for a variety of reasons, some of which are:

- System complexity.
- Volatile code.
- The effects of change on change.
- Development staff experience.
- Development staff inexperience.

This is the application of the Pareto principle to software testing: approximately 80 per cent of the problems are found in about 20 per cent of the modules. It is useful if testing activity reflects this spread of defects, and targets areas of the application under test where a high proportion of defects can be found. However, it must be remembered that testing should not concentrate exclusively on these parts. There may be fewer defects in the remaining code, but testers still need to search diligently for them.

The pesticide paradox

Running the same set of tests continually will not continue to find new defects. Developers will soon know that the test team always tests the boundaries of conditions, for example, so they will test these conditions before the software is delivered. This does not make defects elsewhere in the code less likely, so continuing to use the same test set will result in decreasing effectiveness of the tests. Using other techniques will find different defects.

For example, a small change to software could be specifically tested and an additional set of tests performed, aimed at showing that no additional problems have been introduced (this is known as regression testing). However, the software may fail in production because the regression tests are no longer relevant to the requirements of the system or the test objectives. Any regression test set needs to change to reflect business needs, and what are now seen as the most important risks. Regression testing will be discussed later in this chapter, but is covered in more detail in **Chapter 2**.

Testing is context dependent

Different testing is necessary in different circumstances. A website where information can merely be viewed will be tested in a different way to an ecommerce site, where goods can be bought using credit/debit cards. We need to test an air traffic control system with more rigour than an application for calculating the length of a mortgage.

Risk can be a large factor in determining the type of testing that is needed. The higher the possibility of losses, the more we need to invest in testing the software before it is implemented. A fuller discussion of risk is given in **Chapter 5**.

For an ecommerce site, we should concentrate on security aspects. Is it possible to bypass the use of passwords? Can 'payment' be made with an invalid credit card, by entering excessive data into the card number field? Security testing is an example of a specialist area, not appropriate for all applications. Such types of testing may require specialist staff and software tools. Test tools are covered in more detail in **Chapter 6**.

Absence of errors fallacy

Software with no known errors is not necessarily ready to be shipped. Does the application under test match up to the users' expectations of it? The fact that no defects are outstanding is not a good reason to ship the software.

Before dynamic testing has begun, there are no defects reported against the code delivered. Does this mean that software that has not been tested (but has no outstanding defects against it) can be shipped? We think not.

CHECK OF UNDERSTANDING

1. Why is 'zero defects' an insufficient guide to software quality?
2. Give three reasons why defect clustering may exist.
3. Briefly justify the idea of early testing.

FUNDAMENTAL TEST PROCESS

We previously determined that testing is a process, discussed above. This process is detailed in what has become known as the fundamental test process, a key element of what testers do, and is applicable at all stages of testing.

The most visible part of testing is running one or more tests: test execution. We also have to prepare for running tests, analyse the tests that have been run, and see whether testing is complete. Both planning and analysing are very necessary activities that enhance and amplify the benefits of the test execution itself. It is no good testing without deciding how, when and what to test. Planning is also required for the less formal test approaches such as exploratory testing, covered in more detail in **Chapter 4**.

The fundamental test process consists of five parts that encompass all aspects of testing (Figure 1.4):

1. Planning and control.
2. Analysis and design.
3. Implementation and execution.
4. Evaluating exit criteria and reporting.
5. Test closure activities.

Figure 1.4 Fundamental test process

Although the main activities are in a broad sequence, they are not undertaken in a rigid way. An earlier activity may need to be revisited. A defect found in test execution can sometimes be resolved by adding functionality that was originally not present (either missing in error, or the new facilities are needed to make the other part correct). The new features themselves have to be tested, so even though implementation and execution are in progress, the 'earlier' activity of analysis and design has to be performed for the new features (Figure 1.5).

Figure 1.5 Iteration of activities

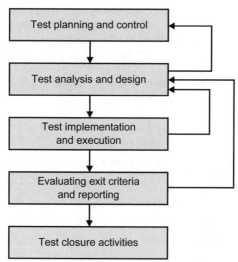

We sometimes need to do two or more of the main activities in parallel. Time pressure can mean that we begin test execution before all tests have been designed.

Test planning and control

Planning is determining what is going to be tested, and how this will be achieved. It is where we draw a map; how activities will be done; and who will do them. Test planning is also where we define the test completion criteria. Completion criteria are how we know when testing is finished. Control, on the other hand, is what we do when the activities do not match up with the plans. It is the ongoing activity where we compare the progress against the plan. As progress takes place, we may need to adjust plans to meet the targets, if this is possible. Therefore we need to undertake both planning and control throughout the testing activities. We plan at the outset, but as testing progresses, undertake monitoring and control activities (monitoring to measure what has happened, control to adjust future activities in the light of experience). Monitoring and control feed back into the continual activity of planning. The activities of planning and control are developed in more detail in **Chapter 5**.

Test analysis and design

Analysis and design are concerned with the fine detail of what to test (test conditions), and how to combine test conditions into test cases, so that a small number of test cases can cover as many of the test conditions as possible. The analysis and design stage is the bridge between planning and test execution. It is looking backward to the planning (schedules, people, what is going to be tested) and forward to the execution activity (test expected results, what environment will be needed).

A part of the design process needs to consider the test data that will be required for the test conditions and test cases that have been drawn up.

21

Test design involves predicting how the software under test should behave in a given set of circumstances. Sometimes the expected outcome of a test is trivial: when ordering books from an online book retailer, for instance, under no circumstances should money be refunded to the customer's card without intervention from a supervisor. If we do not detail expected outcomes before starting test execution, there is a real danger that we will miss the one item of detail that is vital, but wrong.

These topics will be discussed in more detail in **Chapter 4**, when test case design techniques are presented. The main points of this activity are as follows:

- Reviewing requirements, architecture, design, interface specifications and other parts, which collectively comprise the test basis.
- Analysing test items, the specification, behaviour and structure to identify test conditions and test data required.
- Designing the tests, including assigning priority.
- Determining whether the requirements and the system are testable.
- Detailing what the test environment should look like, and whether there are any infrastructure and tools required.
- Highlighting the test data required for the test conditions and test cases.
- Creating bidirectional traceability between test basis and test cases.

Test implementation and execution

The test implementation and execution activity involves running tests, and this will include where necessary any set-up/tear-down activities for the testing. It will also involve checking the test environment before testing begins. Test execution is the most visible part of testing, but it is not possible without other parts of the fundamental test process. It is not just about running tests. As we have already mentioned, the most important tests need to be run first. How do we know what are the most important tests to run? This is determined during the planning stages, and refined as part of test design.

One important aspect undertaken at this stage is combining test cases into an overall run procedure, so that test time can be utilised efficiently. Here the logical ordering of tests is important so that, where possible, the outcome of one test creates the preconditions for one or more tests that are later in the execution sequence.

As tests are run, their outcome needs to be logged, and a comparison made between expected results and actual results. Whenever there is a discrepancy between the expected and actual results, this needs to be investigated. If necessary a test incident should be raised. Each incident requires investigation, although corrective action will not be necessary in every case. Test incidents will be discussed in **Chapter 5**.

When anything changes (software, data, installation procedures, user documentation etc.), we need to do two kinds of testing on the software. First of all, tests should be run to make sure that the problem has been fixed. We also need to make sure that the changes have not broken the software elsewhere. These two types are usually called retesting and regression testing, respectively. In retesting we are looking in fine detail at the changed area of functionality, whereas regression testing should cover all the main functions to ensure that no unintended changes have occurred. On a financial system, we should include end of day/end of month/end of year processing, for example, in a regression test pack.

Test implementation and execution is where the most visible test activities are undertaken, and usually have the following parts:

- Developing and prioritising test cases, creating test data, writing test procedures and, optionally, preparing test harnesses and writing automated test scripts.
- Collecting test cases into test suites, where tests can be run one after another for efficiency.
- Checking the test environment set-up is correct.
- Running test cases in the determined order. This can be manually or using test execution tools.
- Keeping a log of testing activities, including the outcome (pass/fail) and the versions of software, data, tools and testware (scripts etc.).
- Comparing actual results with expected results.
- Reporting discrepancies as incidents with as much information as possible, including if possible causal analysis (code defect, incorrect test specification, test data error or test execution error).
- Where necessary, repeating test activities when changes have been made following incidents raised. This includes re-execution of a test that previously failed in order to confirm a fix (retesting), execution of a corrected test and execution of previously passed tests to check that defects have not been introduced (regression testing).

Evaluating exit criteria and reporting

Remember that exit criteria were defined during test planning and before test execution started. At the end of test execution, the test manager checks to see if these have been met. If the criterion was that there would be 85 per cent statement coverage (i.e. 85 per cent of all executable statements have been executed (see **Chapter 4** for more detail)), and as a result of execution the figure is 75 per cent, there are two possible actions: change the exit criteria, or run more tests. It is possible that even if the preset criteria were met, more tests would be required. Also, writing a test summary for stakeholders would say what was planned, what was achieved, highlight any differences and in particular things that were not tested.

The fourth stage of the fundamental test process, evaluating exit criteria, comprises the following:

- Checking whether the previously determined exit criteria have been met.
- Determining if more tests are needed or if the specified exit criteria need amending.
- Writing up the result of the testing activities for the business sponsors and other stakeholders.

More detail is given on this subject in **Chapter 5**.

Test closure activities

Testing at this stage has finished. Test closure activities concentrate on making sure that everything is tidied away, reports written, defects closed, and those defects deferred for another phase clearly seen to be as such.

At the end of testing, the test closure stage is composed of the following:

- Ensuring that the documentation is in order; what has been delivered is defined (it may be more or less than originally planned), closing incidents and raising changes for future deliveries, documenting that the system has been accepted.
- Closing down and archiving the test environment, test infrastructure and testware used.
- Passing over testware to the maintenance team.
- Writing down the lessons learned from this testing project for the future, and incorporating lessons to improve the testing process ('testing maturity').

The detail of the test closure activities is discussed in **Chapter 5**.

Agile methodologies and the fundamental test process

Thus far we have concentrated on 'traditional' methodologies when discussing the fundamental test process. We now want to focus on Agile methodologies.

The use of Agile methodologies and the relationship with the fundamental test process is not a syllabus topic for the Foundation Certificate, but in the following discussion our understanding of both the fundamental test process and Agile methodologies will grow.

We use the term 'Agile methodologies' because there is not a single variant or 'flavour' of Agile. Any distinctions between these are unimportant here, but the principles are important. Agile software development life cycles aim to have frequent deliveries of software, where each iteration or sprint will build on any previously made available. The aim is to have software that could be implemented into the production environment at the end of each sprint – although a delivery into production might not happen as frequently as this.

From the brief introduction to Agile above, it follows that an Agile project has a beginning and an end, but the processes that go between these stages can be repeated many times. Agile projects can be successfully progressing over the course of many months or even years, with a continuous stream of (same length) iterations producing production-quality software, typically every two, three or four weeks. In terms of the fundamental test process, there is a part of the planning and control stage that takes place at the start of the project, and the test closure activities take place at the end of the project. However, some planning and control, and all of the middle three stages of the fundamental test process are present in each and every sprint.

Some planning and control activities take place at the beginning of the project. This would typically include resourcing activities, some outline planning on the length of the project, and an initial attempt at ordering the features to be implemented (although this could change significantly as the project progresses, sprint by sprint). Infrastructure planning, together with the identification and provision of any specific testing tools is usually undertaken at this stage, together with a clear understanding within the whole team of what is 'done' (i.e. a definition of 'done').

At the start of each sprint, planning activity takes place, to determine items to include in the sprint. This is a whole team activity based on reaching a consensus of how long each potential deliverable will take. As sprint follows sprint, so the accuracy of estimation increases. The sprint is a fixed length, so throughout the duration of the development, items could be added or removed, to ensure that, at the conclusion, there is tested code 'on the shelf' and available for implementation as required.

Also the three middle stages of the fundamental test process are accomplished in each sprint. A daily stand-up meeting should result in a short feedback loop, to enable any adjustments to take place and items that prevent progress to be resolved. The whole time for development and testing is limited, so the preparation for testing and the testing itself have to be undertaken in parallel. Towards the end of the sprint, it is possible that most or all of the team are involved in testing, with a focus of delivering all that was agreed at the time of the sprint planning meeting.

Automated testing tools are frequently used in Agile projects. Tests can be very low level, and a tester on such a project can provide very useful input to developers in defining tests to be used to identify specific conditions. The earlier in a sprint that this is done the more advantages can be gained within that sprint.

The proposed deliverables are sometimes used in conjunction with the definition of 'done' to enable a burn-down chart to be drawn up. This enables a track to be kept of progress for all to see – in itself usually a motivating factor. As sprint follows sprint, the subject of regression testing previously delivered, working software becomes more important. Part of the test analysis and design stage will involve selecting regression tests that are appropriate for the current sprint. Tests that previously worked might now (correctly) not pass because the new sprint has changed the intention of previously delivered software. The conclusion of the sprint might often be a sprint review meeting, which can include a demonstration to user representatives and/or the project sponsor.

For development using Agile methodologies, the final stage in the fundamental test process – 'test closure activities' – is scheduled after the end of the last sprint. This should not be done before, because testing collateral that was used in the last-but-three sprint might no longer be appropriate at the conclusion of the final sprint. As we discussed earlier, even the regression tests might have changed, or a more suitable set of regression tests identified.

Further information about Agile methodologies is given in **Chapter 2**.

CHECK OF UNDERSTANDING

1. What are the stages in the fundamental test process (in the correct sequence)?
2. Briefly compare regression testing and retesting.
3. When should the expected outcome of a test be defined?

THE PSYCHOLOGY OF TESTING

A variety of different people may be involved in the total testing effort, and they may be drawn from a broad set of backgrounds. Some will be developers, some professional testers, and some will be specialists, such as those with performance testing skills, while others may be users drafted in to assist with acceptance testing. Who ever is involved in testing needs at least some understanding of the skills and techniques of testing to make an effective contribution to the overall testing effort.

Testing can be more effective if it is not undertaken by the individual(s) who wrote the code, for the simple reason that the creator of anything (whether it is software or a work of art) has a special relationship with the created object. The nature of that relationship is such that flaws in the created object are rendered invisible to the creator. For that reason it is important that someone other than the creator should test the object. Of course we do want the developer who builds a component or system to debug it, and even to attempt to test it, but we accept that testing done by that individual cannot be assumed to be complete. Developers can test their own code, but it requires a mindset change, from that of a developer (to prove it works) to that of a tester (trying to show that it does not work). If there are separate individuals involved, there are no potential conflicts of interest. We therefore aim to have the software tested by someone who was not involved in its creation; this approach is called test independence. Below are people who could test software, listed in order of increasing independence:

- Those who wrote the code.
- Members of the same development team.
- Members of a different group (independent test team).
- Members of a different company (a testing consultancy/outsourced).

Of course independence comes at a price; it is much more expensive to use a testing consultancy than to test a program oneself.

Testers and developers think in different ways. However, although we know that testers should be involved from the beginning, it is not always good to get testers involved in code execution at an early stage; there are advantages and disadvantages. Getting developers to test their own code has advantages (as soon as problems are discovered, they can be fixed, without the need for extensive error logs), but also difficulties (it is hard to find your own mistakes). People and projects have objectives, and we all modify actions to blend in with the goals. If a developer has a goal of producing acceptable software by certain dates, then any testing is aimed towards that goal.

If a defect is found in software, the software author may see this as criticism. Testers need to use tact and diplomacy when raising defect reports. Defect reports need to be raised against the software, not against the individual who made the mistake. The mistake may be in the code written, or in one of the documents on which the code is based (requirement documents or system specification). When we raise defects in a constructive way, bad feeling can be avoided.

We all need to focus on good communication, and work on team building. Testers and developers are not opposed, but working together, with the joint target of better quality systems. Communication needs to be objective, and expressed in impersonal ways:

- The aim is to work together rather than be confrontational. Keep the focus on delivering a quality product.

- Results should be presented in a non-personal way. The work-product may be wrong, so say this in a non-personal way.

- Attempt to understand how others feel; it is possible to discuss problems and still leave all parties feeling positive.

- At the end of discussions, confirm that you have both understood and been understood. 'So, am I right in saying that your aim was to deliver on Friday by 12:00, even if you knew there were problems?'

As testers and developers, one of our goals is better quality systems delivered in a timely manner. Good communication between testers and the development teams is one way that this goal can be reached.

CHECK OF UNDERSTANDING

1. When testing software, who has the highest level of independence?
2. Contrast the advantages and disadvantages of developers testing their own code.
3. Suggest three ways that confrontation can be avoided.

CODE OF ETHICS

One last topic that we need to address before we move onto the more detailed coverage of topics in the following chapters is that testers must adhere to a code of ethics: they are required to act in a professional manner. Testers can have access to confidential and/or privileged information, and they are to treat any information with care and attention, and act responsibly to the owner(s) of this information, employers and the wider public interest. Of course, anyone can test software, so the declaration of this code of conduct applies to those who have achieved software testing certification. The code of ethics applies to the following areas:

- Public – certified software testers shall consider the wider public interest in their actions.

- Client and employer – certified software testers shall act in the best interests of their client and employer (being consistent with the wider public interest).

- Product – certified software testers shall ensure that the deliverables they provide (for any products and systems they work on) meet the highest professional standards possible.

- Judgement – certified software testers shall maintain integrity and independence in their professional judgement.

- Management – certified software test managers and leaders shall subscribe to and promote an ethical approach to the management of software testing.

- Profession – certified software testers shall advance the integrity and reputation of the profession consistent with the public interest.

- Colleagues – certified software testers shall be fair to and supportive of their colleagues, and promote cooperation with software developers.

- Self – certified software testers shall participate in lifelong learning regarding the practice of their profession, and shall promote an ethical approach to the practice of the profession.

The code of ethics is far-reaching in its aims, and a quick review of the eight points reveals interaction with other areas of the syllabus. The implementation of this code of ethics is expanded on in all chapters of this book, and perhaps is the reason for the whole book itself.

CHECK OF UNDERSTANDING

1. Why do testers need to consider how they treat the information they use?
2. What eight areas should testers consider when conducting themselves in the workplace?
3. What other sections of this chapter have described how testers should conduct themselves with colleagues?

SUMMARY

In this chapter, we have looked at key ideas that are used in testing, and introduced some terminology. We examined some of the types of software problems that can occur, and why the blanket explanation of 'insufficient testing' is unhelpful. The problems encountered then led us through some questions about the nature of testing, why errors and mistakes are made, and how these can be identified and eliminated. Individual examples enabled us to look at what testing can achieve, and the view that testing does not improve software quality, but provides information about that quality.

We have examined both general testing principles and a standard template for testing: the fundamental test process. These are useful and can be effective in identifying the types of problems we considered at the start of the chapter. The chapter finished by examining how developers and testers think, and looked at different levels of test independence, and how testers should behave by adhering to a code of ethics.

This chapter is an introduction to testing, and to themes that are developed later in the book. It is a chapter in its own right, but also points to information that will come later. A rereading of this chapter when you have worked through the rest of the book will place all the main topics into context.

Example examination questions with answers

E1. K1 question
Which of the following is correct?

Debugging is:

    a. Testing/checking whether the software performs correctly.

    b. Checking that a previously reported defect has been corrected.

    c. Identifying the cause of a defect, repairing the code and checking the fix is correct.

    d. Checking that no unintended consequences have occurred as a result of a fix.

E2. K2 question
Which of the following are aids to good communication, and which hinder it?

    i.   Try to understand how the other person feels.

    ii.   Communicate personal feelings, concentrating on individuals.

    iii. Confirm the other person has understood what you have said and vice versa.

    iv. Emphasise the common goal of better quality.

    v.   Each discussion is a battle to be won.

    a. i, ii and iii *aid*, iv and v *hinder*.

    b. iii, iv and v *aid*, i and ii *hinder*.

    c. i, iii and iv *aid*, ii and v *hinder*.

    d. ii, iii and iv *aid*, i and v *hinder*.

E3. K1 question
Which option is part of the 'implementation and execution' area of the fundamental test process?

    a. Developing the tests.

    b. Comparing actual and expected results.

    c. Writing a test summary.

    d. Analysing lessons learnt for future releases.

E4. K1 question
The five parts of the fundamental test process have a broad chronological order. Which of the options gives three different parts in the correct order?

    a.   Implementation and execution, planning and control, analysis and design.

    b.   Analysis and design, evaluating exit criteria and reporting, test closure activities.

    c.   Evaluating exit criteria and reporting, implementation and execution, analysis and design.

    d.   Evaluating exit criteria and reporting, test closure activities, analysis and design.

E5. K2 question
Which pair of definitions is correct?

    a.   Regression testing is checking that the reported defect has been fixed; retesting is testing that there are no additional problems in previously tested software.

    b.   Regression testing is checking there are no additional problems in previously tested software; retesting enables developers to isolate the problem.

    c.   Regression testing involves running all tests that have been run before; retesting runs new tests.

    d.   Regression testing is checking that there are no additional problems in previously tested software, retesting is demonstrating that the reported defect has been fixed.

E6. K1 question
Which statement is *most* true?

    a.   Different testing is needed depending on the application.

    b.   All software is tested in the same way.

    c.   A technique that finds defects will always find defects.

    d.   A technique that has found no defects is not useful.

E7. K1 question
When is testing complete?

    a.   When time and budget are exhausted.

    b.   When there is enough information for sponsors to make an informed decision about release.

    c.   When there are no remaining high priority defects outstanding.

    d.   When every data combination has been exercised successfully.

E8. K1 question
Which list of levels of tester independence is in the correct order, starting with the *most* independent first?

    a.   Tests designed by the author; tests designed by another member of the development team; tests designed by someone from a different company.

    b.   Tests designed by someone from a different department within the company; tests designed by the author; tests designed by someone from a different company.

    c.   Tests designed by someone from a different company; tests designed by someone from a different department within the company; tests designed by another member of the development team.

    d.   Tests designed by someone from a different department within the company; tests designed by someone from a different company; tests designed by the author.

E9. K2 question
The following statements relate to activities that are part of the fundamental test process.

    i.   Evaluating the testability of requirements.

    ii.   Repeating testing activities after changes.

    iii.   Designing the test environment set-up.

    iv.   Developing and prioritising test cases.

    v.   Verifying the environment is set up correctly.

Which statement below is true?

    a.   i and ii are part of analysis and design, iii, iv and v are part of test implementation and execution.

    b.   i and iii are part of analysis and design, ii, iv and v are part of test implementation and execution.

    c.   i and v are part of analysis and design, ii, iii and iv are part of test implementation and execution.

    d.   i and iv are part of analysis and design, ii, iii and v are part of test implementation and execution.

E10. K2 question
Which of the following is true?

    a.   The developer misunderstood the specification, introducing a mistake into the software that caused a run-time error.

    b.   The specification was incorrect (resulting from a mistake) – this carried forward into the software and resulted in a failure when the code was executed.

    c.   A failure in the writing of the specification gave rise to an error in the code that was implemented.

    d.   A run-time failure in the software was caused by a mistake in the code as written by the developer.

E11. K1 question
Which of the following describes why testing is necessary?

    a.   To show that there are no defects in the software.

    b.   To reduce the risk of problems occurring when code is implemented.

    c.   To decide when the software should be implemented.

    d.   To enable the project plan to be followed.

E12. K2 question
Which one of the following definition pairs is correct?

    a.   Retesting is rerunning previously successful tests to ensure that there are no unintended consequences; regression testing is ensuring the previously failed test now performs correctly.

    b.   Regression testing is rerunning previously successful tests to ensure that there are no unintended consequences; retesting testing is ensuring the previously failed test now performs correctly.

    c.   Retesting is identifying and correcting the cause of a defect; regression testing is rerunning previously successful tests to ensure that there are no unintended consequences.

    d.   Retesting is rerunning a failed test to identify the cause of the failure; regression testing is selecting the tests that need to be rerun.

E13. K1 question
How does software testing lead to higher quality?

    a.   By identifying defects, enabling these to be investigated.

    b.   By preventing software being implemented whilst it is unstable.

    c.   By ensuring that correct processes are followed.

    d.   By ensuring software developers know their work will be examined.

E14. K2 question
When has enough testing been done?

    a.   When all tests have been run.

    b.   When there are no outstanding high priority defects.

    c.   When the most important tests have been successfully run.

    d.   When sufficient information is available for sponsors to make an informed decision about release.

E15. K1 question
Which one of the following is *not* part of the test analysis and design stage of the fundamental test process?

    a.   Identifying test data to support test conditions and test cases.
    b.   Creating bidirectional traceability between the test basis and test cases.
    c.   Examining the testability of the test basis.
    d.   Verifying that the test environment has been set up correctly.

E16. K1 question
Why might developer-only testing be less effective than using testing professionals?

    a.   Testers have had training in test techniques, developers have not.
    b.   Developers are only doing testing because it is one of their assigned tasks.
    c.   It is harder to see your own errors than those of someone else.
    d.   Testers have a greater understanding of how the software is meant to work.

E17. K2 question
Which of the following test objectives are *particularly* relevant to operational testing?

    i.   Assessing system reliability.
    ii.   To cause as many failures as possible.
    iii.   To give as much information to stakeholders of the risk of releasing at a given time.
    iv.   Checking that no new defects have been introduced during the development of changes.
    v.   To provide an assessment of the system availability.

    a.   i and ii.
    b.   iii and v.
    c.   ii and iv.
    d.   i and v.

E18. K1 question
Which *one* item below hinders good communication within the team?

    a.   Try to understand how the other person feels.
    b.   Communicate personal feelings, concentrating on individuals.
    c.   Confirm the other person has understood what you have said and vice versa.
    d.   Emphasise the common goal of better quality.

E19. K2 question
Which of the following are applicable to debugging?

    i.   Identifying a failure.

    ii.   Performed by a tester.

    iii.   Locating the cause of failure.

    iv.   Fixing the defect.

    v.   Performed by a developer.

    vi.   Checking the fix has resolved the failure.

    a.   iii, iv and v.

    b.   i, ii and iv.

    c.   i, v and vi.

    d.   ii, iii and vi.

Answers to questions in the chapter

SA1.   The correct answer is c.
SA2.   The correct answer is b.
SA3.   The correct answer is d.

Answers to example questions

E1. The correct answer is c.

a.   is a brief definition of testing.
b.   is retesting.
d.   is regression testing.

E2. The correct answer is c.
If you are unsure why, revisit the section in this chapter on the psychology of testing.

E3. The correct answer is b.

a.   is part of 'analysis and design'.
c.   is part of 'evaluating exit criteria and reporting'.
d.   is part of 'test closure activities'.

E4. The correct answer is b.
All other answers have at least one stage of the fundamental test process in the wrong sequence.

E5. The correct answer is d.
Regression testing is testing that nothing has **regressed**. Retesting (or confirmation testing) **confirms** the fix is correct by running the same test after the fix has been made. No other option has both of these as true.

E6. The correct answer is a.
This is a restatement of the testing principle 'testing is context dependent'.

E7. The correct answer is b.
Sometimes time/money does signify the end of testing, but it is really complete when everything that was set out in advance has been achieved.

E8. The correct answer is c.
This option has someone **nearer** to the written code in each statement. All other options are not in this order.

E9. The correct answer is b.
All other answers contain an activity identified as analysis and design that is part of implementation and test execution.

E10. The correct answer is b.
This relies on the 'mistake–defect–failure' or 'error–fault–failure' sequence. A mistake is the result of a person – it introduces a defect into the work-product, resulting in a failure when the observed behaviour is not as expected. Other options do not have the correct terms.

E11. The correct answer is b.
It is not possible to show that there are no defects in the software (a). Testing does not decide when software is implemented (c), although the information from testing might help others decide. Option d is not applicable.

E12. The correct answer is b.
The definitions in b are applicable for retesting and regression testing. If you are unsure, revisit the section in the chapter that goes through these definitions.

E13. The correct answer is a.
Testing has as a central aim to uncover as many defects as possible. Quality improves as these are uncovered and investigated (and in many cases, fixed). None of the other answers encompasses this central point.

E14. The correct answer is d.
There being no high priority defects, b is not an indication of enough testing – this might be the case when no tests have been run (and could be the case when the first 10 per cent of tests have been completed). Option a (all tests being run) can be discounted – what about any tests that failed? All high priority tests could have been successfully run, but **all** the low priority tests might have failed. Option d gives an indication of enough testing – sufficient information is available to enable the sponsors (not 'testers') to make a decision based on the information provided.

E15. The correct answer is d.
Verifying that the test environment has been set up is part of the test implementation and execution stage of the fundamental test process.

E16. The correct answer is c.
Testers bring a sense of 'independence', and do not have the same assumptions as any developer who created the software.

E17. The correct answer is d.
Other answers give objectives for other phases of testing: finding as many defects as possible is development testing; giving information to assess the risk of releasing is acceptance testing; and checking no defects have been introduced during the development of a change is maintenance testing.

E18. The correct answer is b.
The other options help good communication within the overall team.

E19. The correct answer is a.
All other answers contain something that is more appropriate to 'testing' rather than 'debugging'.

2 LIFE CYCLES

Angelina Samaroo

INTRODUCTION

In the previous chapter, we looked at testing as a concept – what it is and why we should do it. In this chapter we will look at testing as part of overall software development. Clearly testing does not take place in isolation; there must be a product first.

We will refer to work-products and products. A work-product is an intermediate deliverable required to create the final product. Work-products can be documentation or code. The code and associated documentation will become the product when the system is declared ready for release. In software development, work-products are generally created in a series of defined stages, from capturing a customer requirement, to creating the system, to delivering the system. These stages are usually shown as steps within a software development life cycle.

In this chapter we will look at two life cycle models – sequential and iterative. For each one, the testing process will be described, and the objectives at each stage of testing explained.

Finally, we will look at the different types of testing that can take place throughout the development life cycle.

Learning objectives

The learning objectives for each section are as follows. Each section has been categorised as K2 overall, but individual K1 elements are shown where applicable.

Software development models (K2)

- Understanding of the relationship between development, test activities and work-products in the development life cycle, giving examples based on project and product characteristics and context.

- Recognition that software development models must be adapted to the context of project and product characteristics. (K1)

- Recall of reasons for different levels of testing, and characteristics of good testing in any life cycle model. (K1)

Test levels (K2)

- Be able to compare the different levels of testing, considering for each the:
  - Major objectives.
  - Typical objectives of testing.
  - Typical targets of testing (e.g. functional or structural) and related work-products.
  - People who test.
  - Types of defects and failures to be identified.

Test types (K2)

- Comparison of the four requirement types (functional, non-functional, structural and change-related) by example.
- Recognition that functional and structural tests can occur at any level. (K1)
- Identification and description of non-functional test types based on non-functional requirements.
- Identification and description of test types based on the analysis of a software system's structure or architecture.
- Explanation of the purpose of confirmation and regression testing.

Maintenance testing (K2)

- Recognition of differences between testing existing systems and new systems, considering:
  - Test types
  - Triggers for testing
  - Amount of testing
- Recall of reasons for maintenance testing (K1):
  - Modification
  - Migration
  - Retirement
- Description of the role of regression testing and impact analysis in maintenance testing.

Self-assessment questions

The following questions have been designed to assess the reader's current knowledge of this topic. The answers are provided at the end of the chapter.

Question SA1 (K2)
Which of the following is true about the V-model?

    a.   It has the same steps as the waterfall model for software development.

    b.   It is referred to as a cyclical model for software development.

    c.   It enables the production of a working version of the system as early as possible.

    d.   It enables test planning to start as early as possible.

Question SA2 (K2)
Which of the following is true of iterative development?

    a.   It uses fully defined specifications from the start.

    b.   It involves the users in the testing throughout.

    c.   Changes to the system do not need to be formally recorded.

    d.   It is not suitable for developing websites.

Question SA3 (K1)
Which of the following is in the correct order (typically)?

    a.   Unit testing, system testing, acceptance testing, maintenance testing.

    b.   System testing, unit testing, acceptance testing, maintenance testing.

    c.   Acceptance testing, system testing, maintenance testing, unit testing.

    d.   Unit testing, maintenance testing, system testing, acceptance testing.

SOFTWARE DEVELOPMENT MODELS

A development life cycle for a software product involves capturing the initial requirements from the customer, expanding on these to provide the detail required for code production, writing the code and testing the product, ready for release.

A simple development model is shown in Figure 2.1. This is known traditionally as the waterfall model.

Figure 2.1 Waterfall model

The waterfall model in Figure 2.1 shows the steps in sequence where the customer requirements are progressively refined to the point where coding can take place. This type of model is often referred to as a linear or sequential model. Each work-product or activity is completed before moving on to the next.

In the waterfall model, testing is carried out once the code has been fully developed. Once this is completed, a decision can be made on whether the product can be released into the live environment.

This model for development shows how a fully tested product can be created, but it has a significant drawback: what happens if the product fails the tests? Let us look at a simple case study.

CASE STUDY – DEVELOPMENT PROCESS

Let us consider the manufacture of a smartphone. Smartphones have become an essential part of daily life for many. They must be robust enough to withstand the rigours of being thrown into bags or on floors and must be able to respond quickly to commands.

Many phones now have touchscreens. This means that the apps on the phone must be accessible via a tap on the screen. This is done via a touchscreen driver. The driver is a piece of software that sits between the screen (hardware) and the apps (software), allowing the app to be accessed from a touch on an icon on the screen.

If a waterfall model were to be used to manufacture and ship a touchscreen phone, then all functionality would be tested at the very end, just prior to shipping.

If it is found that the phone can be dropped from a reasonable height without breaking, but that the touchscreen driver is defective, then the phone will have failed in its core required functionality. This is a very late stage in the life cycle to uncover such a fault.

In the waterfall model, the testing at the end serves as a quality check. The product can be accepted or rejected at this point. In the smartphone manufacturing example, this model could be adopted to check that the phone casings after manufacture are crack free, rejecting those that have failed.

In software development, however, it is unlikely that we can simply reject the parts of the system found to be defective, and release the rest. The nature of software function- ality is such that removal of software is often not a clean-cut activity – this action could cause other areas to function incorrectly. It might even cause the system to become unusable. If the touchscreen driver is not functioning correctly, then some of the apps might not be accessible via a tap on the icon. On a touchscreen phone this would be an intolerable fault in the live environment.

What is needed is a process that assures quality throughout the development life cycle. At every stage, a check should be made that the work-product for that stage meets its objectives. This is a key point, work-product evaluation taking place at the point where the product has been declared complete by its creator. If the work-product passes its evaluation (test), we can progress to the next stage in confidence. In addition, finding problems at the point of creation should make fixing any problems cheaper than fixing them at a later stage. This is the cost escalation model, described in **Chapter 1**.

The checks throughout the life cycle include verification and validation.

> **Verification** – checks that the work-product meets the requirements set out for it. An example of this would be to ensure that a website being built follows the guidelines for making websites usable by as many people as possible. Verification helps to ensure that we are building the product in the right way.
>
> **Validation** – changes the focus of work-product evaluation to evaluation against user needs. This means ensuring that the behaviour of the work-product matches the customer needs as defined for the project. For example, for the same website above, the guidelines may have been written with people familiar with websites in mind. It may be that this website is also intended for novice users. Validation would include these users checking that they too can use the website easily. Validation helps to ensure that we are building the right product as far as the users are concerned.

There are two types of development model that facilitate early work-product evaluation.

The first is an extension to the waterfall model, known as the V-model. The second is a cyclical model, where the coding stage often begins once the initial user needs have been captured. Cyclical models are often referred to as iterative models.

We will consider first the V-model.

V-model (sequential development model)

There are many variants of the V-model. One of these is shown in Figure 2.2.

Figure 2.2 V-model for software development

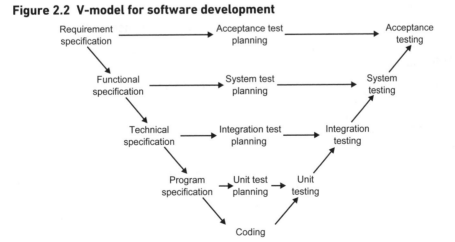

As for the waterfall model, the left-hand side of the model focuses on elaborating the initial requirements, providing successively more technical detail as the development progresses. In the model shown, these are:

- Requirement specification – capturing of user needs.

- Functional specification – definition of functions required to meet user needs.

- Technical specification – technical design of functions identified in the functional specification.

- Program specification – detailed design of each module or unit to be built to meet required functionality.

These specifications could be reviewed to check for the following:

- Conformance to the previous work-product (so in the case of the functional specification, verification would include a check against the requirement specification).

- That there is sufficient detail for the subsequent work-product to be built correctly (again, for the functional specification, this would include a check that there is sufficient information in order to create the technical specification).

- That it is testable – is the detail provided sufficient for testing the work-product?

Formal methods for reviewing documents are discussed in **Chapter 3**.

The middle of the V-model shows that planning for testing should start with each work-product. Thus, using the requirement specification as an example, acceptance testing would be planned for, right at the start of the development. Test planning is discussed in more detail in **Chapter 5**.

The right-hand side focuses on the testing activities. For each work-product, a testing activity is identified. These are shown in Figure 2.2:

- Testing against the requirement specification takes place at the acceptance testing stage.

- Testing against the functional specification takes place at the system testing stage.

- Testing against the technical specification takes place at the integration testing stage.

- Testing against the program specification takes place at the unit testing stage.

This allows testing to be concentrated on the detail provided in each work-product, so that defects can be identified as early as possible in the life cycle, when the work-product has been created. The different stages of testing are discussed later.

Remembering that each stage must be completed before the next one can be started, this approach to software development pushes validation of the system by the user representatives right to the end of the life cycle. If the customer needs were not captured accurately in the requirement specification, or if they change, then these issues may not be uncovered until the user testing is carried out. As we saw in **Chapter 1**, fixing problems at this stage could be very costly; in addition, it is possible that the project could be cancelled altogether.

Iterative–incremental development models

Let us now look at a different model for software development – iterative development. This is one where the requirements do not need to be fully defined before coding can start. Instead, a working version of the product is built, in a series of stages, or iterations – hence the name iterative or incremental development. Each stage encompasses requirements definition, design, code and test. This is shown diagrammatically in Figure 2.3.

Figure 2.3 Iterative development

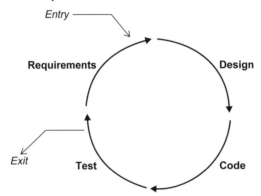

This type of development is often referred to as cyclical – we go 'round the development cycle a number of times', within the project. The project will have a defined timescale and cost. Within this, the cycles will be defined. Each cycle will also have a defined timescale and cost. The cycles are commonly referred to as time-boxes. For each time-box, a require-ment is defined and a version of the code is produced, which will allow testing by the user representatives. At the end of each time-box, a decision is made on what extra functionality needs to be created for the next iteration. This process is then repeated until a fully working system has been produced.

A key feature of this type of development is the involvement of user representatives in the testing. Having the users represented throughout minimises the risk of developing an unsatisfactory product. The user representatives are empowered to request changes to the software, to meet their needs.

This approach to software development can pose problems, however.

The lack of formal documentation makes it difficult to test. To counter this, developers may use test-driven development. This is where functional tests are written first, and code is then created and tested. It is reworked until it passes the tests.

In addition, the working environment may be such that developers make any changes required, without formally recording them. This approach could mean that changes cannot be traced back to the requirements or to the parts of the software that have changed. Thus, traceability as the project progresses is reduced. To mitigate this, a robust process must be put in place at the start of the project to manage these changes (often part of a configuration management process – this is discussed further in **Chapter 5**).

Another issue associated with changes is the amount of testing required to ensure that implementation of the changes does not cause unintended changes to other parts of the software (this is called regression testing, discussed later in this chapter).

Forms of iterative development include prototyping, Rapid Application Development (RAD), the Dynamic Systems Development Methodology (DSDM), the Rational Unified Process (RUP) and Agile software development.

Agile methods of developing software have gained significant ground in recent years. Organisations across sectors have embraced this collaborative way of working and many qualifications focusing on Agile methodologies now exist. The syllabus for this qualification does not dwell on Agile; however, for completeness of learning, a summary will now be provided.

The Agile development methodology is supported through the Agile Alliance, www.agilealliance.org. The alliance has created an Agile manifesto with four points, supported by 12 principles. The essence of these is to espouse the value of adopting a can-do and collaborative approach to creating a product. The idea is that the development teams work closely with the business, responding to their needs at the time, rather than attempting to adhere to a contract for requirements that might well need to be changed prior to the launch date. Many examples can be drawn to suggest that this is a suitable way of working. Going back to our smartphone example, there are many well-known phone manufacturers who failed to move with consumer demands, costing them significant market share.

A popular framework for Agile is Scrum. Scrum is not an acronym; it was taken from the game of rugby. In rugby the team huddles to agree tactics; the ball is then passed back and forth until a sprint to the touchline is attempted. In Scrum, there is a daily stand-up meeting to agree tactics for the day; an agreed set of functionality to be delivered at the end of a time-box (Sprint); periodic reviews of functionality by the customer representatives; and a team retrospective to reflect on the previous Sprint in order to improve on the next. In Agile the term 'user story' is common when referring to requirements, as is the term 'backlog' when referring to a set of requirements or tasks for a particular Sprint.

The ISTQB now offer a qualification in Agile testing as an extension to this Foundation in software testing. Further information can be found at www.istqb.org

TEST LEVELS

For both types of development, testing plays a significant role. Testing helps to ensure that the work-products are being developed in the right way (verification) and that the product will meet the user needs (validation).

Characteristics of good testing across the development life cycle include:

- Early test design – in the V-model, we saw that test planning begins with the specification documents. This activity is part of the fundamental test process discussed in **Chapter 1**. After test planning, the documents are analysed and test cases designed. This approach ensures that testing starts with the development of the requirements, that is a proactive approach to testing is undertaken. Proactive approaches to test design are discussed further in **Chapter 5**. As we saw in iterative development, test-driven development may be adopted, pushing testing to the front of the development activity.

- Each work-product is tested – in the V-model, each document on the left is tested by an activity on the right. Each specification document is called the test basis, that is it is the basis on which tests are created. In iterative development, each release is tested before moving on to the next.

- Testers are involved in reviewing requirements before they are released – in the V-model, testers are invited to review all documents from a testing perspective. Techniques for reviewing documents are outlined in **Chapter 3**.

In Figure 2.2, the test stages of the V-model are shown. They are often called test levels. The term test level provides an indication of the focus of the testing, and the types of problems it is likely to uncover. The typical levels of testing are:

- Unit (component) testing.
- Integration testing.
- System testing.
- Acceptance testing.

Each of these test levels will include tests designed to uncover problems specifically at that stage of development. These levels of testing can also be applied to iterative development. In addition, the levels may change depending on the system. For instance, if the system includes some software developed by external parties, or bought off the shelf, acceptance testing on these may be conducted before testing the system as a whole.

Let us now look at these levels of testing in more detail.

Unit (component) testing

Before testing of the code can start, clearly the code has to be written. This is shown at the bottom of the V-model. Generally, the code is written in component parts, or units. The units are usually constructed in isolation, for integration at a later stage. Units are also called programs, modules or components.

Unit testing is intended to ensure that the code written for the unit meets its specification, prior to its integration with other units.

In addition to checking conformance to the program specification, unit testing also verifies that all of the code that has been written for the unit can be executed. Instead of using the specification to decide on inputs and expected outputs, the developer uses the code that has been written for this. Testing based on code is discussed in detail in **Chapter 4**. Thus the test bases for unit testing can include: the component requirements; the detailed design; the code itself.

Unit testing requires access to the code being tested. Thus test objects (i.e. what is under test) can be the components, the programs, data conversion/migration programs and database modules. Unit testing is often supported by a unit test framework (e.g. Kent Beck's Smalltalk Testing Framework: http://xprogramming.com/testfram.htm). In addition, debugging tools are often used.

An approach to unit testing is called test-driven development. As its name suggests, test cases are written first, and then the code is built, tested and changed until the unit passes its tests. This is an iterative approach to unit testing.

Unit testing is usually performed by the developer who wrote the code (and who may also have written the program specification). Defects found and fixed during unit testing are often not recorded.

Integration testing

Once the units have been written, the next stage is to put them together to create the system. This is called integration. It involves building something large from a number of smaller pieces.

The purpose of integration testing is to expose defects in the interfaces and in the inter-actions between integrated components or systems.

Thus the test bases for integration testing can include: the software and system design; a diagram of the system architecture; workflows; and use cases.

The test objects are essentially the interface code. This can include subsystems' data-base implementations.

Before integration testing can be planned, an integration strategy is required. This involves making decisions on how the system will be put together prior to testing. There are three commonly quoted integration strategies, as follows.

Big-bang integration

This is where all units are linked at once, resulting in a complete system. When the testing of this system is conducted, it is difficult to isolate any errors found, because attention is not paid to verifying the interfaces across individual units.

This type of integration is generally regarded as a poor choice of integration strategy. It introduces the risk that problems may be discovered late in the project, where they are more expensive to fix.

Top-down integration

This is where the system is built in stages, starting with components that call other components. Components that call others are usually placed above those that are called. Top-down integration testing permits the tester to evaluate component inter-faces, starting with those at the 'top'.

Let us look at the diagram in Figure 2.4 to explain this further.

The control structure of a program can be represented in a chart. In Figure 2.4, compo-nent 1 can call components 2 and 3. Thus in the structure, component 1 is placed above components 2 and 3. Component 2 can call components 4 and 5. Component 3 can call components 6 and 7. Thus in the structure, components 2 and 3 are placed above com-ponents 4 and 5 and components 6 and 7, respectively.

Figure 2.4 Top-down control structure

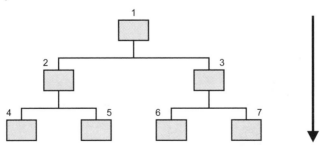

In this chart, the order of integration might be:

- 1,2
- 1,3
- 2,4
- 2,5
- 3,6
- 3,7

Top-down integration testing requires that the interactions of each component must be tested when it is built. Those lower down in the hierarchy may not have been built or integrated yet. In Figure 2.4, in order to test component 1's interaction with component 2, it may be necessary to replace component 2 with a substitute since component 2 may not have been integrated yet. This is done by creating a skeletal implementation of the component, called a stub. A stub is a passive component, called by other components. In this example, stubs may be used to replace components 4 and 5, when testing component 2.

The use of stubs is commonplace in top-down integration, replacing components not yet integrated.

Bottom-up integration

This is the opposite of top-down integration and the components are integrated in a bottom-up order. This is shown in Figure 2.5.

The integration order might be:

- 4,2
- 5,2
- 6,3
- 7,3

Figure 2.5 Bottom-up integration

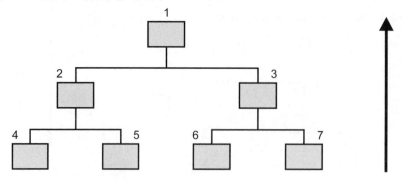

- 2,1
- 3,1

So, in bottom-up integration, components 4–7 would be integrated before components 2 and 3. In this case, the components that may not be in place are those that actively call other components. As in top-down integration testing, they must be replaced by specially written components. When these special components call other components, they are called drivers. They are so called because, in the functioning program, they are active, controlling other components.

Components 2 and 3 could be replaced by drivers when testing components 4–7. They are generally more complex than stubs.

There may be more than one level of integration testing. For example:

- Component integration testing focuses on the interactions between software components and is done after component (unit) testing. This type of integration testing is usually carried out by developers.

- System integration testing focuses on the interactions between different systems and may be done after system testing each individual system. For example, a trading system in an investment bank will interact with the stock exchange to get the latest prices for its stocks and shares on the international market. This type of integration testing is usually carried out by testers.

It should be noted that testing at system integration level carries extra elements of risk. These can include: at a technical level, cross-platform issues; at an operational level, business workflow issues; and at a business level, risks associated with ownership of regression issues associated with change in one system possibly having a knock-on effect on other systems.

System testing

Having checked that the components all work together at unit level, the next step is to consider the functionality from an end-to-end perspective. This activity is called system testing.

System testing is necessary because many of the criteria for test selection at unit and integration testing result in the production of a set of test cases that are unrepresentative of the operating conditions in the live environment. Thus testing at these levels is unlikely to reveal errors due to interactions across the whole system, or those due to environmental issues.

System testing serves to correct this imbalance by focusing on the behaviour of the whole system/product as defined by the scope of a development project or programme, in a representative live environment. It is usually carried out by a team that is independent of the development process. The benefit of this independence is that an objective assessment of the system can be made, based on the specifications as written, and not the code.

In the V-model, the behaviour required of the system is documented in the functional specification. It defines what must be built to meet the requirements of the system.

The functional specification should contain definitions of both the functional and non-functional requirements of the system.

A functional requirement is a requirement that specifies a function that a system or system component must perform. Functional requirements can be specific to a system. For instance, you would expect to be able to search for flights on a travel agent's website, whereas you would visit your online bank to check that you have sufficient funds to pay for the flight.

Thus functional requirements provide detail on what the application being developed will do.

Non-functional system testing looks at those aspects that are important but not directly related to what functions the system performs. These tend to be generic requirements, which can be applied to many different systems. In the example above, you can expect that both systems will respond to your inputs in a reasonable time frame, for instance. Typically, these requirements will consider both normal operations and behaviour under exceptional circumstances.

Thus non-functional requirements detail how the application will perform in use.

Examples of non-functional requirements include:

- Installability – installation procedures.
- Maintainability – ability to introduce changes to the system.
- Performance – expected normal behaviour.
- Load handling – behaviour of the system under increasing load.
- Stress handling – behaviour at the upper limits of system capability.
- Portability – use on different operating platforms.
- Recovery – recovery procedures on failure.
- Reliability – ability of the software to perform its required functions over time.
- Usability – ease with which users can engage with the system.

Note that security and interoperability with specific systems are regarded as functional requirements in this syllabus.

The amount of testing required at system testing, however, can be influenced by the amount of testing carried out (if any) at the previous stages. In addition, the amount of testing advisable would also depend on the amount of verification carried out on the requirements (this is discussed further in **Chapter 3**).

Test bases for system testing can include: system and software requirement specifications; use cases; functional specifications; risk analysis reports; and system, user and operation manuals.

The test object will generally be the system under test.

Acceptance testing

The next step after system testing is often acceptance testing. The purpose of acceptance testing is to provide the end users with confidence that the system will function according to their expectations. Referring once more to the V-model, acceptance testing will be carried out using the requirement specification as a basis for test.

The requirement specification is typically the first document to be written, after initial capture of the user requirement. An example of a requirement could be to create a website that enables users to buy airline tickets online.

The subsequent documentation (functional, technical and program specifications) will expand on this in increasing levels of detail, in order to facilitate development of the system, as seen earlier. Thus, it is paramount that these requirements are fully documented and correct before further development activity is carried out. Again, this is the V-model approach. You may well be aware that having such an ideal set of requirements is a rare thing. This does not mean, however, that the need for correctness and completeness should be ignored. Techniques for verifying requirements are given in **Chapter 3**.

As for system testing, no reference is made to the code from which the system is constructed. Thus the test bases can include: user requirements; system requirements; use cases; business processes; and risk analysis reports.

The test objects can include: the fully integrated system; forms and reports produced by the system.

Unlike system testing, however, the testing conducted here should be independent of any other testing carried out. Its key purpose is to demonstrate system conformance to, for example, the customer requirements and operational and maintenance processes. For instance, acceptance testing may assess the system's readiness for deployment and use.

Acceptance testing is often the responsibility of the customers or users of a system, although other project team members may be involved as well.

Typical forms of acceptance testing include the following:

- User acceptance testing – testing by user representatives to check that the system meets their business needs. This can include factory acceptance testing, where the system is tested by the users before moving it to their own site. Site acceptance testing could then be performed by the users at their own site.
- Operational acceptance testing – often called operational readiness testing. This involves checking that the processes and procedures are in place to allow the system to be used and maintained. This can include checking:
  - back-up facilities;
  - procedures for disaster recovery;
  - training for end users;

- maintenance procedures;
- data load and migration tasks;
- security procedures.

- Contract and regulation acceptance testing

  - Contract acceptance testing – sometimes the criteria for accepting a system are documented in a contract. Testing is then conducted to check that these criteria have been met, before the system is accepted.

  - Regulation acceptance testing – in some industries, systems must meet governmental, legal or safety standards. Examples of these are the defence, banking and pharmaceutical industries.

- Alpha and beta testing

  - Alpha testing takes place at the developer's site – the operational system is tested while still at the developer's site by internal staff, before release to external customers. Note that testing here is still independent of the development team.

  - Beta testing takes place at the customer's site – the operational system is tested by a group of customers, who use the product at their own locations and provide feedback, before the system is released. This is often called 'field testing'.

CHECK OF UNDERSTANDING

1. In the V-model, which document would be used as the test basis for unit testing?
2. Describe three typical integration strategies.
3. Identify why stubs and drivers are usually used.
4. In the V-model, which document is used as the test basis for system testing?
5. Compare a functional requirement with a non-functional requirement.
6. List three non-functional requirements.
7. What is the purpose of acceptance testing?
8. In the V-model, what is the test basis for acceptance testing?
9. Identify three types of acceptance testing.

TEST TYPES

In the last section we saw that each test level has specific testing objectives. In this section we will look at the types of testing required to meet these objectives.

Test types fall into the following categories:

- Functional testing.
- Non-functional testing.
- Structural testing.
- Testing after code has been changed.

To facilitate different types of testing, models may be used as follows:

- Functional testing: process flows; state transition models; security threat models; plain language specifications.
- Non-functional testing: performance model; usability model.
- Structural testing: control flow model; menu structure model.

Functional testing

As you saw in the section on system testing, functional testing looks at the specific functionality of a system, such as searching for flights on a website, or perhaps calculating employee pay correctly using a payroll system. Note that security testing is a functional test type. Another type of functional testing is interoperability testing – this evaluates the capability of the system to interact with other specified components.

Functional testing is also called specification-based testing: testing against a specification.

Non-functional testing

This is where the behavioural aspects of the system are tested. As you saw in the section on system testing, examples are usability, performance under load and stress, among others. As for functional testing, these requirements are usually documented in a functional specification. Thus, mainly black-box testing techniques are used for this type of testing.

These tests can be referenced against a quality model, such as the one defined in ISO 9126 *Software engineering – Product Quality*. Note that a detailed understanding of this standard is not required for the exam.

Structural testing

This type of testing is used to measure how much testing has been carried out. In functional testing, this could be the number of functional requirements tested against the total number of requirements.

In structural testing, we change our measure to focus on the structural aspects of the system. This could be the code itself, or an architectural definition of the system. We want to do this to check the thoroughness of the testing carried out on the system that has actually been built. A common measure is to look at how much of the actual code that has been written has been tested. Further detail on code coverage measures is provided in **Chapter 4**.

Note that structural testing can be carried out at any test level.

Testing related to changes

The previous sections detail the testing to be carried out at the different stages in the development life cycle. At any level of testing, it can be expected that defects will be discovered. When these are found and fixed, the quality of the system being delivered is improved.

After a defect is detected and fixed the changed software should be retested to confirm that the problem has been successfully removed. This is called retesting or confirmation testing. Note that when the developer removes the defect, this activity is called debugging, which is not a testing activity. Testing finds a defect, debugging fixes it.

The unchanged software should also be retested to ensure that no additional defects have been introduced as a result of changes to the software. This is called regression testing. Regression testing should also be carried out if the environment has changed.

Regression testing involves the creation of a set of tests which serve to demonstrate that the system works as expected. These are run again many times over a testing project, when changes are made, as discussed above. This repetition of tests makes regression testing suitable for automation in many cases. Test automation is covered in detail in **Chapter 6**.

CHECK OF UNDERSTANDING

Which of the following is correct?

    a. Regression testing checks that a problem has been successfully addressed, while confirmation testing is done at the end of each release.

    b. Regression testing checks that all problems have been successfully addressed, while confirmation testing refers to testing individual fixes.

    c. Regression testing checks that fixes to errors do not introduce unexpected functionality into the system, while confirmation testing checks that fixes have been successful.

    d. Regression testing checks that all required testing has been carried out, while confirmation testing checks that each test is complete.

MAINTENANCE TESTING

For many projects (though not all) the system is eventually released into the live environment. Hopefully, once deployed, it will be in service as long as intended, perhaps for years or decades.

During this deployment, it may become necessary to change the system. Changes may be due to:

- Additional features being required.
- The system being migrated to a new operating platform.

- The system being retired – data may need to be migrated or archived.
- Planned upgrade to commercial off-the-shelf (COTS)-based systems.
- New faults being found requiring fixing (these can be 'hot fixes').

Once changes have been made to the system, they will need to be tested (retesting), and it also will be necessary to conduct regression testing to ensure that the rest of the system has not been adversely affected by the changes. Testing that takes place on a system which is in operation in the live environment is called maintenance testing.

When changes are made to migrate from one platform to another, the system should also be tested in its new environment. When migration includes data being transferred in from another application, then conversion testing also becomes necessary.

As we have suggested, all changes must be tested, and, ideally, all of the system should be subject to regression testing. In practice, this may not be feasible or cost-effective. An understanding of the parts of the system that could be affected by the changes could reduce the amount of regression testing required. Working this out is termed impact analysis, that is analysing the impact of the changes on the system.

Impact analysis can be difficult for a system that has already been released. This is because the specifications may be out of date (or non-existent), and/or the original development team may have moved on to other projects, or left the organisation altogether.

CHECK OF UNDERSTANDING

1. What is the purpose of maintenance testing?
2. Give examples of when maintenance testing would be necessary.
3. What is meant by the term impact analysis?

SUMMARY

In this chapter we have explored the role of testing within the software development life cycle. We have looked at the basic steps in any development model, from understanding customer needs to delivery of the final product. These were built up into formally recognisable models, using distinct approaches to software development.

The V-model, as we have seen, is a stepwise approach to software development, meaning that each stage in the model must be completed before the next stage can be started, if a strict implementation of the model is required. This is often the case in safety-critical developments. The V-model typically has the following work-products and activities:

1. Requirement specification.
2. Functional specification.
3. Technical specification.
4. Program specification.
5. Code.

6. Unit testing.
7. Integration testing.
8. System testing.
9. Acceptance testing.

Work-products 1–5 are subject to verification, to ensure that they have been created following the rules set out. For example, the program specification is assessed to ensure that it meets the requirements set out in the technical specification, and that it contains sufficient detail for the code to be produced.

In activities 6–9, the code is assessed progressively for compliance to user needs, as captured in the specifications for each level.

An iterative model for development has fewer steps, but involves the user from the start. These steps are typically:

1. Define iteration requirement.
2. Build iteration.
3. Test iteration.

This sequence is repeated for each iteration until an acceptable product has been developed.

An explanation of each of the test levels in the V-model was given. For unit testing the focus is the code within the unit itself, for integration testing it is the interfacing between units, for system testing it is the end-to-end functionality, and for acceptance testing it is the user perspective.

An explanation of test types was then given and by combining alternative test types with test levels we can construct a test approach that matches a given system and a given set of test objectives very closely. The techniques associated with test types are covered in detail in **Chapter 4** and the creation of a test approach is covered in **Chapter 5**.

Finally, we looked at the testing required when a system has been released, but a change has become necessary – maintenance testing. We discussed the need for impact analysis in deciding how much regression testing to do after the changes have been implemented. This can pose an added challenge, if the requirements associated with the system are missing or have been poorly defined.

In the next chapter, techniques for improving requirements will be discussed.

Example examination questions with answers

E1. K1 question
Which of the following is usually the test basis for integration testing?

    a.   Program specification.

    b.   Functional specification.

    c.   Technical specification.

    d.   Requirement specification.

E2. K2 question
A top-down development strategy affects which level of testing most?

    a.   Component testing.

    b.   Integration testing.

    c.   System testing.

    d.   User acceptance testing.

E3. K2 question
Which of the following is a non-functional requirement?

    a.   The system will enable users to buy books.

    b.   The system will allow users to return books.

    c.   The system will ensure security of the customer details.

    d.   The system will allow up to 100 users to log in at the same time.

E4. K1 question
Which of the following are examples of iterative development models?

    i.   V-model.

    ii.   Rapid Application Development model.

    iii.   Waterfall model.

    iv.   Agile development model.

    a.   i and ii.

    b.   ii and iii.

    c.   ii and iv.

    d.   iii and iv.

E5. K2 question
Which of the following statements are true?

i. For every development activity there is a corresponding testing activity.
ii. Each test level has the same test objectives.
iii. The analysis and design of tests for a given test level should begin after the corresponding development activity.
iv. Testers should be involved in reviewing documents as soon as drafts are available in the development life cycle.

a. i and ii.
b. iii and iv.
c. ii and iii.
d. i and iv.

E6. K1 question
Which of the following is not true of regression testing?

a. It can be carried out at each stage of the life cycle.
b. It serves to demonstrate that the changed software works as intended.
c. It serves to demonstrate that software has not been unintentionally changed.
d. It is often automated.

Answers to questions in the chapter

SA1.   The correct answer is d.
SA2.   The correct answer is b.
SA3.   The correct answer is a.

Answers to example questions

E1. The correct answer is c.
Option a is used for unit testing. Option b is used for system testing and option d is used for acceptance testing.

E2. The correct answer is b.
The development strategy will affect component testing (option a), in so far as it cannot be tested unless it has been built. Options c and d require the system to have been delivered; at these points the development strategy followed is not important to the tester. Option b needs knowledge of the development strategy in order to determine the order in which components will be integrated and tested.

E3. The correct answer is d.
The other options are functional requirements. Note that security is regarded as a functional requirement in this syllabus.

E4. The correct answer is c.
The other two models are sequential models.

E5. The correct answer is d.
Option ii is incorrect: each test level has a different objective. Option iii is also incorrect: test analysis and design should start once the documentation has been completed.

E6. The correct answer is b.
This is a definition of confirmation testing. The other three options are true of regression testing.

3 STATIC TESTING

Geoff Thompson

INTRODUCTION

This chapter provides an introduction to an important area of software testing – static techniques. Static techniques test software without executing it. They are important because they can find errors and defects before code is executed and therefore earlier in the life cycle of a project, making corrections easier and cheaper to achieve than for the same defects found during test execution. Review techniques are central to the static testing approach, and in this chapter we will look at the alternative types of review and how they fit with the test process that was defined in **Chapter 2**.

The chapter also considers static analysis of the developed code, which is a technique for examining code without executing it to identify actual and potential problems. With the advances in coding languages and the legacy status of many older systems, static testing is often impossible to achieve manually, so our focus will therefore be on the types of static testing that can be completed using tools. In this chapter we focus on the techniques of static testing; the tools that are referred to are described in **Chapter 6**.

Learning objectives

The learning objectives for this chapter are listed below. You can confirm that you have achieved these by using the self-assessment questions at the start of the chapter, the 'Check of understanding' boxes distributed throughout the text, and the example examination questions provided at the end of the chapter. The chapter summary will remind you of the key ideas.

The sections are allocated a K number to represent the level of understanding required for that section; where an individual element has a lower K number than the section as a whole this is indicated for that topic; for an explanation of the K numbers see the **Introduction**.

Static techniques and the test process (K2)

- Recognise software work-products that can be examined by the different static techniques. (K1)
- Describe the importance and value of considering static techniques for the assessment of software work-products.

- Explain the difference between static and dynamic techniques, considering objectives, types of defects to be identified, and the role of these techniques within the software life cycle.

Review process (K2)

- Recall the phases, roles and responsibilities of a typical formal review. (K1)
- Explain the differences between different types of review: informal review, technical review, walkthrough and inspection.
- Explain the factors for successful performance of reviews.

Static analysis by tools (K2)

- Recall typical defects and errors identified by static analysis and compare them with reviews and dynamic testing. (K1)
- Describe, using examples, the typical benefits of static analysis.
- List typical code and design defects that may be identified by static analysis tools. (K1)

Self-assessment questions

The following questions have been designed to enable you to check your current level of understanding for the topics in this chapter. The answers are at the end of the chapter.

Question SA1 (K1)
One of the roles in a review is that of moderator. Which of the following best describes this role?

    a. Plans the review, runs the review meeting and ensures that follow-up activities are completed.

    b. Allocates time in the plan, decides which reviews will take place and that the benefits are delivered.

    c. Writes the document to be reviewed, agrees that the document can be reviewed, and updates the document with any changes.

    d. Documents all issues raised in the review meeting, records problems and open points.

Question SA2 (K2)
Which of the following statements are correct for walkthroughs?

    i. Often led by the author.

    ii. Documented and defined results.

    iii. All participants have defined roles.

    iv. Used to aid learning.

    v. Main purpose is to find defects.

    a. i and v are correct.

    b. ii and iii are correct.

    c. i and iv are correct.

    d. iii and iv are correct.

Question SA3 (K1)
What do static analysis tools analyse?

    a.   Design.
    b.   Test cases.
    c.   Requirements.
    d.   Program code.

BACKGROUND TO STATIC TECHNIQUES

Static testing techniques are those techniques that test software and work-products without executing the code. Typically, this includes requirements or specification documents, and the testing of code without actually executing it. The first of these is known as a review and is typically used to find and remove errors and ambiguities in documents before they are used in the development process, thus reducing one source of defects in the code; the second is known as static analysis, and it enables code to be analysed for structural defects or systematic programming weaknesses that may lead to defects.

Static techniques find the causes of failures rather than the failure itself, which would be found during test execution.

Reviews are normally completed manually; static analysis is normally completed automatically using tools. The tools used for static analysis will be described in **Chapter 6**.

REVIEWS AND THE TEST PROCESS

A review is a systematic examination of a document by one or more people with the main aim of finding and removing errors. Giving a draft document to a colleague to read is the simplest example of a review, and one which can yield a larger crop of errors than often anticipated (see **Chapter 5** regarding 'world view' to understand why).

Reviews can be used to test anything that is written or typed; this can include documents such as requirement specifications, system designs, code, test plans and test cases. Reviews represent the first form of testing that can take place during a software development life cycle, since the documents such as design documentation – in Agile development this would mean user stories – should be ready long before the code has been written. The practice of testing specification documents by reviewing them early on in the life cycle helps to identify defects before they become part of the executable code, and so makes those defects cheaper and easier to remove. The same defect, if found during dynamic test execution, would incur the extra cost of initially creating and testing the defective code, diagnosing the source of the defect, correcting the problem and rewriting the code to eliminate the defect.

Reviewing code against development standards can also prevent defects from appearing in test execution, though in this case, because the code has already been written, not all the additional costs and delays are avoided.

Benefits of finding defects early in the life cycle include the following:

- Development productivity can be improved and timescales reduced because the correction of defects in early work-products will help to ensure that those work-products are clear and unambiguous. This should enable a developer to move more quickly through the process of writing code. Also, if defects are removed before they become executable code there will be fewer errors to find and fix during test execution.

- Testing costs and time can be reduced by removing the main delays in test execution, which arise when defects are found after they have become failures and the tester has to wait for a fix to be delivered. By reviewing the code and removing defects before they become failures the tester can move more swiftly through test execution.

- Reductions in lifetime costs can be achieved because fewer defects in the final software ensure that ongoing support costs will be lower.

- Improved communication results as authors and their peers discuss and refine any ambiguous content discovered during review to ensure that all involved understand exactly what is being delivered.

The types of defects most typically found by reviews are:

- Deviations from standards either internally defined and managed or regulatory/ legally defined by government or perhaps a trade organisation, for example the Motor Industry Software Reliability Association (MISRA) standards for the testing of technology in a car.

- Requirements defects – for example, the requirements are ambiguous, or there are missing elements.

- Design defects – for example, the design does not match the requirements.

- Insufficient maintainability – for example, the code is too complex to maintain.

- Incorrect interface specifications – for example, the interface specification does not match the design or the receiving or sending interface.

All reviews aim to find defects, but some types of review find certain types of defects more effectively and efficiently than others.

Review process

Review processes can vary widely in their level of formality, where formality relates to the level of structure and documentation associated with the activity. Some types of review are completely informal, while others are very formal. The decision on the appropriate level of formality for a review is usually based on combinations of the following factors:

- The maturity of the development process. The more mature the process is, the more formal reviews tend to be.

- Legal or regulatory requirements. These are used to govern the software development activities in certain industries, notably in safety-critical areas such as railway signalling, and determine what kinds of review should take place.

- The need for an audit trail. Formal review processes ensure that it is possible to trace backwards throughout the software development life cycle. The level of formality in the types of review used can help to raise the level of audit trail.

Reviews can also have a variety of objectives, where the term 'review objective' identifies the main focus for a review. Typical review objectives include:

- Finding defects.
- Gaining understanding.
- Generating discussion.
- Decision making by consensus.

The way a review is conducted will depend on what its specific objective is, so a review aimed primarily at finding defects will be quite different from one that is aimed at gaining understanding of a document.

Basic review process

All reviews, formal and informal alike, exhibit the same basic elements of process:

- The document under review is studied by the reviewers.
- Reviewers identify issues or problems and inform the author either verbally or in a documented form, which might be as formal as raising a defect report or as informal as annotating the document under review.
- The author decides on any action to take in response to the comments and updates the document accordingly.

This basic process is always present, but in the more formal reviews it is elaborated to include additional stages and more attention to documentation and measurement.

Activities of a formal review

Reviews at the more formal end of the spectrum, such as technical reviews and inspections, share certain characteristics that differentiate them from the less formal reviews, of which walkthroughs are a typical example.

Figure 3.1 shows the key stages that characterise formal reviews.

The following list explains the key stages in more detail:

- Planning
  - Defining the review criteria – the criteria upon which the review will be measured will be defined, for example the time that should be taken for the review, and an expectation of the number of pages to be reviewed together with an expectation of the number of defects to be found.
  - Selecting the personnel – ensuring that those selected can and will add value to the process. There is little point in selecting a reviewer who will agree with everything written by the author without question. As a rule of

Figure 3.1 Stages of a formal review

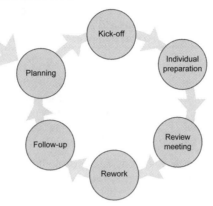

thumb it is best to include some reviewers who are from a different part of the organisation, who are known to be 'picky', and known to be dissenters. Reviews, like weddings, are enhanced by including 'something old, something new, something borrowed, something blue'. In this case 'something old' would be an experienced practitioner; 'something new' would be a new or inexperienced team member; 'something borrowed' would be someone from a different team; 'something blue' would be the dissenter who is hard to please. At the earliest stage of the process a moderator (review leader) must be identified. This is the person who will coordinate all of the review activity.

- Allocating roles – each reviewer is given a role to provide them with a unique focus on the document under review. Someone in a tester role might be checking for testability and clarity of definition, while someone in a user role might look for simplicity and a clear relationship to business values. This approach ensures that, although all reviewers are working on the same document, each individual is looking at it from a different perspective.

- Defining the entry and exit criteria, especially for the most formal review types (e.g. inspections) – before a review can start certain criteria have to be met. These are defined by the moderator, and could include: all reviewers must have received the review papers; all reviewers have a kick-off meeting booked in their diaries; any training of reviewers has been completed.

- Selecting the parts of documents to be reviewed (not always required – this will depend on the size of the document: a large document might need to be split into smaller parts and each part reviewed by a different person to ensure the whole document is reviewed fully).

- Checking entry criteria (mainly used for more formal review types such as inspections) – this stage is where the entry criteria agreed earlier are checked to ensure that they have been met so that the review can continue.

- Kick-off

  - Distributing documents – the moderator distributes all of the required documents to all reviewers.

- Explaining the objectives, process and documents to the participants – this can be run as a meeting or simply by sending out the details to the reviewers. The method used will depend on timescales and the volume of information to pass on. A lot of information can be disseminated better by a meeting rather than expecting reviewers to read pages of text.

- Individual preparation

  - Preparing for the review meeting by reviewing the documents – work done by each of the participants on their own before the review meeting, which would include reading the source documents, noting potential defects, questions and comments. This is a key task and may be time-boxed, for example participants might be given 2 hours to complete the preparation.

  - Noting potential defects, questions and comments – in this stage the potential defects, questions and comments found during individual preparation are logged.

- Examination, evaluation, recording results (Review meeting)

  - Discussing or logging with documented results or minutes (for more formal review types) – this might include discussion regarding any defects found or might be a log of defects found. The more formal review types like inspections will have documented results or minutes.

  - Noting defects, making recommendations regarding handling the defects, making decisions about the defects – the meeting participants might simply note defects for the author to correct; they might also make recommendations for handling or correcting the defects. The approach taken will have been decided at the kick-off stage so that all participants are aware of what is required of them. The decision about which approach to take may be based on one or all of the following factors:

    - Time available (if time is short the meeting may only collect defects).

    - Requirements of the author (if the author would like help in correcting defects).

    - Type of review (in an inspection only the collection of defects is allowed – there is never any discussion).

  - Examining/evaluating and recording issues during any physical meetings or tracking and group electronic communications.

- Rework

  - Fixing defects found – here typically the author will be fixing defects that were found and agreed as requiring a fix.

  - Recording updated status of defects – always done during more formal review techniques; optional for others.

- Follow-up

  - Checking the defects have been addressed – the moderator will check that the agreed defects have been addressed.

  - Metrics, such as how much time was spent on the review and how many defects were found, are collected to show notionally how the quality of the reviewed item has increased, but also the value added by the review to later stages of the life cycle, for example how much the defect would have cost if it hadn't been found until user acceptance testing.

- Checking on exit criteria – the moderator will also check the exit criteria (for more formal review types such as inspections) to ensure that they have been met so that the review can be officially closed as finished.

Roles and responsibilities

The role of each reviewer is to look at documents belonging to them from their assigned perspective; this may include the use of checklists. For example, a checklist based on a particular perspective (such as user, maintainer, tester or operations) may be used, or a more general checklist (such as typical requirements problems) may be used to identify defects.

In addition to these assigned review roles the review process itself defines specific roles and responsibilities that should be fulfilled for formal reviews. They are:

- Manager: the manager decides on what is to be reviewed (if not already defined), ensures there is sufficient time allocated in the project plan for all of the required review activities, and determines if the review objectives have been met. Managers do not normally get involved in the actual review process unless they can add real value, for example they have technical knowledge key to the review.

- Moderator: the moderator is sometimes known as the review leader. This is the person who leads the review of the document or set of documents, including planning the review, running the meeting, and follow-ups after the meeting. If necessary, the moderator may mediate between the various points of view and is often the person on whom the success of the review rests. The moderator will also make the final decision as to whether to release an updated document.

- Author: the author is the writer or person with chief responsibility for the development of the document(s) to be reviewed. The author will in most instances also take responsibility for fixing any agreed defects.

- Reviewers: these are individuals with a specific technical or business background (also called checkers or inspectors) who, after the necessary preparation, identify and describe findings (e.g. defects) in the product under review. As discussed above, reviewers should be chosen to represent different perspectives and roles in the review process and take part in any review meetings.

- Scribe (or recorder): the scribe attends the review meeting and documents all of the issues and defects, problems and open points that were identified during the meeting.

An additional role not normally associated with reviews is that of the tester. Testers have a particular role to play in relation to document reviews. In their test analysis role they will be required to analyse a document to enable the development of tests. In analysing the document they will also review it, for example in starting to build end-to-end scenarios they will notice if there is a 'hole' in the requirements that will stop the business functioning, such as a process that is missing or some data that is not available at a given point. So effectively a tester can either be formally invited to review a document or may do so by default in carrying out the tester's normal test analysis role.

Types of review

A single document or related work-product may be subject to many different review types: for example, an informal review may be carried out before the document is subjected to a technical review or, depending on the level of risk, a technical review or inspection may take place before a walkthrough with a customer.

Figure 3.2 shows the different levels of formality by review type.

Figure 3.2 Formality of reviews

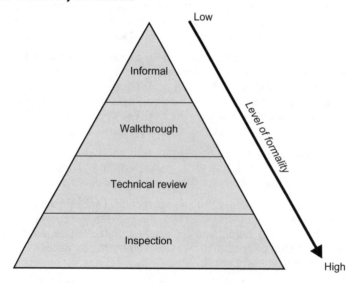

Each type of review has its own defining characteristics. We identify four review types to cover the spectrum of formality. These are usually known as:

1. Informal review (least formal). Key characteristics:

   • There is no formal process underpinning the review.

   • The review may be documented but this is not required; many informal reviews are not documented.

- There may be some variations in the usefulness of the review depending on the reviewer, for example the reviewer does not have the technical skills but is just available to check quickly and ensure that the document makes sense.
- The main purpose is to find defects and this is an inexpensive way to achieve some limited benefit.
- The review may be implemented by pair programming (where one programmer reviews the code of the other 'pair programmer') or by a technical lead reviewing designs and code.

2. Walkthrough. Key characteristics:

- The meeting is led by the author of the document under review and attended by members of the author's peer group.
- Review sessions are open-ended and may vary in practice from quite informal to very formal.
- Preparation by reviewers before the walkthrough meeting, production of a review report or a list of findings, and appointment of a scribe who is not the author are all optional components.
- The main purposes are to enable learning about the content of the document under review, to help team members gain an understanding of the content of the document, and to find defects.
- Walkthroughs typically explore scenarios, or conduct dry runs of code or processes.

3. Technical review. Key characteristics:

- Technical reviews are documented and use a well-defined defect detection process that includes peers and technical experts.
- The review is usually performed as a peer review without management participation and is ideally led by a trained moderator who is not the author.
- Reviewers prepare for the review meeting, optionally using checklists, and prepare a review report with a list of findings.
- Technical reviews may vary in practice from the quite informal to very formal and have a number of purposes, including: discussion, decision making, evaluation of alternatives, finding defects, solving technical problems and checking conformance to specifications and standards.

4. Inspection (most formal). Key characteristics:

- Inspections are led by a trained moderator who is not the author and usually involve peer examination of a document; individual inspectors work within defined roles.
- The inspection process is formal, based on rules and checklists, and uses entry and exit criteria.
- Pre-meeting preparation is essential, which includes reading of any source documents to ensure consistency.

- An inspection report, with a list of findings, is produced, which includes metrics that can be used to aid improvements to the process as well as correcting defects in the document under review.

- After the meeting a formal follow-up process is used to ensure that corrective action is completed and timely.

- The main purpose is to find defects, and process improvement may be a secondary purpose.

In reality the lines between the review types often get blurred and what is seen as a technical review in one company may be seen as an inspection in another. The above is the 'classic view' of reviews. The key for each company is to agree the objectives and benefits of the reviews that they plan to carry out.

Success factors for reviews

When measuring the success of a particular review the following suggested success factors should be considered:

- Each review should have a clearly predefined and agreed objective and the right people should be involved to ensure the objective is met. For example, in an inspection, if the objective is technically based, each reviewer will have a defined role and have the experience to complete the technical review; this should include testers as valued reviewers.

- Any defects found are welcomed, and expressed objectively.

- The review should be seen as being conducted within an atmosphere of trust, so that the outcome will not be used for the evaluation of the participants, and that the people issues and psychological aspects are dealt with (e.g. making it a positive experience for the author and all participants).

- Review techniques (both formal and informal) that are suitable to the type and level of software work-products and reviewers (this is especially important in inspections).

- Checklists or roles should be used, where appropriate, to increase effectiveness of defect identification; for example, in an inspection, roles such as data entry clerk or technical architect may be required to review a particular document.

- Management support is essential for a good review process (e.g. by incorporating adequate time for review activities in project schedules).

- There should be an emphasis on learning and process improvement.

Other more quantitative approaches to success measurement could also be used:

- How many defects found.

- Time taken to review/inspect.

- Percentage of project budget used/saved.

In his original paper on the benefits of inspections in 1976,[2] Michael Fagan of IBM, who developed the Fagan Inspection Method, reported a 23 per cent increase in 'coding productivity alone' by using inspections. Success can be measured in many ways; however, the key is to keep measuring to ensure success is still being achieved and, more importantly, reported to a wider audience.

CHECK OF UNDERSTANDING

1. Compare the differences between a walkthrough and an inspection.
2. Name three characteristics of a walkthrough.
3. Identify at least five success factors for a review.

STATIC ANALYSIS BY TOOLS

Like reviews, static analysis looks for defects without executing the code. However, unlike reviews static analysis is carried out once the code has been written. Its objective is to find defects in software source code and software models.

Source code is any series of statements written in some human-readable computer programming language that can then be converted to equivalent computer executable code – it is normally generated by the developer.

A software model is an image of the final solution developed using techniques such as Unified Modeling Language (UML); it is normally generated by a software designer.

Static analysis can find defects that are hard to find during test execution by analysing the program code, for example instructions to the computer can be in the form of control flow graphs (how control passes between modules) and data flows (ensuring data is identified and correctly used).

The value of static analysis is:

• Early detection of defects prior to test execution. As with reviews, the earlier the defect is found, the cheaper and easier it is to fix.

• Early warning about suspicious aspects of the code or design, by the calculation of metrics, such as a high-complexity measure. If code is too complex it can be more prone to error or less dependent on the focus given to the code by developers. If they understand that the code has to be complex, then they are more likely to check and double check that it is correct; however, if it is unexpectedly complex there is a higher chance that there will be a defect in it.

---

[2] Fagan, M.E. (1976) Design and code inspeections to reduce errors in program development. *IBM Systems Journal*, 15 (3). 182–211.

- Identification of defects not easily found by dynamic testing, such as development standard breaches as well as detecting dependencies and inconsistencies in software models, such as links or interfaces that were either incorrect or unknown before static analysis was carried out.

- Improved maintainability of code and design. By carrying out static analysis, defects will be removed that would otherwise have increased the amount of maintenance required after 'go live'. It can also recognise complex code that if corrected will make the code more understandable and therefore easier to maintain.

- Prevention of defects. By identifying the defect early in the life cycle it is a lot easier to identify why it was there in the first place (root cause analysis) than during test execution, thus providing information on possible process improvement that could be made to prevent the same defect appearing again.

Typical defects discovered by static analysis tools include:

- Referencing a variable with an undefined value, for example using a variable as part of a calculation before the variable has been given a value.

- Inconsistent interface between modules and components, for example module X requests three values from module Y, which has only two outputs.

- Variables that are never used. This is not strictly an error, but if a programmer declares a variable in a program and does not use it, there is a chance that some intended part of the program has inadvertently been omitted.

- Unreachable (dead) code. This means lines of code that cannot be executed because the logic of the program does not provide any path in which that code is included.

- Programming standards violations, for example if the standard is to add comments only at the end of the piece of code, but there are notes throughout the code, this would be a violation of standards.

- Security vulnerabilities, for example password structures that are not secure.

- Syntax violations of code and software models, for example incorrect use of the programming or modelling language.

Static analysis tools add the greatest value when used during component and integration testing. This will normally involve their use by developers to check against predefined rules or development standards, and by designers during software modelling.

A static analysis tool runs automatically and reports all defects it identifies, some of which may be insignificant and require little or no work to correct, while others could be critical and need urgent correction. These defects therefore require strong management to ensure that the full benefit is obtained from using the tool in the first place.

Software compilers are computer programs (or a set of programs) that translate codes written in one computer language (the source language) into another computer language (the target language). As part of the compile process certain static analysis can be undertaken that will identify some defects and provide the calculation of software metrics.

Static analysis tools are explained in **Chapter 6**.

CHECK OF UNDERSTANDING

1. What is static analysis looking for?
2. Name the five benefits of static analysis.
3. What is the name of the type of defect that relates to password checks?

SUMMARY

In this chapter we have looked at how review techniques and static analysis fit within the test process defined in **Chapter 2**. We have understood that a review is a static test, that is it is a test carried out without executing any code (by reading and commenting on any document (work-product) such as a requirement specification, a piece of code or a test plan/test case). We have also looked at the different types of review techniques available, such as walkthroughs and inspections, as well as spending time understanding the benefits of reviews themselves.

Reviews vary in formality. The formality governs the amount of structure and documentation that surround the review itself.

To obtain the most benefit from reviews, they should be carried out as early in the project life cycle as possible, preferably as soon as the document to be reviewed has been written and definitely, in the case of work-products such as requirement specifications and designs, before any code is written or executed. The roles of the participant reviewers need to be defined and, in the more structured review techniques, written output from reviews is expected.

We have learnt that static analysis is checking the developed software code before it is executed, checking for defects such as unreachable (dead code) and the misuse of development standards. We have also learnt that static analysis is best carried out using tools, which are described in detail in **Chapter 6**.

Like reviews, the greatest benefits of static analysis are realised when it is carried out as soon as possible after the code is written.

Example examination questions with answers

E1. K1 question
Which of the following is most likely to be a benefit of using static techniques?

    a. Fewer performance defects.

    b. Productivity improvements in the development process.

    c. More efficient regression testing.

    d. Quick return on investment in static analysis tools.

E2. K2 question
Which of the following has the typical formal review activities in the correct sequence?

    a. Kick-off, review meeting, planning, follow-up.

    b. Kick-off, planning, review meeting, rework.

    c. Planning, kick-off, individual preparation, review meeting.

    d. Planning, individual preparation, follow-up, rework.

E3. K2 question
Which of the following statements are true?

    i.   Defects are likely to be found earlier in the development process by using reviews rather than static analysis.

    ii.   Walkthroughs require code but static analysis does not require code.

    iii. Informal reviews can be performed on code and specifications.

    iv. Dynamic techniques are generally used before static techniques.

    v.   Dynamic techniques can only be used after code is ready to be executed.

    a. i, ii, vi.

    b. ii, iii, v.

    c. i, iv, v.

    d. i, iii, v.

E4. K1 question
Which of the following are static techniques?

    a. Walkthrough.

    b. State transition testing.

    c. Decision table testing.

    d. Statement testing.

E5. K1 question
Which *one* of the following roles is typically used in a review?

    a. Champion.
    b. Author.
    c. Project sponsor.
    d. Custodian.

E6. K2 question
Which of the following is most likely to be performed by developers?

    a. Technical review of a functional specification.
    b. Walkthrough of a requirements document.
    c. Informal review of a program specification.
    d. Static analysis of a software model.

Answers to questions in the chapter

SA1. The correct answer is a.
SA2. The correct answer is c.
SA3. The correct answer is d.

Answers to example questions

E1. The correct answer is b.
Although the other options might be seen as benefits they are not among the most likely benefits. Option b is the benefit that is most likely to be realised.

E2. The correct answer is c.
The correct sequence is: planning, kick-off, individual preparation, review meeting, rework, follow-up. All of the other options have either the activities in the wrong order or activities missing from the strict flow.

E3. The correct answer is d.
The other answers are incorrect because:

ii. Walkthroughs do not require code and static analysis does require code.
iv. Static techniques do not execute the code and therefore can be run before and after the code is ready for execution.

E4. The correct answer is a.
Options b, c and d are all dynamic test techniques.

E5. The correct answer is b.
The Author is the only role that is typically used in a review. A Champion might sponsor the review process but is not a defined role within an actual review; a Project sponsor, if technically competent, might be asked to play a defined role within the review process, but while using that role they will not be a Project sponsor; finally, a Custodian might ensure the results are stored safely but would not be involved in the actual review itself.

E6. The correct answer is d.
Static analysis is done almost exclusively by developers. The other review types would be performed using a combination of developers, testers and other interested stake-holders.

4 TEST DESIGN TECHNIQUES

Brian Hambling

INTRODUCTION

This chapter covers the very large topic of test case design techniques. Beginning with an introduction to the key terms and the basic process of creating a suite of tests for execution, the chapter explores the three categories of test case design techniques: specification-based, structure-based and experience-based. In each case specific techniques are explained and examples are given of their use. In the section on structure-based techniques we go beyond the basic requirements of the Foundation syllabus to introduce the skills needed to analyse code and to draw both flow charts and control flow graphs to represent code structure and facilitate analysis. The control flow graph format used in Foundation examinations is also introduced and examples and exercises based on this format are provided to make exam preparation as effective as possible. A final section on the selection of techniques completes the chapter.

Learning objectives

The learning objectives for this chapter are listed below. You can confirm that you have achieved these by using the self-assessment questions at the start of the chapter, the 'Check of understanding' boxes distributed throughout the text, and the example examination questions provided at the end of the chapter. The chapter summary will remind you of the key ideas.

The sections are allocated a K number to represent the level of understanding required for that section; where an individual topic has a lower K number than the section as a whole this is indicated for that topic; for an explanation of the K numbers see the **Introduction**.

The test development process (K3)

- Differentiate between a test design specification, test case specification and test procedure specification. (K2)

- Compare the terms test condition, test case and test procedure. (K2)

- Evaluate the quality of test cases in terms of clear traceability to the requirements and expected results. (K2)

- Translate test cases into a well-structured test procedure specification at a level of detail relevant to the knowledge of the testers.

Categories of test design techniques (K2)

- Recall reasons that both specification-based (black-box) and structure-based (white-box) approaches to test case design are useful, and list the common techniques for each. (K1)

- Explain the characteristics, commonalities and differences between specification-based testing, structure-based testing and experience-based testing.

Specification-based or black-box techniques (K3)

- Write test cases from given software models using equivalence partitioning, boundary value analysis, decision tables and state transition diagrams/tables.

- Explain the main purpose of each of the four techniques, what level and type of testing could use the technique, and how coverage may be measured. (K2)

- Explain the concept of use case testing and its benefits. (K2)

Structure-based or white-box techniques (K4)

- Describe the concept and importance of code coverage. (K2)

- Explain the concepts of statement and decision coverage, and give reasons why these concepts can also be used at test levels other than component testing (e.g. on business procedures at system level). (K2)

- Write test cases from given control flows using statement and decision test design techniques. (K3)

- Assess statement and decision coverage for completeness with respect to defined exit criteria.

Experience-based techniques (K2)

- Recall reasons for writing test cases based on intuition, experience and knowledge about common defects. (K1)

- Compare experience-based techniques with specification-based testing techniques.

Choosing test techniques (K2)

- Classify test design techniques according to their fitness to a given context, for the test basis, respective models and software characteristics.

Self-assessment questions

The following questions have been designed to enable you to check your current level of understanding for the topics in this chapter. The answers are at the end of the chapter. If you struggled with the K3 question you probably need more practice with applying the techniques; you can get this by working through the examples and exercises and attempting the additional practice questions at the end of the chapter. If you struggled with the K2 question it suggests that, while your recall of key ideas might be reasonable, your ability to apply the ideas needs developing. You need to study this chapter carefully and be careful to recognise all the connections between individual topics.

Question SA1 (K2)
Which of the following statements is true?

    a. Test cases give rise to test conditions, which are elaborated into test procedures.

    b. Test procedures contain test cases and test conditions.

    c. Test procedures elaborate test cases that are derived from test conditions.

    d. Test conditions are elaborated in test procedures and consist of collections of test cases.

Question SA2 (K2)
Which of the following statements is true?

    a. A test case specification includes a definition of test conditions.

    b. A test case specification defines the expected results of each test.

    c. A test execution schedule defines the sequence of actions for the execution of a test.

    d. A test procedure specification is only required for automated tests and defines the test script.

Question SA3 (K1)
Which of the following statements correctly defines structure-based testing?

    a. Structure-based testing systematically derives test cases from a model of the software.

    b. Structure-based testing derives test cases from knowledge of likely defects and their distribution.

    c. Structure-based testing derives test cases from knowledge of how the software is constructed.

    d. Structure-based testing enables the extent of coverage of the technical specification to be measured.

THE TEST DEVELOPMENT PROCESS

The specification of test cases is the second step in the fundamental test process (FTP) defined in **Chapter 1**. The terms specification and design are used interchangeably in this context; in this section we discuss the creation of test cases by design.

The design of tests comprises three main steps:

    1. Identify test conditions.
    2. Specify test cases.
    3. Specify test procedures.

Our first task is to become familiar with the terminology.

> **A test condition – an item or event of a component or system that could be verified by one or more test cases, for example a function, transaction, feature, quality attribute or structural element.**

In other words, a test condition is some characteristic of our software that we can check with a test or a set of tests.

> **A test case – a set of input values, execution preconditions, expected results and execution postconditions, developed for a particular objective or test condition, such as to exercise a particular program path or to verify compliance with a specific requirement.**

In other words, a test case: gets the system to some starting point for the test (execution preconditions); then applies a set of input values that should achieve a given outcome (expected result), and leaves the system at some end point (execution postcondition).

Our test design activity will generate the set of input values and we will predict the expected outcome by, for example, identifying from the specification what should happen when those input values are applied.

We have to define what state the system is in when we start so that it is ready to receive the inputs and we have to decide what state it is in after the test so that we can check that it ends up in the right place.

> **A test procedure specification – a sequence of actions for the execution of a test.**

A test procedure therefore identifies all the necessary actions in sequence to execute a test. Test procedure specifications are often called test scripts (or sometimes manual test scripts to distinguish them from the automated scripts that control test execution tools, introduced in **Chapter 6**).

So, going back to our three step process above, we:

1. decide on a test condition, which would typically be a small section of the specification for our software under test;
2. design a test case that will verify the test condition;
3. write a test procedure to execute the test, that is get it into the right starting state, input the values, and check the outcome.

In spite of the technical language, this is quite a simple set of steps. Of course we will have to carry out a very large number of these simple steps to test a whole system, but the basic process is still the same. To test a whole system we write a test execution schedule, which puts all the individual test procedures in the right sequence and sets up the system so that they can be run.

Bear in mind as well that the test development process may be implemented in more or less formal ways. In some situations it may be appropriate to produce very little documentation and in others a very formal and documented process may be appropriate. It all depends on the context of the testing, taking account of factors such as maturity of development and test processes, the amount of time available and the nature of the system under test. Safety-critical systems, for example, will normally require a more formal test process.

The best way to clarify the process is to work through a simple example.

TEST CASE DESIGN BASICS

Suppose we have a system that contains the following specification for an input screen:

1.2.3 The input screen shall have three fields: a title field with a drop-down selector; a surname field that can accept up to 20 alphabetic characters and the hyphen (-) character; a first name field which can accept up to 20 alphabetic characters. All alphabetic characters shall be case insensitive. All fields must be completed. The data is validated when the Enter key is pressed. If the data is valid the system moves on to the job input screen; if not, an error message is displayed.

This specification enables us to define test conditions; for example, we could define a test condition for the surname field (i.e. it can accept up to 20 alphabetic characters and the hyphen (-) character) and define a set of test cases to test that field.

To test the surname field we would have to navigate the system to the appropriate input screen, select a title, tab to the surname field (all this would be setting the test precondition), enter a value (the first part of the set of input values), tab to the first name field and enter a value (the second part of the set of input values that we need because all fields must be completed), then press the Enter key. The system should either move on to the job input screen (if the data we input was valid) or display an error message (if the input data was not valid). Of course, we would need to test both of these cases.

The preceding paragraph is effectively the test procedure, though we might lay it out differently for real testing.

A good test case needs some extra information. First, it should be traceable back to the test condition and the element of the specification that it is testing; we can do this by applying the specification reference to the test, for example by identifying this test as T1.2.3.1 (because it is the first test associated with specification element 1.2.3).

Secondly, we would need to add a specific value for the input, say 'Hambling' and 'Brian'. Finally we would specify that the system should move to the job input screen when 'Enter' is pressed.

TEST CASE DESIGN EXAMPLE

As an example, we could key in the following test cases:

Mr	Hambling	Brian
Ms	Samaroo	Angelina
Ms	Simmonite	Compo
Mr	Hyde-White	Wilfred

All these would be valid test cases; even though Compo Simmonite was an imaginary male character in a TV series, the input is correct according to the specification.

We should also test some invalid inputs, such as:

Mr	Thompson1	Geoff
Mr	"Morgan"	Peter
Mr	Williams	'Pete'
Miss	Ruby	Very-long-firstname-rejected

There are many more possibilities that infringe the rules in the specification, but these should serve to illustrate the point. You may be thinking that this simple specification could generate a very large number of test cases – and you would be absolutely right. One of our aims in using systematic test case design techniques will be to cut down the number of tests we need to run to achieve a given level of confidence in the software we are testing.

The test procedure would need to add some details along the following lines:

1. Select the <Name or Personal Details> option from the main menu.
2. Select the 'input' option from the <Name or Personal Details> menu.
3. Select 'Mr' from the 'Title' drop-down menu.
4. Check that the cursor moves to the 'surname' field.
5. Type in 'Hambling' and press the tab key once; check that the cursor moves to the 'first name' field.
6. Type in 'Brian' and press the Enter key.
7. Check that the Job Input screen is displayed.
8. ...

That should be enough to demonstrate what needs to be defined, and also how slow and tedious such a test would be to run, and we have only completed one of the test cases so far!

The test procedure would collect together all the test cases related to this specification element so that they can all be executed together as a block; there would be several to test valid and non-valid inputs, as you have seen in the example.

In the wider process (the FTP) we would move on to the test execution step next. In preparation for execution the test execution schedule collects together all the tests and sequences them, taking into account any priorities (highest priority tests would be run first) and any dependencies between tests. For example, it would make sense to do all the tests on the input screen together and to do all the tests that use input data afterwards; that way we get the input screen tests to do the data entry that we will need for the later tests. There might also be technical reasons why we run tests in a particular sequence; for example, a test of the password security needs to be done at the beginning of a sequence of tests because we need to be able to get into the system to run the other tests.

THE IDEA OF TEST COVERAGE

Test coverage is a very important idea because it provides a quantitative assessment of the extent and quality of testing. In other words, it answers the question 'how much testing have you done?' in a way that is not open to interpretation. Statements such as 'I'm nearly finished', or 'I've done two weeks' testing' or 'I've done everything in the test plan' generate more questions than they answer. They are statements about how much testing has been done or how much effort has been applied to testing, rather than statements about how effective the testing has been or what has been achieved. We need to know about test coverage for two very important reasons:

- It provides a quantitative measure of the quality of the testing that has been done by measuring what has been achieved.

- It provides a way of estimating how much more testing needs to be done. Using quantitative measures we can set targets for test coverage and measure progress against them.

Statements like 'I have tested 75 per cent of the decisions' or 'I've tested 80 per cent of the requirements' provide useful information. They are neither subjective nor qualitative; they provide a real measure of what has actually been tested. If we apply coverage measures to testing based on priorities, which are themselves based on the risks addressed by individual tests, we will have a reliable, objective and quantified framework for testing.

Test coverage can be applied to any systematic technique; in this chapter we will apply it to specification-based techniques to measure how much of the functionality has been tested, and to structure-based techniques to measure how much of the code has been tested. Coverage measures may be part of the completion criteria defined in the test plan (step 1 of the FTP) and used to determine when to stop testing in the final step of the FTP.

CATEGORIES OF TEST CASE DESIGN TECHNIQUES

There are very many ways to design test cases. Some are general, others are very specific. Some are very simple to implement, others are difficult and complex to implement. The many excellent books published on software testing techniques every year testify to the rate of development of new and interesting approaches to the challenges that confront the professional software tester.

There is, however, a collection of test case design techniques that has come to be recognised as the most important ones for a tester to learn to apply, and these have been selected as the representatives of test case design for the Foundation Certificate, and hence for this book.

The test case design techniques we will look at are grouped into three categories:

- Those based on deriving test cases directly from a specification or a model of a system or proposed system, known as specification-based or black-box techniques. So black-box techniques are based on an analysis of the test basis documentation, including both functional and non-functional aspects. They do not use any information regarding the internal structure of the component or system under test.

- Those based on deriving test cases directly from the structure of a component or system, known as structure-based, structural or white-box techniques. We will concentrate on tests based on the code written to implement a component or system in this chapter, but other aspects of structure, such as a menu structure, can be tested in a similar way.

- Those based on deriving test cases from the tester's experience of similar systems and general experience of testing, known as experience-based techniques.

It is convenient to categorise techniques for test case design in this way (it is easier for you to remember, for one thing) but do not assume that these are the only categories or the only techniques; there are many more that can be added to the tester's 'tool kit' over time.

The category now known as specification-based was originally called 'black-box' because the techniques in it take a view of the system that does not need to know what is going on 'inside the box'. Those of us born in the first half of the 20th century will recognise 'black box' as the name of anything technical that you can use but about which you know nothing or next to nothing. 'Specification-based' is a more descriptive title for those who may not find the 'black-box' image helpful. The natural alternative to 'black box' is 'white box' and so 'white box' techniques are those that are based on internal structure rather than external function.

Experience-based testing was not really treated as 'proper' testing in testing prehistory, so it was given a disdainful name such as 'ad hoc'; the implication that this was not a systematic approach was enough to exclude it from many discussions about testing. Both the intellectual climate and the sophistication of experience-based techniques have moved on from those early days. It is worth bearing in mind that many systems are still tested in an experience-based way, partly because the systems are not specified in enough detail or in a sufficiently structured way to enable other categories of technique to be applied, or because neither the development team nor the testing team have been trained in the use of specification-based or structure-based techniques.

Before we look at these categories in detail, think for a moment about what we are trying to achieve. We want to try to check that a system does everything that its specification says it should do and nothing else. In practice the 'nothing else' is the hardest part and generates the most tests; that is because there are far more ways of getting something wrong than there are ways of getting it right. Even if we just concentrate on testing that the system does what it is supposed to do, we will still generate a very large number of tests. This will be expensive and time-consuming, which means it probably will not happen, so we need to ensure that our testing is as efficient as possible. As you will see, the best techniques do this by creating the smallest set of tests that will achieve a given objective, and they do that by taking advantage of certain things we have learned about testing; for example, that defects tend to cluster in interesting ways.

Bear this in mind as we take a closer look at the categories of test case design techniques.

SPECIFICATION-BASED (BLACK-BOX) TECHNIQUES

The main thing about specification-based techniques is that they derive test cases directly from the specification or from some other kind of model of what the system should do. The source of information on which to base testing is known as the 'test basis'. If a test basis is well defined and adequately structured we can easily identify test conditions from which test cases can be derived.

The most important point about specification-based techniques is that specifications or models do not (and should not) define how a system should achieve the specified behaviour when it is built; it is a specification of the required (or at least desired) behaviour. One of the hard lessons that software engineers have learned from experience is that it is important to separate the definition of what a system should do (a specification) from the definition of how it should work (a design). This separation allows the two specialist groups (testers for specifications and designers for design) to work independently so that we can later check that they have arrived at the same place, that is they have together built a system and tested that it works according to its specification.

If we set up test cases so that we check that desired behaviour actually occurs then we are acting independently of the developers. If they have misunderstood the specification or chosen to change it in some way without telling anyone then their implementation will deliver behaviour that is different from what the model or specification said the system behaviour should be. Our test, based solely on the specification, will therefore fail and we will have uncovered a problem.

Bear in mind that not all systems are defined by a detailed formal specification. In some cases the model we use may be quite informal. If there is no specification at all, the tester may have to build a model of the proposed system, perhaps by interviewing key stakeholders to understand what their expectations are. However formal or informal the model is, and however it is built, it provides a test basis from which we can generate tests systematically.

Remember, also, that the specification can contain non-functional elements as well as functions; topics such as reliability, usability and performance are examples. These need to be systematically tested as well.

What we need, then, are techniques that can explore the specified behaviour systematically and thoroughly in a way that is as efficient as we can make it. In addition, we use what we know about software to 'home in' on problems; each of the test case design techniques is based on some simple principles that arise from what we know in general about software behaviour.

You need to know five specification-based techniques for the Foundation Certificate:

- Equivalence partitioning.
- Boundary value analysis.
- Decision table testing.
- State transition testing.
- Use case testing.

You should be capable of generating test cases for the first four of these techniques.

CHECK OF UNDERSTANDING

1. What do we call the category of test case design techniques that requires knowledge of how the system under test actually works?
2. What do black-box techniques derive their test cases from?
3. How do we make specification-based testing work when there is no specification?

Equivalence partitioning

Input partitions

Equivalence partitioning is based on a very simple idea: it is that in many cases the inputs to a program can be 'chunked' into groups of similar inputs. For example, a program that accepts integer values can accept as valid any input that is an integer (i.e. a whole number) and should reject anything else (such as a real number or a character). The range of integers is infinite, though the computer will limit this to some finite value in both the negative and positive directions (simply because it can only handle numbers of a certain size; it is a finite machine). Let us suppose, for the sake of an example, that the program accepts any value between −10,000 and +10,000 (computers actually represent numbers in binary form, which makes the numbers look much less like the ones we are familiar with, but we will stick to a familiar representation). If we imagine a program that separates numbers into two groups according to whether they are positive or negative the total range of integers could be split into three 'partitions': the values that are less than zero; zero; and the values that are greater than zero. Each of these is known as an 'equivalence partition' because every value inside the partition is exactly equivalent to any other value as far as our program is concerned. So if the computer accepts −2,905 as a valid negative integer we would expect it also to accept −3. Similarly, if it accepts 100 it should also accept 2,345 as a positive integer. Note that we are treating zero as a special case. We could, if we chose to, include zero with the positive integers, but my rudimentary specification did not specify that clearly, so it is really left as an undefined value (and it is not untypical to find such ambiguities or undefined areas in specifications). It often suits us to treat zero as a special case for testing where ranges of numbers are involved; we treat it as an equivalence partition with only one member. So we have three valid equivalence partitions in this case.

The equivalence partitioning technique takes advantage of the properties of equivalence partitions to reduce the number of test cases we need to write. Since all the values in an equivalence partition are handled in exactly the same way by a given program, we need only test one of them as a representative of the partition. In the example given, then, we need any positive integer, any negative integer and zero. We generally select values somewhere near the middle of each partition, so we might choose, say, −5,000, 0 and 5,000 as our representatives. These three test inputs would exercise all three partitions and the theory tells us that if the program treats these three values correctly it is very likely to treat all of the other values, all 19,998 of them in this case, correctly.

The partitions we have identified so far are called valid equivalence partitions because they partition the collection of valid inputs, but there are other possible inputs to this program that would not be valid − real numbers, for example. We also have two input partitions of integers that are not valid: integers less than −10,000 and integers greater than 10,000. We should test that the program does not accept these, which is just as important as the program accepting valid inputs.

If you think about the example we have been using you will soon recognise that there are far more possible non-valid inputs than valid ones, since all the real numbers (e.g. numbers containing decimals) and all characters are non-valid in this case. It is generally the case that there are far more ways to provide incorrect input than there are to provide correct input; as a result, we need to ensure that we have tested the program against the possible non-valid inputs. Here again equivalence partitioning comes to our aid: all real numbers are equally non-valid, as are all alphabetic characters. These represent two non-valid partitions that we should test, using values such as 9.45 and 'r' respectively. There will be many other possible non-valid input partitions, so we may have to limit the test cases to the ones that are most likely to crop up in a real situation.

EXAMPLE EQUIVALENCE PARTITIONS

- Valid input: integers in the range 100 to 999.
  - Valid partition: 100 to 999 inclusive.
  - Non-valid partitions: less than 100, more than 999, real (decimal) numbers and non-numeric characters.
- Valid input: names with up to 20 alphabetic characters.
  - Valid partition: strings of up to 20 alphabetic characters.
  - Non-valid partitions: strings of more than 20 alphabetic characters, strings containing non-alphabetic characters.

Exercise 4.1

Suppose you have a bank account that offers variable interest rates: 0.5 per cent for the first £1,000 credit; 1 per cent for the next £1,000; 1.5 per cent for the rest. If you wanted to check that the bank was handling your account correctly what valid input partitions might you use?

The answer can be found at the end of the chapter.

Output partitions

Just as the input to a program can be partitioned, so can the output. The program in the exercise above could produce outputs of 0.5 per cent, 1 per cent and 1.5 per cent, so we could use test cases that generate each of these outputs as an alternative to generating input partitions. An input value in the range £0.00–£1,000.00 would generate the 0.5 per cent output; a value in the range £1,001.00–£2,000.00 would generate the 1 per cent output; a value greater than £2,000.00 would generate the 1.5 per cent output.

Other partitions

If we know enough about an application we may be able to partition other values instead of or as well as input and output. For example, if a program handles input requests by placing them on one of a number of queues we could, in principle, check that requests end up on the right queue. In this case a stream of inputs can be partitioned according to the queue we anticipate it will be placed into. This is more technical and difficult than input or output partitioning but it is an option that can be considered when appropriate.

PARTITIONS – EXAMPLE 4.1

A mail-order company charges £2.95 postage for deliveries if the package weighs less than 2 kg, £3.95 if the package weighs 2 kg or more but less than 5 kg, and £5 for packages weighing 5 kg or more. Generate a set of valid test cases using equivalence partitioning.

The valid input partitions are: under 2 kg; 2 kg or over but less than 5 kg; and 5 kg or over.

Input values could be 1 kg, 3.5 kg, 7.5 kg. These would produce expected results of £2.95, £3.95 and £5 respectively.

In this case there are no non-valid inputs (unless the scales fail).

Exercise 4.2

A mail-order company selling flower seeds charges £3.95 for postage and packing on all orders up to £20 value and £4.95 for orders above £20 value and up to £40 value. For orders above £40 value there is no charge for postage and packing.

If you were using equivalence partitioning to prepare test cases for the postage and packing charges what valid partitions would you define?

What about non-valid partitions?

The answer can be found at the end of the chapter.

Boundary value analysis

One thing we know about the kinds of mistakes that programmers make is that errors tend to cluster around boundaries. For example, if a program should accept a sequence of numbers between 1 and 10, the most likely fault will be that values just outside this range are incorrectly accepted or that values just inside the range are incorrectly rejected. In the programming world these faults coincide with particular programming structures such as the number of times a program loop is executed or the exact point at which a loop should stop executing.

This works well with our equivalence partitioning idea because partitions must have boundaries. (Where partitions do not have boundaries, for example in the set of days of the week, the boundary analysis technique cannot be used.) A partition of integers between 1 and 99, for instance, has a lowest value, 1, and a highest value, 99. These are called boundary values. Actually they are called valid boundary values because they are the boundaries on the inside of a valid partition. What about the values on the outside? Yes, they have boundaries too. So the boundary of the non-valid values at the lower end will be zero because it is the first value you come to when you step outside the partition at the bottom end. (You can also think of this as the highest value inside the non-valid partition of integers that are less than one, of course.) At the top end of the range we also have a non-valid boundary value, 100.

This is the boundary value technique, more or less. For most practical purposes the boundary value analysis technique needs to identify just two values at each boundary. For reasons that need not detain us here there is an alternative version of the technique that uses three values at each boundary. For this variant, which is the one documented in BS 7925-2, we include one more value at each boundary when we use boundary value analysis: the rule is that we use the boundary value itself and one value (as close as you can get) either side of the boundary.

So, in this case lower boundary values will be 0, 1, 2 and upper boundary values will be 98, 99, 100. What does 'as close as we can get' mean? It means take the next value in sequence using the precision that has been applied to the partition. If the numbers are to a precision of 0.01, for example, the lower boundary values would be 0.99, 1.00, 1.01 and the upper boundary values would be 98.99, 99.00, 99.01.

When you come to take your exam you will find that the exam recognises that there are two possible approaches to boundary value analysis. For this reason any questions about boundary value analysis will clearly signal whether you are expected to identify 2 or 3 values at any boundary. You will find that this causes no problems, but there are examples below using both the 2 value and the 3 value approach, just to be on the safe side and ensure that you do not get taken by surprise in the exam.

The best way to consolidate the idea of boundaries is to look at some examples.

BOUNDARY VALUES – EXAMPLE 4.2

- The boiling point of water – the boundary is at 100 degrees Celsius, so for the 3 value boundary approach the boundary values will be 99 degrees, 100 degrees, 101 degrees – unless you have a very accurate digital thermometer, in which case they could be 99.9 degrees, 100.0 degrees, 100.1 degrees. For the 2 value approach the corresponding values would be 100 and 101.

- Exam pass – if an exam has a pass boundary at 40 per cent, merit at 60 per cent and distinction at 80 per cent the 3 value boundaries would be 39, 40, 41 for pass, 59, 60, 61 for merit, 79, 80, 81 for distinction. It is unlikely that marks would be recorded at any greater precision than whole numbers. The 2 value equivalents would be 39 and 40, 59 and 60, and 79 and 80 respectively.

Exercise 4.3

A system is designed to accept scores from independent markers who have marked the same examination script. Each script should have 5 individual marks, each of which is out of 20, and a total for the script. Two markers' scores are compared and differences greater than three in any question score or 10 overall are flagged for further examination.

Using equivalence partitioning and boundary value analysis identify the boundary values that you would explore for this scenario.

(In practice, some of the boundary values might actually be in other equivalence partitions, and we do not need to test them twice, so the total number of boundary values requiring testing might be less than you might expect.)

The answer can be found at the end of the chapter.

CHECK OF UNDERSTANDING

1. What is the relationship between a partition and a boundary?
2. Why are equivalence partitioning and boundary value analysis often used together?
3. Explain what is meant by 'as close as possible to a boundary'?

Decision table testing

Specifications often contain business rules to define the functions of the system and the conditions under which each function operates. Individual decisions are usually simple, but the overall effect of these logical conditions can become quite complex. As testers we need to be able to assure ourselves that every combination of these conditions that might occur has been tested, so we need to capture all the decisions in a way that enables us to explore their combinations. The mechanism usually used to capture the logical decisions is called a decision table.

A decision table lists all the input conditions that can occur and all the actions that can arise from them. These are structured into a table as rows, with the conditions at the top of the table and the possible actions at the bottom. Business rules, which involve combinations of conditions to produce some combination of actions, are arranged across the top. Each column therefore represents a single business rule (or just 'rule') and shows how input conditions combine to produce actions. Thus each column represents a possible test case, since it identifies both inputs and expected outputs. This is shown schematically in the box below.

DECISION TABLE STRUCTURE

	Business rule 1	Business rule 2	Business rule 3
Condition 1	T	F	T
Condition 2	T	T	T
Condition 3	T	–	F
Action 1	Y	N	Y
Action 2	N	Y	Y

Business rule 1 requires all conditions to be true to generate action 1. Business rule 2 results in action 2 if condition 1 is false and condition 2 is true but does not depend on condition 3. Business rule 3 requires conditions 1 and 2 to be true and condition 3 to be false.

In reality the number of conditions and actions can be quite large, but usually the number of combinations producing specific actions is relatively small. For this reason we do not enter every possible combination of conditions into our decision table, but restrict it to those combinations that correspond to business rules – this is called a limited entry decision table to distinguish it from a decision table with all combinations of inputs identified. In this chapter we will always mean the limited entry kind when we refer to a decision table.

As usual, we use an example to clarify what we mean.

DECISION TABLE TESTING – EXAMPLE 4.3

A supermarket has a loyalty scheme that is offered to all customers. Loyalty cardholders enjoy the benefits of either additional discounts on all purchases (rule 3) or the acquisition of loyalty points (rule 4), which can be converted into vouchers for the supermarket or to equivalent points in schemes run by partners. Customers without a loyalty card receive an additional discount only if they spend more than £100 on any one visit to the store (rule 2), otherwise only the special offers offered to all customers apply (rule 1).

	Rule 1	Rule 2	Rule 3	Rule 4
Conditions:				
Customer without loyalty card	T	T	F	F
Customer with loyalty card	F	F	T	T
Extra discount selected	–	–	T	F
Spend > £100	F	T	–	–
Actions:				
No discount	T	F	F	F
Extra discount	F	T	T	F
Loyalty points	F	F	F	T

From the decision table we can determine test cases by setting values for the conditions and determining the expected output, for example from rule 1 we could input a normal customer with a £50 transaction and check that no discount was applied. The same customer with a £150 transaction (rule 2) should attract a discount. Thus we can see that each column of the decision table represents a possible test case.

CHECK OF UNDERSTANDING

1. What is a decision table derived from?
2. Why does decision table testing use limited entry decision tables?
3. Describe how test cases are identified from decision tables.
4. Which element of a decision table defines the expected output for a test case?

Exercise 4.4

A mutual insurance company has decided to float its shares on the stock exchange and is offering its members rewards for their past custom at the time of flotation. Anyone with a current policy will benefit provided it is a 'with-profits' policy and they have held it since 2001. Those who meet these criteria can opt for either a cash payment or an allocation of shares in the new company; those who have held a qualifying policy for less than the required time will be eligible for a cash payment but not for shares. Here is a decision table reflecting those rules.

	Rule 1	Rule 2	Rule 3	Rule 4
Conditions:				
Current policy holder	Y	Y	Y	N
Policy holder since 2001	N	Y	N	–
'With-profits' policy	Y	Y	N	–
Actions:				
Eligible for cash payment	Y	Y	N	N
Eligible for share allocations	N	Y	N	N

What expected result would you expect to get for the following test case?

Billy Bunter is a current policy holder who has held a 'with-profits' policy since 2003.

The answer can be found at the end of the chapter.

State transition testing

The previous technique, decision table testing, is particularly useful in systems where combinations of input conditions produce various actions. Now we consider a similar technique, but this time we are concerned with systems in which outputs are triggered by changes to the input conditions, or changes of 'state'; in other words, behaviour depends on current state and past state, and it is the transitions that trigger system behaviour. It will be no surprise to learn that this technique is known as state transition testing or that the main diagram used in the technique is called a state transition diagram.

Look at the box to see an example of a state transition diagram.

STATE TRANSITION DIAGRAMS

A state transition diagram is a representation of the behaviour of a system. It is made up from just two symbols.

The first is

which is the symbol for a state. A state is just what it says it is: the system is 'static', in a stable condition from which it will only change if it is stimulated by an event of some kind. For example, a TV stays 'on' unless you turn it 'off'; a multifunction watch tells the time unless you change mode.

The second is

which is the symbol for a transition, that is a change from one state to another. The state change will be triggered by an event (e.g. pressing a button or switching a switch). The transition will be labelled with the event that caused it and any action that arises from it. So we might have 'mode button pressed' as an event and 'presentation changes' as the action. Usually (but not necessarily) the start state will have a double arrowhead pointing to it. Often the start state is obvious anyway.

If we have a state transition diagram representation of a system we can analyse the behaviour in terms of what happens when a transition occurs.

Transitions are caused by events and they may generate outputs and/or changes of state. An event is anything that acts as a trigger for a change; it could be an input to the system, or it could be something inside the system that changes for some reason, such as a database field being updated.

In some cases an event generates an output, in others the event changes the system's internal state without generating an output, and in still others an event may cause an output and a change of state. What happens for each change is always deducible from the state transition diagram.

STATE TRANSITION DIAGRAM – EXAMPLE 4.4

A hill-walker's watch has two modes: Time and Altimeter. In Time mode, pressing the Mode switch causes the watch to switch to Alt mode; pressing Mode again returns to Time mode. While the watch is in Alt mode the Set button has no effect.

When the watch is in Time mode pressing the Set button transitions the watch into Set Hrs, from which the Hrs display can be incremented by pressing the Set button. If the Mode switch is pressed while the watch is in Set Hrs mode the watch transitions to Set Mins mode, in which pressing the Set button increments the Mins display. If the Mode button is pressed in this mode the watch transitions back to Time mode (Figure 4.1).

Note that not all events have an effect in all states. Where an event does not have an effect on a given state it is usually omitted, but it can be shown as an arrow starting from the state and returning to the same state to indicate that no transition takes place; this is sometimes known as a 'null' transition or an 'invalid' transition.

Rather than work out what happens for each event each time we want to initiate a test, we can take the intermediate step of creating what is known as a state table (ST). An ST records all the possible events and all the possible states; for each combination of event and state it shows the outcome in terms of the new state and any outputs that are generated.

The ST is the source from which we usually derive test cases. It makes sense to do it this way because the analysis of state transitions takes time and can be a source of errors; it is better to do this task once and then have a simple way of generating tests from it than to do it every time we want to generate a new test case.

Table 4.1 provides an example of what an ST looks like.

Figure 4.1 State transition diagram of the hill-walker's watch

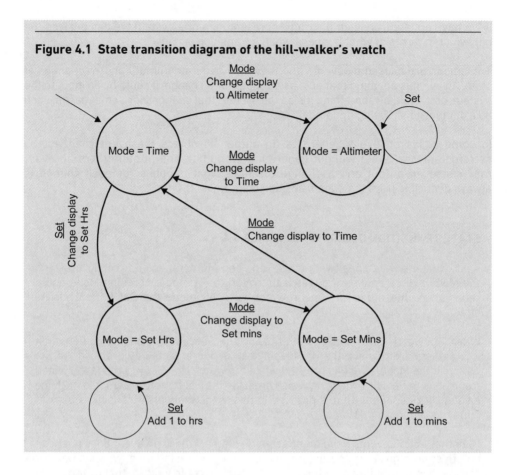

STATE TABLE – EXAMPLE 4.4

An ST has a row for each state in the state transition diagram and a column for every event. For a given row and column intersection we read off the state from the state transition diagram and note what effect (if any) each event has. If the event has no effect we label the table entry with a symbol that indicates that nothing happens; this is sometimes called a 'null' transition or an 'invalid' transition. If the event does have an effect label the table entry with the state to which the system transitions when the given event occurs; if there is also an output (there is sometimes but not always) the output is indicated in the same table entry separated from the new state by the '/' symbol. The example shown in Table 4.1 is the ST for Figure 4.1, which we drew in the previous box.

Table 4.1 ST for the hill-walker's watch

	Mode	Set
Mode = Time	Mode = Altimeter/Change Display to Altimeter	Mode = Set Hrs/Change Display to Set Hrs
Mode = Altimeter	Mode = Time/Change Display to Time	Null
Set Hrs	Mode = Set Mins/Change display to Set Mins	Set Hrs/Add 1 to Hrs
Set Mins	Mode = Time/Change Display to Time	Set Mins/Add 1 to Mins

Once we have an ST it is a simple exercise to generate the test cases that we need to exercise the functionality by triggering state changes.

STATE TRANSITION TESTING – EXAMPLE 4.4

We generate test cases by stepping through the ST. If we begin in Time mode then the first test case might be to press Mode and observe that the watch changes to Alt state; pressing Mode again becomes test case 2, which returns the watch to Time state. Test case 3 could press Set and observe the change to Set Hrs mode and then try a number of presses of Set to check that the incrementing mechanism works. In this way we can work our way systematically round the ST until every single transition has been exercised. If we want to be more sophisticated we can exercise pairs of transitions, for example pressing Set twice as a single test case, to check that Hrs increments correctly. We should also test all the negative cases, that is those cases where the ST indicates there is no valid transition.

CHECK OF UNDERSTANDING

1. What is the main use of an ST for testers?
2. Name three components of a state transition diagram.
3. How are negative tests identified from an ST?
4. What is meant by the term 'invalid' transition'?

Exercise 4.5

In the state transition diagram in Figure 4.2, which of the sequences of transitions below would be valid?

    a.   ABCDE
    b.   FEABC
    c.   ABCEF
    d.   EFADC

The answer can be found at the end of the chapter.

Figure 4.2 State transition diagram

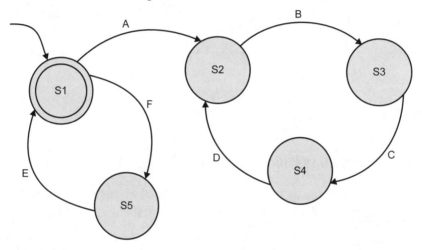

Use case testing

Use cases are one way of specifying functionality as business scenarios or process flows. They capture the individual interactions between 'actors' and the system. An actor represents a particular type of user and the use cases capture the interactions that each user takes part in to produce some output that is of value. Test cases based on use cases at the business process level, often called scenarios, are particularly useful in exercising business rules or process flows and will often identify gaps or weaknesses in these that would not be found by exercising individual components in isolation. This makes use case testing very effective in defining acceptance tests because the use cases represent actual likely use.

Use cases may also be defined at the system level, with preconditions that define the state the system needs to be in on entry to a use case to enable the use case to complete successfully, and postconditions that define the state of the system on completion of the use case. Use cases typically have a mainstream path, defining the expected behaviour, and one or more alternative paths related to such aspects as error conditions. Well-defined use cases can therefore be an excellent basis for system level testing, and they can also help to uncover integration defects caused by incorrect interaction or communication between components.

In practice, writing a test case to represent each use case is often a good starting point for testing, and use case testing can be combined with other specification-based testing.

Figure 4.3 Use case example

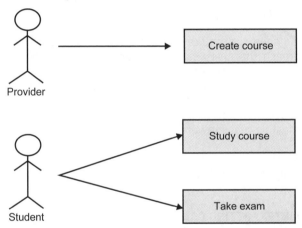

Use case testing has the major benefit that it relates to real user processes, so it offers an opportunity to exercise a complete process flow. The principles applied elsewhere can be applied here: first test the highest priority (highest value) use cases by taking typical examples; then exercise some attempts at incorrect process flows; and then exercise the boundaries.

STRUCTURE-BASED (WHITE-BOX) TECHNIQUES

Structure-based test techniques are used to explore system or component structures at several levels. At the component level, the structures of interest will be program structures such as decisions; at the integration level we may be interested in exploring the way components interact with other components (in what is usually termed a calling structure); at the system level we may be interested in how users will interact with a menu structure. All these are examples of structures and all may be tested using white-box test case design techniques. Instead of exercising a component or system to see if it functions correctly white-box tests focus on ensuring that particular elements of the structure itself are correctly exercised. For example, we can use structural testing techniques to ensure that each statement in the code of a component is executed at least once. At the component level, where structure-based testing is most commonly used, the test case design techniques involve generating test cases from code, so we need to be able to read and analyse code. As you will see later, in **Chapter 6**, code analysis and structure-based testing at the component level are mostly done by specialist tools, but a knowledge of the techniques is still valuable. You may wish to run simple test cases on code to ensure that it is basically sound before you begin detailed functional testing, or you may want to interpret test results from programmers to ensure that their testing adequately exercises the code.

The CTFL syllabus does not require this complete level of understanding and takes a simplified approach that uses simplified control flow graphs (introduced in the section on **Simplified control flow graphs**). The following paragraphs can therefore be considered optional for readers whose interest is solely to pass the CTFL exam at this stage, but, for anyone intending to progress to the more advanced levels, they provide an essential introduction to code analysis that will be required for these exams and that will be needed in testing real software.

Our starting point, then, is the code itself. The best route to a full understanding of white-box techniques is to start here and work through the whole section.

READING AND INTERPRETING CODE

In a Foundation-level examination the term 'code' will always mean pseudo code. Pseudo code is a much more limited language than any real programming language but it enables designers to create all the main control structures needed by programs. It is sometimes used to document designs before they are coded into a programming language.

In the next few boxes we will introduce all the essential elements of pseudo code that you will need to be able to analyse code and create test cases for the Foundation examination.

Wherever you see the word 'code' from here on in this chapter read it as 'pseudo code'.

Real programming languages have a wide variety of forms and structures – so many that we could not adequately cover them all. The advantage of pseudo code in this respect is that it has a simple structure.

OVERALL PROGRAM STRUCTURE

Code can be of two types, executable and non-executable. Executable code instructs the computer to take some action; non-executable code is used to prepare the computer to do its calculations but it does not involve any actions. For example, reserving space to store a calculation (this is called a declaration statement) involves no actions. In pseudo code non-executable statements will be at the beginning of the program; the start of the executable part is usually identified by BEGIN, and the end of the program by END. So we get the following structure:

```
1    Non-executable statements
2    BEGIN
3
4    Executable statements
5
6    END
```

If we were counting executable statements we would count lines 2, 4 and 6. Line 1 is not counted because it is non-executable. Lines 3 and 5 are ignored because they are blank.

If there are no non-executable statements there may be no BEGIN or END either, but there will always be something separating non-executable from executable statements where both are present.

Now we have a picture of an overall program structure we can look inside the code. Surprisingly, there are only three ways that executable code can be structured, so we only have three structures to learn. The first is simple and is known as sequence: that just means that the statements are exercised one after the other as they appear on the page. The second structure is called selection: in this case the computer has to decide if a condition (known as a Boolean condition) is true or false. If it is true the computer takes one route, and if it is false the computer takes a different route. Selection structures therefore involve decisions. The third structure is called iteration: it simply involves the computer exercising a chunk of code more than once; the number of times it exercises the chunk of code depends on the value of a condition (just as in the selection case). Let us look at that a little closer.

PROGRAMMING STRUCTURES

SEQUENCE

The following program is purely sequential:

```
1    Read A
2    Read B
3    C = A + B
```

The BEGIN and END have been omitted in this case since there were no non-executable statements; this is not strictly correct but is common practice, so it is wise to be aware of it and remember to check whether there are any non-executable statements when you do see BEGIN and END in a program. The computer would execute those three statements in sequence, so it would read (input) a value into A (this is just a name for a storage location), then read another value into B, and finally add them together and put the answer into C.

SELECTION

```
1    IF P > 3
2    THEN
3        X = X + Y
4    ELSE
5        X = X - Y
6    ENDIF
```

Here we ask the computer to evaluate the condition P > 3, which means compare the value that is in location P with 3. If the value in P is greater than 3 then the condition is true; if not, the condition is false. The computer then selects which statement to execute next. If the condition is true it will execute the part labelled THEN, so it executes line 3. If the condition is false it will execute line 5. After it has executed either line 3 or line 5 it will go to line 6, which is the end of the selection (IF THEN ELSE) structure. From there it will continue with the next line in sequence.

There may not always be an ELSE part, as below:

```
1    IF P > 3
2    THEN
3        X = X + Y
4    ENDIF
```

In this case the computer executes line 3 if the condition is true, or moves on to line 4 (the next line in sequence) if the condition is false.

ITERATION

Iteration structures are called loops. The most common loop is known as a DO WHILE (or WHILE DO) loop and is illustrated below:

```
1    X = 15
2    Count = 0
3    WHILE X < 20 DO
4        X = X + 1
5        Count = Count + 1
6    END DO
```

As with the selection structures there is a decision. In this case the condition that is tested at the decision is X < 20. If the condition is true the program 'enters the loop' by executing the code between DO and END DO. In this case the value of X is increased by one and the value of Count is increased by one. When this is done the program goes back to line 3 and repeats the test. If X < 20 is still true the program 'enters the loop' again. This continues as long as the condition is true. If the condition is false the program goes directly to line 6 and then continues to the next sequential instruction. In the program fragment above, the loop will be executed five times before the value of X reaches 20 and causes the loop to terminate. The value of Count will then be 5.

There is another variation of the loop structure known as a REPEAT UNTIL loop. It looks like this:

```
1    X = 15
2    Count = 0
3    REPEAT
4        X = X + 1
5        Count = Count + 1
6    UNTIL X = 20
```

The difference from a DO WHILE loop is that the condition is at the end, so the loop will always be executed at least once. Every time the code inside the loop is executed the program checks the condition. When the condition is true the program continues with the next sequential instruction. The outcome of this REPEAT UNTIL loop will be exactly the same as the DO WHILE loop above.

CHECK OF UNDERSTANDING

1. What is meant by the term executable statement?
2. Briefly describe the two forms of looping structure introduced in this section.
3. What is a selection structure?
4. How many different paths are there through a selection structure?

Flow charts

Now that we can read code we can go a step further and create a visual representation of the structure that is much easier to work with. The simplest visual structure to draw is the flow chart, which has only two symbols. Rectangles represent sequential statements and diamonds represent decisions. More than one sequential statement can be placed inside a single rectangle as long as there are no decisions in the sequence. Any decision is represented by a diamond, including those associated with loops.

Let us look at our earlier examples again.

To create a flow chart representation of a complete program (see Example 4.5) all we need to do is to connect together all the different bits of structure.

Figure 4.4 Flow chart for a sequential program

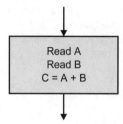

Figure 4.5 Flow chart for a selection (decision) structure

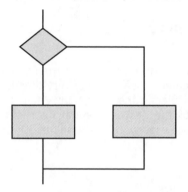

Figure 4.6 Flow chart for an iteration (loop) structure

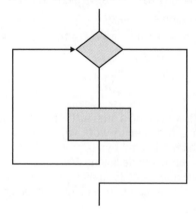

PROGRAM ANALYSIS – EXAMPLE 4.5

Here is a simple program for calculating the mean and maximum of three integers.

```
1    Program MaxandMean
2
3    A, B, C, Maximum: Integer
4    Mean: Real
5
6    Begin
7
8    Read A
9    Read B
10   Read C
11   Mean = (A + B + C)/3
12
13   If A > B
14   Then
15       If A > C
16       Then
17           Maximum = A
18       Else
19           Maximum = C
20       Endif
21   Else
22       If B > C
23       Then
24           Maximum = B
25       Else
26           Maximum = C
27       Endif
28   Endif
29
30   Print ("Mean of A, B and C is ", Mean)
31   Print ("Maximum of A, B, C is ", Maximum)
32
33   End
```

Note one important thing about this code: it has some non-executable statements (those before the **Begin** and those after the **Begin** that are actually blank lines) that we will have to take account of when we come to count the number of executable statements later. The line numbering makes it a little easier to do the counting.

By the way, you may have noticed that the program does not recognise if two of the numbers are the same value, but simplicity is more important than sophistication at this stage.

This program can be expressed as a flow chart; have a go at drawing it before you look at the solution in the text.

Figure 4.7 shows the flow chart for Example 4.5.

Figure 4.7 Flow chart representation for Example 4.5

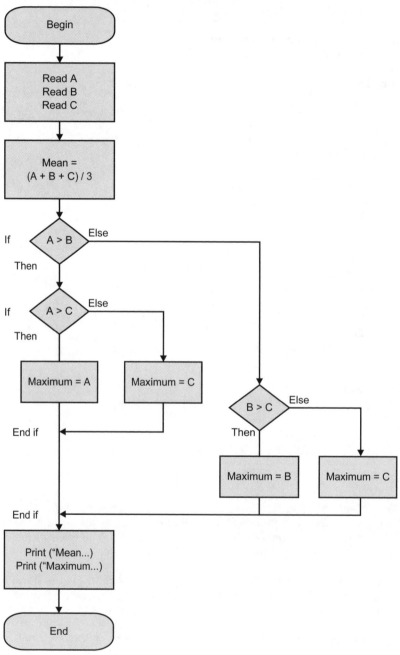

Before we move on to look at how we generate test cases for code, we need to look briefly at another form of graphical representation called the control flow graph.

Control flow graphs

A control flow graph provides a method of representing the decision points and the flow of control within a piece of code, so it is just like a flow chart except that it only shows decisions. A control flow graph is produced by looking only at the statements affecting the flow of control.

The graph itself is made up of two symbols: nodes and edges. A node represents any point where the flow of control can be modified (i.e. decision points), or the points where a control structure returns to the main flow (e.g. END WHILE or ENDIF). An edge is a line connecting any two nodes. The closed area contained within a collection of nodes and edges, as shown in the diagram, is known as a region.

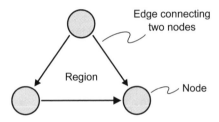

We can draw 'subgraphs' to represent individual structures. For a flow graph the representation of sequence is just a straight line, since there is no decision to cause any branching.

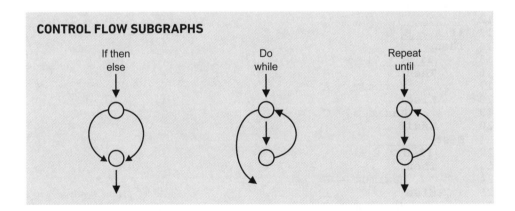

The subgraphs show what the control flow graph would look like for the program structures we are already familiar with.

DRAWING A CONTROL FLOW GRAPH

The steps are as follows:

1. Analyse the component to identify all control structures, that is all statements that can modify the flow of control, ignoring all sequential statements.
2. Add a node for any decision statement.
3. Expand the node by substituting the appropriate subgraph representing the structure at the decision point.

Any chunk of code can be represented by using these subgraphs.

As an example, we will return to Example 4.5.

Step 1 breaks the code into statements and identifies the control structures, ignoring the sequential statements, in order to identify the decision points; these are highlighted below.

```
1    Program MaxandMean
2
3    A, B, C, Maximum: Integer
4    Mean: Real
5
6    Begin
7
8    Read A
9    Read B
10   Read C
11   Mean = (A + B + C)/3
12
13   If A > B
14   Then
15        If A > C
16        Then
17             Maximum = A
18        Else
19             Maximum = C
20        Endif
21   Else
22        If B > C
23        Then
24             Maximum = B
25        Else
26             Maximum = C
27        Endif
28   Endif
29
30   Print ("Mean of A, B and C is ", Mean)
31   Print ("Maximum of A, B, C is ", Maximum)
32
33   End
```

Step 2 adds a node for each branching or decision statement (Figure 4.8).

Step 3 expands the nodes by substituting the appropriate subgraphs (Figure 4.9).

Figure 4.8 Control flow graph showing subgraphs as nodes

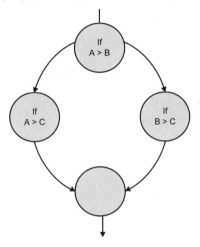

Figure 4.9 Control flow graph with subgraphs expanded

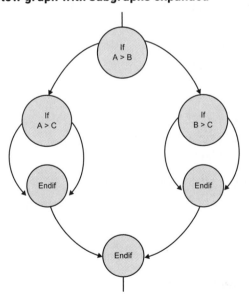

Exercise 4.6

Draw a flow chart and a control flow graph to represent the following code:

```
1    Program OddandEven
2
3    A, B: Real;
4    Odd: Integer;
5
6    Begin
7        Read A
8        Read B
9        C = A + B
10       D = A - B
11       Odd = 0
12
13       If A/2 DIV 2 <> 0  (DIV gives the remainder after division)
14       Then Odd = Odd + 1
15       Endif
16
17       If B/2 DIV 2 <> 0
18       Then Odd = Odd + 1
19       Endif
20
21       If Odd = 1
22       Then
23           Print ("C is odd")
24           Print ("D is odd")
25       Else
26           Print ("C is even")
27           Print ("D is even")
28       Endif
29   End
```

The answer can be found at the end of the chapter.

Statement testing and coverage

Statement testing is testing aimed at exercising programming statements. If we aim to test every executable statement we call this full or 100 per cent statement coverage. If we exercise half the executable statements this is 50 per cent statement coverage, and so on. Remember: we are only interested in executable statements, so we do not count non-executable statements at all when we are measuring statement coverage.

Why measure statement coverage? It is a very basic measure that testing has been (relatively) thorough. After all, a suite of tests that had not exercised all of the code would not be considered complete. Actually, achieving 100 per cent statement coverage does not tell us very much, and there are much more rigorous coverage measures that we can apply, but it provides a baseline from which we can move on to more useful coverage measures. Look at the following pseudo code:

```
1    Program Coverage example
2    A, X: Integer
3    Begin
4        Read A
5        Read X
6        If A > 1 AND X = 2
7        Then
8            X = X/A
9        Endif
10       If A = 2 OR X = 2
11       Then
12           X = X + 1
13       Endif
14   End
```

A flow chart can represent this, as in Figure 4.10.

Having explored flow charts and flow graphs a little, you will see that flow charts are very good at showing you where the executable statements are; they are all represented by diamonds or rectangles and where there is no rectangle there is no executable code. A flow graph is less cluttered, showing only the structural details, in particular where the program branches and rejoins. Do we need both diagrams? Well, neither has everything that we need. However, we can produce a version of the flow graph that allows us to determine statement coverage.

To do this we build a conventional control flow graph but then we add a node for every branch in which there is one or more statements. Take the Coverage example; we can produce its flow graph easily as shown in Figure 4.11.

Before we proceed, let us confirm what happens when a program runs. Once the program starts it will run through to the end executing every statement that it comes to in sequence. Control structures will be the only diversion from this end-to-end sequence, so we need to understand what happens with the control structures when the program runs. The best way to do that is to 'dry run' the program with some inputs; this means writing down the inputs and then stepping through the program logic noting what happens at each step and what values change. When you get to the end you will know what the output values (if any) will be and you will know exactly what path the program has taken through the logic.

Figure 4.10 Flow chart for Coverage example

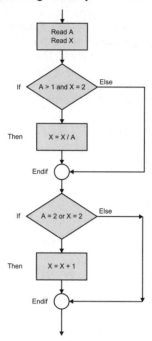

THE HYBRID FLOW GRAPH

Figure 4.11 The hybrid flow graph

Note the additional nodes that represent the edges with executable statements in them; they make it a little easier to identify what needs to be counted for statement coverage.

PATHS THROUGH A PROGRAM

Flow charts, control flow graphs and hybrid flow graphs all show essentially the same information, but sometimes one format is more helpful than another. We have identified the hybrid flow graph as a useful combination of the control flow graph and the control flow chart. To make it even more useful we can add to it labels to indicate the paths that a program can follow through the code. All we need to do is to label each edge; paths are then made up from sequences of the labels, such as abeh, which make up a path through the code (see Figure 4.12).

Figure 4.12 Paths through the hybrid flow graph

In the Coverage example, for which we drew the flow chart in Figure 4.10, 100 per cent statement coverage can be achieved by writing a single test case that follows the path acdfgh (using lower case letters to label the arcs on the diagram that represent path fragments). By setting A = 2 and X = 2 at point a, every statement will be executed once. However, what if the first decision should be an OR rather than an AND? The test would not have detected the error, since the condition will be true in both cases. Similarly, if the second decision should have stated X > 2 this error would have gone undetected because the value of A guarantees that the condition is true. Also, there is a path through the program in which X goes unchanged (the path abeh). If this were an error it would also go undetected.

Remember that statement coverage takes into account only executable statements. There are 12 in the Coverage example if we count the **BEGIN** and **END** statements, so statement coverage would be 12/12 or 100 per cent. There are alternative ways to count executable statements: some people count the **BEGIN** and **END** statements; some count the lines containing **IF, THEN** and **ELSE**; some count none of these. It does not matter as long as:

- You exclude the non-executable statements that precede **BEGIN**.

- You ignore blank lines that have been inserted for clarity.

- You are consistent about what you do or do not include in the count with respect to control structures.

As a general rule, for the reasons given above, statement coverage is too weak to be considered an adequate measure of test effectiveness.

STATEMENT TESTING – EXAMPLE 4.6

Here is an example of the kind you might see in an exam. Try to answer the question, but if you get stuck the answer follows immediately in the text.

Here is a program. How many test cases will you need to achieve 100 per cent statement coverage and what will the test cases be?

```
1    Program BestInterest
2    Interest, Base Rate, Balance: Real
3
4    Begin
5    Base Rate = 0.035
6    Interest = Base Rate
7
8    Read (Balance)
9    If Balance > 1000
10   Then
11       Interest = Interest + 0.005
12       If Balance < 10000
13       Then
14           Interest = Interest + 0.005
15       Else
16           Interest = Interest + 0.010
17       Endif
18   Endif
19
20   Balance = Balance × (1 + Interest)
21
22   End
```

Figure 4.13 shows what the flow graph looks like. It is drawn in the hybrid flow graph format so that you can see which branches need to be exercised for statement coverage.

Figure 4.13 Paths through the hybrid flow graph

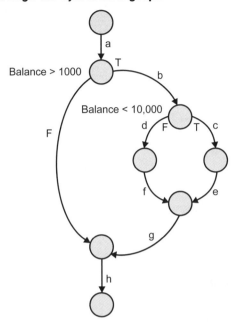

It is clear from the flow graph that the left-hand side (Balance below £1,000) need not be exercised, but there are two alternative paths (Balance between £1,000 and £10,000 and Balance > £10,000) that need to be exercised.

So we need two test cases for 100 per cent statement coverage and Balance = £5,000, Balance = £20,000 will be suitable test cases.

Alternatively we can aim to follow the paths abcegh and abdfgh marked on the flow graph. How many test cases do we need to do that?

We can do this with one test case to set the initial balance value to a value between £1,000 and £10,000 (to follow abcegh) and one test case to set the initial balance to something higher than £10,000, say £12,000 (to follow path abdfgh).

So we need two test cases to achieve 100 per cent statement coverage in this case.

Now look at this example from the perspective of the tester actually trying to achieve statement coverage. Suppose we have set ourselves an exit criterion of 100 per cent statement coverage by the end of component testing. If we ran a single test with an input of Balance = £10,000 we can see that that test case would take us down the path abdfgh, but it would not take us down the path abcegh, and line 14 of the pseudo code would not be exercised. So that test case has not achieved 100 per cent statement coverage and we will need another test case to exercise line 14 by taking path abcegh. We know that Balance = £5000 would do that. We can build up a test suite in this way to achieve any desired level of statement coverage.

CHECK OF UNDERSTANDING

1. What is meant by statement coverage?
2. In a flow chart, how do you decide which paths to include in determining how many test cases are needed to achieve a given level of statement coverage?
3. Does 100 per cent statement coverage exercise all the paths through a program?

Exercise 4.7

For the following program:

```
1    Program Grading
2
3    StudentScore: Integer
4    Result: String
5
6    Begin
7
8    Read StudentScore
9
10   If StudentScore > 79
11   Then Result = "Distinction"
12   Else
13       If StudentScore > 59
14       Then Result = "Merit"
15       Else
16           If StudentScore > 39
17           Then Result = "Pass"
18           Else Result = "Fail"
19           Endif
20       Endif
21   Endif
22   Print ("Your result is", Result)
23   End
```

How many test cases would be needed for 100 per cent statement coverage?

The answer can be found at the end of the chapter.

Exercise 4.8

Now using the program Grading in Exercise 4.7 again, try to calculate whether 100 per cent statement coverage is achieved with a given set of data (this would be a K4 level question in the exam).

Suppose we ran two test cases, as follows:

Test Case 1 StudentScore = 50

Test Case 2 StudentScore = 30

1. Would 100 per cent statement coverage be achieved?
2. If not, which lines of pseudo code will not be exercised?

The answer can be found at the end of the chapter.

Decision testing and coverage

Decision testing aims to ensure that the decisions in a program are adequately exercised. Decisions, as you know, are part of selection and iteration structures; we see them in IF THEN ELSE constructs and in DO WHILE or REPEAT UNTIL loops. To test a decision we need to exercise it when the associated condition is true and when the condition is false; this guarantees that both exits from the decision are exercised.

As with statement testing, decision testing has an associated coverage measure and we normally aim to achieve 100 per cent decision coverage. Decision coverage is measured by counting the number of decision outcomes exercised (each exit from a decision is known as a decision outcome) divided by the total number of decision outcomes in a given program. It is usually expressed as a percentage.

The usual starting point is a control flow graph, from which we can visualise all the possible decisions and their exit paths. Have a look at the following example.

```
1    Program Check
2
3    Count, Sum, Index: Integer
4
5    Begin
6
7    Index = 0
8    Sum = 0
9    Read (Count)
10   Read (New)
11
12   While Index <= Count
13   Do
14       If New < 0
15       Then
16           Sum = Sum + 1
17       Endif
18       Index = Index + 1
19       Read (New)
20   Enddo
21
22   Print ("There were", Sum, "negative numbers in the input
     stream")
23
24   End
```

This program has a WHILE loop in it. There is a golden rule about WHILE loops. If the condition at the WHILE statement is true when the program reaches it for the first time then any test case will exercise that decision in both directions because it will eventually be false when the loop terminates. For example, as long as Index is less than Count when the program reaches the loop for the first time, the condition will be true and the loop will be entered. Each time the program runs through the loop it will increase the value of Index by one, so eventually Index will reach the value of Count and pass it, at which stage the condition is false and the loop will not be entered. So the decision at the start of the loop is exercised through both its true exit and its false exit by a single test case. This makes the assumption that the logic of the loop is sound, but we are assuming that we are receiving this program from the developers who will have debugged it.

Now all we have to do is to make sure that we exercise the **If** statement inside the loop through both its true and false exits. We can do this by ensuring that the input stream has both negative and positive numbers in it.

For example, a test case that sets the variable Count to 5 and then inputs the values 1, 5, −2, −3, 6 will exercise all the decisions fully and provide us with 100 per cent decision coverage. Note that this is considered to be a single test case, even though there is more than one value for the variable New, because the values are all input in a single execution of the program. This example does not provide the smallest set of inputs that would achieve 100 per cent decision coverage, but it does provide a valid example.

Although loops are a little more complicated to understand than programs without loops, they can be easier to test once you get the hang of them.

DECISION TESTING – EXAMPLE 4.7

Let us try an example without a loop now.

```
1    Program Age Check
2
3    CandidateAge: Integer;
4
5    Begin
6
7    Read(CandidateAge)
8
9    If CandidateAge < 18
10   Then
11       Print ("Candidate is too young")
12   Else
13       If CandidateAge > 30
14       Then
15           Print ("Candidate is too old")
16       Else
17           Print("Candidate may join Club 18–30")
18       Endif
19   Endif
20
21   End
```

Have a go at calculating how many test cases are needed for 100 per cent decision coverage and see if you can identify suitable test cases.

Figure 4.14 shows the flow graph drawn in the hybrid flow graph format.

Figure 4.14 Paths through the hybrid flow graph

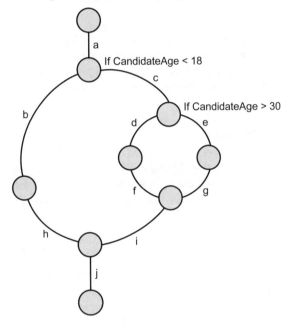

How many test cases will we need to achieve 100 per cent decision coverage? Well each test case will just run through from top to bottom, so we can only exercise one branch of the structure at a time.

We have labelled the path fragments a, b, c, d, e, f, g, h, i, j and you can see that we have three alternative routes through the program – path abhj, path acegij and path acdfij. That needs three test cases.

The first test case needs decision 1 to be true – so CandidateAge = 16 will be OK here. The second needs to make the first decision false and the second decision true, so CandidateAge must be more than 18 and more than 30 – let us say 40. The third test case needs the first decision to be false and the second decision to be false, so CandidateAge of 21 would do here. (You cannot tell which exit is true and which is false in the second decision; if you want to, you can label the exits T and

F, though in this case it does not really matter because we intend to exercise them both anyway.)

So, we need three test cases for 100 per cent decision coverage:

CandidateAge = 16
CandidateAge = 21
CandidateAge = 40

which will exercise all the decisions.

Note that when we are testing decisions, we need to exercise the true and false outcomes of each decision, even if one of these has no statements associated with it. So decision coverage gives us that little bit extra in return for a little more work. One hundred per cent decision coverage guarantees 100 per cent statement coverage, but 100 per cent statement coverage may be less than 100 per cent decision coverage.

CHECK OF UNDERSTANDING

1. What is the purpose of decision testing?
2. How many test cases are needed to exercise a single decision?
3. How many test cases are needed to exercise a loop structure?

Exercise 4.9

This program reads a list of non-negative numbers terminated by –1.

```
1    Program Counting Numbers
2
3    A: Integer
4    Count: Integer
5
6    Begin
7    Count = 0
8    Read A
9    While A <> −1
10   Do
11       Count = Count + 1
12       Read A
13   EndDo
14
15   Print ("There are", Count, "numbers in the list")
16   End
```

How many test cases are needed to achieve 100 per cent decision coverage?

The answer can be found at the end of the chapter.

Exercise 4.10

Using Program Counting Numbers from Exercise 4.9, what level of decision coverage would be achieved by the single input A = –1?

The answer can be found at the end of the chapter.

Simplified control flow graphs

Simplified control flow graphs (CFGs) share the format used for flow charts. They incorporate less detail since their purpose is to identify control structures but not the detail of code. Questions for the CTFL exam are set using simplified CFGs instead of code, so this section deals with the interpretation of simplified CFGs and provides examples and exercises that cover all the learning objectives associated with these structures.

In simplified CFGs, a sequence of code is presented as one or more boxes in a line. Strictly speaking only a single box is needed but additional boxes are sometimes included to make the CFG easier to follow. Decisions are represented by a single box with two exits, usually labelled T and F (for True and False respectively).

Figure 4.15 shows a simplified CFG depicting a sequence of code followed by a decision based on the evaluation of a decision.

Figure 4.15 Simplified control flow graph: a decision

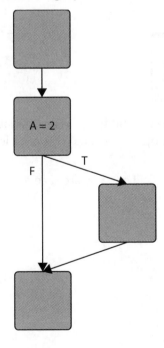

Looping structures can have a decision at the beginning of the loop or at the end (see Figure 4.16).

Figure 4.16 Simplified control flow graph: location of a decision in a loop

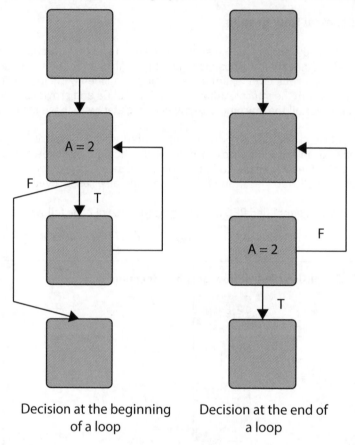

Decision at the beginning
of a loop

Decision at the end of
a loop

Here is an example of how simplified CFGs are read and interpreted for simple structures.

EXAMPLE 4.8

Figure 4.17 Example of how simplified control flow graphs are read and interpreted

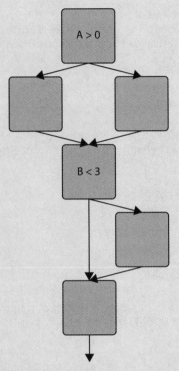

Which of the following pairs of tests would achieve 100 per cent decision coverage for the structure shown in Figure 4.17?

    a. $A = 1, B = 2; A = 0, B = 1$
    b. $A = 2, B = 4; A = 1, B = 2$
    c. $A = 3, B = 0; A = 0, B = 1$
    d. $A = 0, B = 4; A = 1, B = 3$

Answer – The correct answer is d.

Option a. In the first decision A is greater than zero in the first test and equals zero in the second, so this decision has been exercised in both directions. B is less than 3 in both tests, so decision B > 3 is not exercised in both directions. Therefore 100 per cent decision coverage has not been achieved.

Option b. A is greater than zero in both tests, so the decision A > 0 has not been exercised in both directions. Therefore 100 per cent decision coverage has not been achieved.

123

Option c. A is greater than zero in test 1 and equals zero in test 2, so decision A > 0 has been exercised in both directions. B is less than 3 in both tests, so decision B > 3 has not been exercised in both directions. Therefore 100 per cent decision coverage has not been achieved.

Option d. A equals zero on test 1 and equals 1 in test 2, so test A > 0 has been exercised in both directions. B is greater than 3 in test 1, but not in test 2, so decision B > 3 has been exercised in both directions. Therefore 100 per cent decision coverage has been achieved.

EXAMPLE 4.9

Using the same diagram as in Example 4.8, which of the following sets of test cases would achieve 50 per cent decision coverage?

    a.   A = 1, B = 2; A = 0, B = 3
    b.   A = 0, B = 4; A = 1, B = 3
    c.   A = 1, B = 2; A = 2, B = 2
    d.   A = 5, B = 4; A = 0, B = 3

Answer – The correct answer is c.

Option a. The decision A > 0 has been exercised in both directions, but decision B > 3 has been exercised in only one direction. Therefore the decision coverage would be 3/4 or 75 per cent.

Option b. The decision A > 0 has been exercised in both directions and decision B > 3 has been exercised in both directions. Therefore the decision coverage would be 4/4 or 100 per cent.

Option c. The decision A > 0 has not been exercised in both directions and decision B > 3 has not been exercised in both directions. Therefore the decision coverage is 2/4 or 50 per cent.

Option d. The decision A > 0 has been exercised in both directions and decision B > 3 has been exercised in both directions. Therefore the decision coverage would be 4/4 or 100 per cent.

Exercise 4.11

In the simplified CFG shown in Figure 4.18, which of the following sets of test cases would achieve 100 per cent statement coverage?

Figure 4.18 Control flow graph for Exercise 4.11

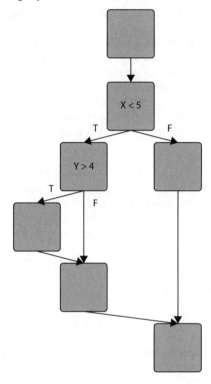

    a.   X = 7, Y = 6; X = 3, Y = 5
    b.   X = 3, Y = 3; X = 4, Y = 4
    c.   X = 6, Y = 5; X = 1, Y = 1
    d.   X = 5, Y = 4; X = 4, Y = 4

The answer can be found at the end of the chapter.

Exercise 4.12

In the same CFG shown in the previous exercise, how many test cases would be required to achieve 100 per cent decision coverage?

    a.   1
    b.   2
    c.   3
    d.   4

The answer can be found at the end of the chapter.

There are further questions for you to try at the end of this chapter.

Other structure-based techniques

More sophisticated techniques are available to provide increasingly complete code coverage. In some applications these are essential: for example, in a safety-critical system it is vital to know that nothing unacceptable happens at any point when the code is executed. Would you like to 'fly by wire' if you did not know what was happening in the software? The many well documented mishaps in computer-controlled systems provide compelling examples of what can happen if code – even code that is not providing essential functionality in some cases – does something unexpected. Measures such as condition coverage and multiple condition coverage are used to reduce the likelihood that code will behave in unpredictable ways by examining more of it in more complex scenarios.

Coverage is also applicable to other types and levels of structure. For example, at the integration level it is useful to know what percentage of modules or interfaces has been exercised by a test suite, while at the functional level it is helpful to step through all the possible paths of a menu structure. We can also apply the idea of coverage to areas outside the computer, for example by exercising all the possible paths through a business process as testing scenarios.

EXPERIENCE-BASED TECHNIQUES

Experience-based techniques are those that you fall back on when there is no adequate specification from which to derive specification-based test cases or no time to run the full structured set of tests. They use the users' and the testers' experience to determine the most important areas of a system and to exercise these areas in ways that are both consistent with expected use (and abuse) and likely to be the sites of errors – this is where the experience comes in. Even when specifications are available it is worth supplementing the structured tests with some that you know by experience have found defects in other similar systems.

Techniques range from the simplistic approach of ad hoc testing or error guessing through to the more sophisticated techniques such as exploratory testing, but all tap the knowledge and experience of the tester rather than systematically exploring a system against a written specification.

Error guessing

Error guessing is a very simple technique that takes advantage of a tester's skill, intuition and experience with similar applications to identify special tests that may not be easy to capture by the more formal techniques. When applied after systematic techniques, error guessing can add value in identifying and exercising test cases that target known or suspected weaknesses or that simply address aspects of the application that have been found to be problematical in the past.

The main drawback of error guessing is its varying effectiveness, depending as it does on the experience of the tester deploying it. However, if several testers and/or users contribute to constructing a list of possible errors and tests are designed to attack each error listed, this weakness can be effectively overcome. Another way to make error guessing more structured is by the creation of defect and failure lists. These lists can use available defect and failure data (where this exists) as a starting point, but the list can be expanded by using the testers' and users' experience of why the application under test in particular is likely to fail. The defect and failure list can be used as the basis of a set of tests that are applied after the systematic techniques have been used. This systematic approach is known as fault attack.

Exploratory testing

Exploratory testing is a technique that combines the experience of testers with a structured approach to testing where specifications are either missing or inadequate and where there is severe time pressure. It exploits concurrent test design, test execution, test logging and learning within time-boxes and is structured around a test charter containing test objectives. In this way exploratory testing maximises the amount of testing that can be achieved within a limited time frame, using test objectives to maintain focus on the most important areas.

SYSTEMATIC AND EXPERIENCE-BASED TECHNIQUES

How do we decide which is the best technique? There are some simple rules of thumb:

1. Always make functional testing the first priority. It may be necessary to test early code products using structural techniques, but we only really learn about the quality of software when we can see what it does.

2. When basic functional testing is complete that is a good time to think about test coverage. Have you exercised all the functions, all the requirements, all the code? Coverage measures defined at the beginning as exit criteria can now come into play. Where coverage is inadequate extra tests will be needed.

3. Use structural methods to supplement functional methods where possible. Even if functional coverage is adequate, it will usually be worth checking statement and decision coverage to ensure that enough of the code has been exercised during testing.

4. Once systematic testing is complete there is an opportunity to use experience-based techniques to ensure that all the most important and most error-prone areas of the software have been exercised. In some circumstances, such as poor specifications or time pressure, experience-based testing may be the only viable option.

The decision of which test technique to use is not a simple one. There are many factors to bear in mind, some of which are listed in the box.

KEY SELECTION FACTORS

- Type of system.
- Regulatory standards.
- Customer or contractual requirements.
- Level of risk.
- Type of risk.
- Test objectives.
- Documentation available.
- Knowledge of the testers.
- Time and budget.
- Development life cycle.
- Use case models.
- Experience of type of defects found.

CHOOSING TEST TECHNIQUES

One or more of these factors may be important on any given occasion. Some leave no room for selection: regulatory or contractual requirements leave the tester with no choice. Test objectives, where they relate to exit criteria such as test coverage, may also lead to mandatory techniques. Where documentation is not available, or where time and budget are limited, the use of experience-based techniques may be favoured. All others provide pointers within a broad framework: level and type of risk will push the tester towards a particular approach, where high risk is a good reason for using systematic techniques; knowledge of testers, especially where this is limited, may narrow down the available choices; the type of system and the development life cycle will encourage testers to lean in one direction or another depending on their own particular experience. There are few clear-cut cases, and the exercise of sound judgement in selecting appropriate techniques is a mark of a good test manager or team leader.

CHECK OF UNDERSTANDING

1. What is meant by experience-based testing?
2. Briefly compare error guessing and exploratory testing.
3. When is the best time to use experience-based testing?

SUMMARY

In this chapter we have considered the most important terminology needed in discussing the specification stage of the fundamental test process, which was introduced in **Chapter 1**. We explained how test conditions are derived and how test cases can be designed and grouped into test procedures for execution.

Test design techniques were categorised into three main groups known as specification-based or black-box techniques, structure-based or white-box techniques, and experience-based techniques.

Specification-based techniques introduced were equivalence partitioning, boundary value analysis, state transition testing, decision table testing and use case testing. Specific worked examples of all except use case testing were given (and this was excluded solely because the examination does not require the ability to generate test cases from use cases). Structure-based techniques were introduced and worked examples were given for statement testing and decision testing. Experience-based techniques introduced included error guessing and exploratory testing.

Finally the factors involved in selecting test case design techniques were discussed and guidance given on the selection criteria to be applied.

Example examination questions with answers

E1. K1 question
Which of the following describes structure-based (white-box) test case design techniques?

a. Test cases are derived systematically from models of the system.
b. Test cases are derived systematically from the tester's experience.
c. Test cases are derived systematically from the delivered code.
d. Test cases are derived from the developers' experience.

E2. K1 question
Which of the following is a structure-based (white-box) technique?

a. Decision table testing.
b. State transition testing.
c. Statement testing.
d. Boundary value analysis.

E3. K3 question
A washing machine has three temperature bands for different kinds of fabrics: fragile fabrics are washed at temperatures between 15 and 30 degrees Celsius; normal fabrics are washed at temperatures between 31 and 60 degrees Celsius; heavily soiled and tough fabrics are washed at temperatures between 61 and 100 degrees Celsius.

Which of the following contains only values that are in *different* equivalence partitions?

a. 15, 30, 60
b. 20, 35, 60
c. 25, 45, 75
d. 12, 35, 55

E4. K3 question

Figure 4.19 Test case for examination question E4

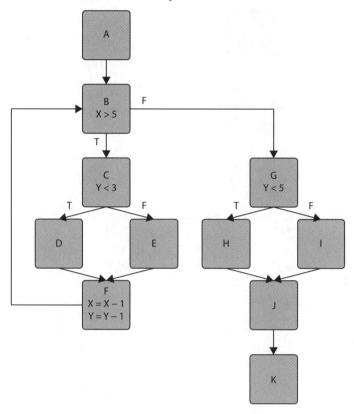

Using Figure 4.19, test case 1 is executed with the values X = 6, Y = 2.

Which of the following paths will be executed by test case 1?

    a.   ABCEFBGIJK

    b.   ABCDFBGIJK

    c.   ABCDFBGHJK

    d.   ABCDFBCEFGHJK

E5. K4 question

Figure 4.20 Test case for examination question E5

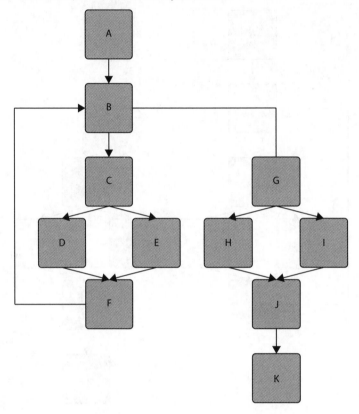

In Figure 4.20, the goal for the project is 100 per cent decision coverage and the following tests have so far been executed:

- Test 1 covers path ABCDFBGHJK.
- Test 2 covers path ABGIJK.

Which of the following statements about decision coverage is correct?

    a.   Decision B has not been tested completely.

    b.   One hundred per cent decision coverage has been achieved.

    c.   Decision G has not been tested completely.

    d.   Decision C has not been tested completely.

E6. K1 question
What is the main purpose of use case testing?

    a.   To identify defects in process flows related to typical use of the system.

    b.   To identify defects in the connections between components.

    c.   To identify defects in the system related to extreme scenarios.

    d.   To identify defects in the system related to the use of unapproved programming practices.

E7. K2 question
Which of the following are the *most* important factors to be taken into account when selecting test techniques?

    i.   Tools available.

    ii.   Regulatory standards.

    iii.   Experience of the development team.

    iv.   Knowledge of the test team.

    v.   The need to maintain levels of capability in each technique.

    a.   i and ii.

    b.   ii and iv.

    c.   iii and iv.

    d.   i and v.

Answers to questions in the chapter

SA1. The correct answer is c.
SA2. The correct answer is b.
SA3. The correct answer is c.

Exercise 4.1

The partitions would be: £0.00–£1,000.00, £1,000.01–£2,000.00, and >= £2,000.01.

Exercise 4.2

The valid partitions would be: £0.00–£20.00, £20.01–£40.00, and >= £40.01. Non-valid partitions would include negative values and alphabetic characters.

Exercise 4.3

The partitions would be: question scores 0–20; total 0–100; question differences: 0–3 and > 3; total differences 0–10 and > 10.

Boundary values would be: –1, 0, 1 and 19, 20, 21 for the question scores; –1, 0, 1 (again) and 99, 100, 101 for the question paper totals; –1, 0, 1 (again) and 2, 3, 4 for differences between question scores for different markers; and –1, 0, 1 (again) and 9, 10, 11 for total differences between different markers.

In this case, although the –1, 0, 1 values occur several times, they may be applied to different parts of the program (e.g. the question score checks will probably be in a different part of the program from the total score checks) so we may need to repeat these values in the boundary tests.

Exercise 4.4

Billy will be eligible for a cash payment but not for a share allocation.

Exercise 4.5

The correct answer is b.

Option a includes the transition DE; option c includes the transition CE; option d includes the transition FA. None of these is valid from the diagram.

Exercise 4.6

The flow chart is shown in Figure 4.21. The control flow graph is shown in Figure 4.22.

Exercise 4.7

The answer is four because there are three decisions and every outcome has an executable statement in it.

Figure 4.21 Flow chart for Exercise 4.6

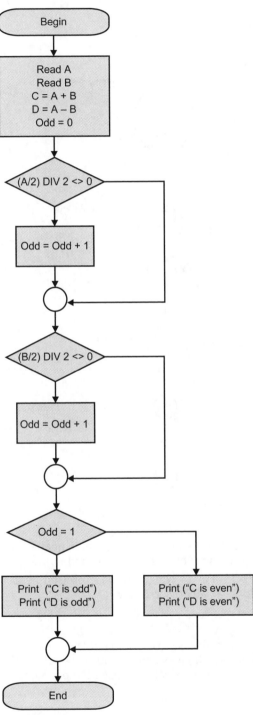

Figure 4.22 Control flow graph for Exercise 4.6

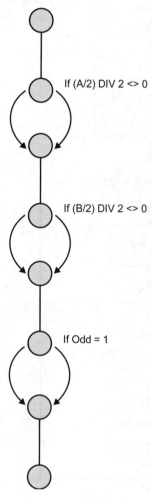

Exercise 4.8

1. No, 100 per cent statement coverage would not be achieved. We know from Exercise 4.7 that four test cases are needed.
2. Statements 11 and 14 would not be exercised because they need inputs higher than 79 and 59 respectively.

Exercise 4.9

The answer is one because a single list terminated by −1 (say 4, 6, 3, −1) will enter the loop the first three times and then exit on the fourth; hence the WHILE decision will be true three times and then false, which exercises the decision in both directions with one test case.

A single test case with values of 1, −1 would also exercise all decisions.

Exercise 4.10

Decision coverage of 50 per cent will be achieved. The −1 input will make the **While** condition False and the loop will not be entered. The program will print the message 'There are 0 integers in the list' and terminate, so the True outcome of the decision will not be exercised.

Exercise 4.11

The correct answer is a.

There are statements in the false exit from decision X < 5 and in the true exit from decision Y > 4, so we need two tests because the test that makes X < 5 false will bypass the decision Y > 4. One of the test cases can be any pair of values that has X >= 5, so X can be 5 or more and Y is irrelevant. In the other test, X must be less than 5 and Y must also be greater than 4. Many pairs of values, such as X = 4, Y = 5, would be suitable. The two tests must have X >= 5 in one test and X < 5 AND Y > 4 in the other. Option a meets these criteria. Option b has X < 5 in both tests, so it cannot be correct. Option c has one test with X > 5 but, although the other test has X < 5, it also sets Y to 1, so Y > 4 is not true. Option d has X = 5 in one test and X < 5 in the other, but in this case the value of Y is 4, so Y > 4 is not true.

Exercise 4.12

The correct answer is c.

In this case we must not only execute every branch with a statement in it, but we must exercise every decision in both its true and false states. We could arrive at the correct answer by recognising that the CFG has two regions and two decisions. The questions regions + 1 and decisions + 1 both give the answer 3. We could also work it out from first principles. The paths we would need to follow would be:

1. False through X < 5
2. True through X < 5 AND True through Y > 4
3. True through X < 5 AND False through Y > 4

These three tests would exercise both decisions in their true and false states and would therefore achieve 100 per cent decision coverage.

Answers to example questions

E1. The correct answer is c.
Option a relates to specification-based testing; option b relates to experience-based testing; option d could relate either to debugging or to experience-based techniques.

E2. The correct answer is c.
All other options are specification-based (black-box) techniques, and the main distracter is option a because decision table testing could be confused with decision testing.

E3. The correct answer is c.
Option a includes two values from the lower partition; option b contains two values from the second partition; option d contains one value that is invalid (out of range).

E4. The correct answer is c.
For a to be true, $Y >= 3$ would have to be true. For b to be true $Y >= 5$ would have to be true. For d to be true $Y >= 3$ would have to be true after one traversal of the loop.

E5. The correct answer is d.
Option a is not true because B was exercised one way in test case 1 and the other way in test case 2. Option b is not true because E has not been traversed, which means that decision E has not been exercised in both directions. Option c is not true because decision G is exercised one way in test case 1 and the other way in test case 2.

E6. The correct answer is a.
Option b relates to integration testing; option c could relate to boundary value analysis or performance testing, but use cases exercise typical process flows rather than extreme examples; option d relates to static analysis.

E7. The correct answer is b.
i looks tempting, and the availability of tools might make the use of a technique more or less attractive, but it would not be decisive in the way that regulatory standards and tester knowledge are. iii is irrelevant because testing should be independent of development anyway, but it could tempt someone who is unsure about the relationship between development and testing. v is a factor in managing the test team, and experience would need to be maintained, but this should not influence the selection of techniques for a live project.

5 TEST MANAGEMENT

Geoff Thompson

INTRODUCTION

This chapter provides a generic overview of how testing is organised and how testing is managed within organisations. A generic view of testing will, inevitably, not match the way testing is organised in specific organisations. The issues addressed are nevertheless important for any organisation and need to be considered by all.

We will start by looking at how testing and risk fit together, as well as providing detailed coverage of test planning and the control of testing, and we will identify how independence assists the test process. One very important area in managing the test process is the understanding of the different roles and tasks associated with the testing role such as the test leader and the tester.

We cannot, in one chapter, provide all the knowledge required to enable the reader to become a practising test leader or test manager, but we do aim to provide the background information necessary for a reader to understand the various facets of the test management role.

Learning objectives

The learning objectives for this chapter are listed below. You can confirm that you have achieved these by using the self-assessment questions at the start of the chapter, the 'Check of understanding' boxes distributed throughout the text, and the example examination questions provided at the end of the chapter. The chapter summary will remind you of the key ideas.

The sections are allocated a K number to represent the level of understanding required for that section; where an individual element has a lower K number than the section as a whole this is indicated for that topic; for an explanation of the K numbers see the **Introduction**.

Test organisation (K2)

- Recognise the importance of independent testing. (K1)
- Explain the benefits and drawbacks of independent testing within an organisation.

- Recognise the different team members to be considered for the creation of a test team. (K1)

- Recall the tasks of typical test leader and tester. (K1)

Test planning and estimation (K3)

- Recognise the different levels and objectives of test planning. (K1)

- Summarise the purpose and content of the test plan, test design specification and test procedure documents according to the *Standard for Software Test Documentation* (IEEE 829-1998). (K2)

- Differentiate between conceptually different test approaches, such as analytical model based methodical, process/standard compliant, dynamic/heuristic, consultative and regression averse. (K2)

- Differentiate between the subject of test planning for a system and for scheduling test execution. (K2)

- Write a test execution schedule for a given set of test cases, considering prioritisation, and technical and logical dependencies.

- List test preparation and execution activities that should be considered during test planning. (K1)

- Recall typical factors that influence the effort related to testing. (K1)

- Differentiate between two conceptually different estimation approaches: the metrics-based approach and the expert-based approach. (K2)

- Recognise/justify adequate exit criteria for specific test levels and groups of test cases (e.g. for integration testing, acceptance testing or test cases for usability testing). (K2)

Test progress monitoring and control (K2)

- Recall common metrics used for monitoring test preparation and execution. (K1)

- Explain and compare test metrics for test reporting and test control (e.g. defects found and fixed, and tests passed and failed) related to purpose and use.

- Summarise the purpose and content of the test summary report document according to the *Standard for Software Test Documentation* (IEEE 829-1998).

Configuration management (K2)

- Summarise how configuration management supports testing.

Risk and testing (K2)

- Describe a risk as a possible problem that would threaten the achievement of one or more stakeholders' project objectives.

- Remember that risks are determined by likelihood (of happening) and impact (harm resulting if it does happen). (K1)

- Distinguish between the project and product risks.

- Recognise typical product and project risks. (K1)

- Describe, using examples, how risk analysis and risk management may be used for test planning.

Incident management (K3)

- Recognise the content of an incident report according to the *Standard for Software Test Documentation* (IEEE 829-1998). (K1)

- Write an incident report covering the observation of a failure during testing.

Self-assessment questions

The following questions have been designed to enable you to check your current level of understanding for the topics in this chapter. The answers are given at the end of the chapter.

Question SA1 (K1)
What is the purpose of exit criteria?

    a.   To identify how many tests to design.
    b.   To identify when to start testing.
    c.   To identify when to stop testing.
    d.   To identify who will carry out the test execution.

Question SA2 (K2)
Which of the following are *most* likely to be used when developing a test strategy or test approach?

    i.   Failure-based approach.
    ii.   Test specification approach.
    iii. Model-based approach.
    iv. Finance-based approach.

    a.   iii and ii.
    b.   i and iv.
    c.   ii and i.
    d.   i and iii.

Question SA3 (K1)
What can a risk-based approach to testing provide?

    a.   The types of test techniques to be employed.
    b.   The total tests needed to provide 100 per cent coverage.
    c.   An estimation of the total cost of testing.
    d.   Only that test execution is effective at reducing risk.

RISK AND TESTING

It is not possible to talk about test management without first looking at risk and how it affects the fundamental test process defined in **Chapter 1**. If there were no risk of adverse future events in software or hardware development then there would be no need for testing. In other words, if defects did not exist then neither would testing.

Risk can be defined as the chance of an event, hazard, threat or situation occurring and its undesirable consequences:

> **Risk – a factor that could result in future negative consequences, usually expressed as impact and likelihood.**

In a project a test leader will manage two different types of risk: project and product. In both instances the calculation of the risk will be:

> **Level of risk = probability of the risk occurring × impact if it did happen**

Project risks

While managing the testing project a test leader will use project risks to manage the capability to deliver.

Project risks include:

- Supplier issues:
  - Failure of a third party to deliver on time or at all.
  - Contractual issues, such as meeting acceptance criteria.
- Organisational factors:
  - Skills, training and staff shortages.
  - Personnel issues.
  - Political issues, such as problems that stop testers communicating their needs and test results.
  - Failure by the team to follow up on information found in testing and reviews (e.g. not improving development and testing practices).
  - Improper attitude toward or expectations of testing (e.g. not appreciating the value of finding defects during testing).

- Technical issues:
  - Problems in defining the right requirements.
  - The extent that requirements can be met given existing project constraints.
  - Test environment not ready on time.
  - Late data conversion, migration planning and development and testing data conversion/migration tools.
  - Low quality of the design, code, configuration data, test data and tests.

For each risk identified a probability (chance of the risk being realised) and impact (what will happen if the risk is realised) should be identified as well as the identification and management of any mitigating actions (actions aimed at reducing the probability of a risk occurring, or reducing the impact of the risk if it did occur).

So, for example, if there was a risk identified that the third-party supplier may be made bankrupt during the development, the test manager would review the supplier's accounts and might decide that the probability of this is medium (3 on a scale of 1 to 5, 1 being a high risk and 5 a low one). The impact on the project if this did happen would be very high (1 using the same scale). The level of risk is therefore $3 \times 1 = 3$. Thus, the lower the number, the more the risk. With 3 being in the medium risk area the test leader would now have to consider what mitigating actions to take to try to stop the risk becoming a reality. This might include not using the third party, or ensuring that payment for third-party deliverables is made efficiently.

When analysing, managing and mitigating these risks the test manager is following well-established project management principles provided within project management methods and approaches. The project risks recognised during test planning should be documented in the IEEE 829 test plan (see later in this chapter for details of the test plan contents); for the ongoing management and control of existing and new project risks a risk register should be maintained by the test leader.

Product risks

When planning and defining tests a test leader or tester using a risk-based testing approach will be managing product risks.

Potential failure areas (adverse future events or hazards) in software are known as product risks because they are a risk to the quality of the product. In other words, the potential of a defect occurring in the live environment is a product risk. Examples of product risks are:

- Failure-prone software delivered.
- The potential that a defect in the software/hardware could cause harm to an individual or company.
- Poor software characteristics (e.g. functionality, security, reliability, usability, performance).

- Poor data integrity and quality (e.g. data migration issues, data conversion problems, data transport problems, violation of data standards).

- Software that does not perform its intended functions.

Risks are used to decide where to start testing in the software development life cycle, for example the risk of poor requirements could be mitigated by the use of formal reviews as soon as the requirements have been documented at the start of a project. Product risks also provide information enabling decisions regarding how much testing should be carried out on specific components or systems, for example the more risk there is, the more detailed and comprehensive the testing may be. In these ways testing is used to reduce the risk of an adverse effect (defect) occurring or being missed.

Mitigating product risks may also involve non-test activities. For example, in the poor requirements situation, a better and more efficient solution may be simply to replace the analyst who is writing the poor requirements in the first place.

As already stated, a risk-based approach to testing provides proactive opportunities to reduce the levels of product risk starting in the initial stages of a project. It involves the identification of product risks and how they are used to guide the test planning, specification and execution. In a risk-based approach the risks identified:

- will determine the test techniques to be employed, and/or the extent of testing to be carried out, for example the MISRA defines which test techniques should be used for each level of risk: the higher the risk, the higher the coverage required from test techniques;

- prioritise testing in an attempt to find the critical defects as early as possible, for example by identifying the areas most likely to have defects (the most complex) the testing can be focused on these areas;

- will determine any non-test activities that could be employed to reduce risk, for example to provide training to inexperienced designers.

Risk-based testing draws on the collective knowledge and insights of the project stakeholders, testers, designers, technical architects, business reps and anyone with knowledge of the solution to determine the risks and the levels of testing required to address those risks.

To ensure that the chance of a product failure is minimised, risk management activities provide a disciplined approach:

- To assess continuously what can go wrong (risks). Reviews of the existing and looking for any new product risks should occur periodically throughout the life cycle.

- To determine what risks are important to deal with (probability × impact). As the project progresses, owing to the mitigation activities risks may reduce in importance, or disappear altogether.

- To implement actions to deal with those risks (mitigating actions).

Testing supports the identification of new risks by continually reviewing risks of the project deliverables throughout the life cycle; it may also help to determine what risks are important to reduce by setting priorities; it may lower uncertainty about risks by, for example, testing a component and verifying that it does not contain any defects; and lastly by running specific tests it may verify other strategies that deal with risks, such as contingency plans.

Testing is a risk control activity that provides feedback about the residual risk in the product by measuring the effectiveness of critical defect removal (see below) and by reviewing the effectiveness of contingency plans.

CHECK OF UNDERSTANDING

1. What are the two types of risks that have to be considered in testing?
2. Compare and contrast these two risk types.
3. How early in the life cycle can risk impact the testing approach?
4. What does MISRA determine when the level of risk is understood?

TEST ORGANISATION

Test organisation and independence

Independent testing is testing carried out by someone other than the creator (developer) of the code being tested. By remaining independent it is possible to improve the effectiveness of testing if implemented correctly.

As humans we are all capable of making mistakes, from the simplest misspelling or wrong use of syntax to fundamental errors at the core of any documents we write. The problem is that as authors we are less able to see our own errors than someone else, who is less directly associated with the document, would be. This is a problem that is made worse, in the world of software development, by the differing 'world view' of testers and developers. A developer, as the creator and owner of documents and code related to development, perceives these deliverables as being correct when they are delivered. The general awareness that we all make mistakes is, at this stage, overridden by the belief that what has been produced is what is required. A tester, by contrast, will take the view that anything delivered for testing is likely to contain errors and will search diligently to identify and locate those errors.

This is where independent testing is important because it is genuinely hard for authors to identify their own errors, but it is easier for others to see them. There are many options for many levels of independence. In general, the more remote a tester is from the production of the document, the greater is the level of independence. Figure 5.1 indicates the most common roles and the levels of independence they bring.

Figure 5.1 Levels of independent testing

The developer
Independent testers ceded to the development team
Independent permanent test team, centre of excellence within the organisation
Independent testers or test team provided by the operational business units
Specialist testers such as usability testers, security testers, or performance testers
Outsourced test team or testers, e.g. contractors or other organisations

Low

Independence

High

Of course independence comes at a price. The greater the level of independence, the greater the likelihood of errors in testing arising from unfamiliarity. Levels of independence will also depend on the size of the organisation. In smaller organisations where everybody contributes to every activity it is harder to differentiate the role of the tester from any other role, and therefore testers may not be very independent at all. The key in these circumstances is for the testers to have independence of mind, not necessarily to be in an independent (separate) team. In organisations where there are clearly defined roles it is a lot easier for a tester to remain independent.

It is also possible to mix and match the levels of independence, for example a test team made up of permanent resources, business unit resources and contractors. For large, complex or safety-critical projects, it is usually best to have multiple levels of testing, with some or all of the levels done by independent testers.

The 'Agile' approach to development challenges the traditional approach to independence. In this approach everybody takes on multiple roles and so maintaining total independence is not always possible. A tester in this situation has to be able to switch to an independent view, at the relevant points in the project. Testers achieve this independence of view by not assuming anything and by not starting to own the software like a developer would, for example the view that was how it was developed to work.

Independence in the implementation of testing has some key benefits and drawbacks, as in Table 5.1.

Table 5.1 Features of independent testing

Benefits	Drawbacks
The tester sees other and different defects to the author	Isolation from the development team (if treated defects as totally independent), which will mean the tester is totally dependent on the test basis to understand what it is the tester is testing (documentation that is rarely up to date)
The tester is unbiased	The tester may be seen as the bottleneck because independent test execution is normally the last stage and affected by any delays earlier in the process
The tester can see what has been built rather than what the developer thought had been built	Developers lose a sense of responsibility for quality because it may be assumed that they need not worry about errors because the independent test team will find them
The tester makes no assumptions regarding quality	The fully independent view sets developers and testers on either side of an invisible fence. This can be a hindrance to communication that would in normal circumstances ensure common understanding and effective working. It can also mean that developers are seen to 'throw' the software over the fence

CHECK OF UNDERSTANDING

1. Why is independent testing more effective at finding errors than simply allowing the developer and author to test their own product?
2. Name three benefits of independence.
3. Which organisation provides the lowest level of independence and which provides the highest?

Tasks of a test leader and tester

Test tasks are traditionally carried out by people who make testing a career; however, test tasks may also be carried out by non-testers such as a project manager, quality manager, developer, business and domain expert, infrastructure personnel or IT operations. The availability of resources usually determines the resource types that are deployed on each project, for example if there are no career testers available an organisation may identify non-testing IT or business resources to carry out the role of tester for a specific project or time period.

The syllabus defines two testing roles, the test leader (or test manager/test coordinator) and the tester. Other roles may exist in your organisation, but they are not covered here.

The testing roles can be undertaken by anyone with the required skills or who is given the right training. For example, the role of a test leader could be undertaken by a project manager. The decision as to who does what will depend on how a project or organisation is structured, as well as the size and number of resources working on a given project.

It is important to understand here the difference between a testing role and a testing job. A role is an activity, or a series of activities given to a person to fulfil, for example the role of test leader. A person may therefore have more than one role at any moment depending on their experience and the level of workload on a project. A job is effectively what an individual is employed to do, so one or many roles could make up a job. For example, a test leader could also be a tester.

The tasks undertaken by a test leader align very closely with those undertaken by a project manager and align closely with standard approaches to project management. In this context a test leader is anyone who leads a team of testers (be that one or many testers). They are also known as test programme managers, test managers, test team leaders and test coordinators.

Typical test leader tasks may include:

- Coordinating the development of the test strategy and plan with project managers and others.

- Writing or reviewing test strategies produced for the project, and test policies produced for the organisation.

- Contributing the testing perspective to other project activities, such as development delivery schedules.

- Planning the development of the required tests – which will include ensuring that the development uses the correct understanding of the risks, selecting the required test approaches (test levels, cycles, objectives and incident management planning), estimating the time and effort and converting to the cost of testing and acquiring the right resources.

- Managing the specification, preparation, implementation and execution of tests, including the monitoring and control of all the specification and execution.

- Taking the required action, including adapting the plan, based on test results and progress (sometimes documented in status reports), and any action necessary to compensate for problems or delays.

- Ensuring that adequate configuration management of testware is in place and that the testware is fully traceable, for example there is a hierarchical relationship established between the requirements and the detailed specification documents.

- Putting in place suitable metrics for measuring test progress and evaluating the quality of the testing delivered and the product.

- Agreeing what should be automated, to what degree, and how, ensuring it is implemented as planned.

- Where required, selecting tools to support testing and ensuring any tool training requirements are met.

- Agreeing the structure and implementation of the test environment.

- Scheduling all testing activity.

- At the end of the project, writing a test summary report based on the information gathered during testing.

These tasks are not, however, all of the tasks that could be carried out by test leaders, just the most common ones. In fact other resources could take on one or more of these tasks as required, or they may be delegated to other resources by the test leader. The key is to ensure that everyone is aware of who is doing what tasks, that they are completed on time and within budget, and that they are tracked through to completion.

The other role covered by the syllabus is that of the tester, also known as test analyst or test executor.

The tasks typically undertaken by a tester may include:

- Reviewing and contributing to the development of test plans.

- Analysing, reviewing and assessing user requirements, specifications and models for testability.

- Creating test specifications from the test basis.

- Setting up the test environment (often coordinating with system administration and network management). In some organisations the setting up and management of the test environment could be centrally controlled; in this situation a tester would directly liaise with the environment management to ensure the test environment is delivered on time and to specification.

- Preparing and acquiring/copying/creating test data.

- Implementing tests on all test levels, executing and logging the tests, evaluating the results and documenting the deviations from expected results as defects.

- Using test administration or management and test monitoring tools as required.

- Automating tests (may be supported by a developer or a test automation expert).

- Where required, running the tests and measuring the performance of components and systems (if applicable).

- Reviewing tests developed by other testers.

If specialist testers are not available, then additional resources could be used at different test levels:

- For component and integration testing, any additional roles would typically be filled by someone from a development background.

- For system and user acceptance testing, any additional roles would typically be filled by someone from a business or user background.

- System operators (sometimes known as production support) would be responsible for operational acceptance testing.

As mentioned earlier, the thing to remember when looking at roles and tasks within a test project is that one person may have more than one role and carry out some or all of the tasks applicable to the role. This is different to having a 'job': a 'job' may contain many roles and tasks.

CHECK OF UNDERSTANDING

1. What other names are given to the test leader role?
2. Detail five possible tasks of a test leader.
3. Detail five possible tasks of a tester.
4. Describe the differences between a test leader role and a test leader task.

TEST APPROACHES (TEST STRATEGIES)

A test approach is the implementation of a test strategy on a particular project. The test approach defines how testing will be implemented. A test approach can reflect testing for a whole organisation, a programme of work or an individual project. It can be:

- developed early in the life cycle, which is known as preventative – in this approach the test design process is initiated as early as possible in the life cycle to stop defects being built into the final solution;

- left until just before the start of test execution, which is known as reactive – this is where testing is the last development stage and is not started until after design and coding have been completed (sometimes it is identified as the waterfall approach, i.e. all development stages are sequential, the next not starting until the previous one has nearly finished).

A test approach includes all of the decisions made on how testing should be implemented, based on the (test) project goals and objectives, as well as the risk assessment. It forms the starting point for test planning, selecting the test design techniques and test types to be employed. It should also define the software under test and test entry and exit criteria.

There are many approaches or strategies that can be employed. All will depend on the context within which the test team is working, and may consider risks, hazards and safety, available resources and skills, the technology, the nature of the system (e.g. custom built versus COTS), test objectives and regulations, and may include:

- Analytical approaches such as risk-based testing where testing is directed to areas of greatest risk (see earlier in this section for an overview of risk-based testing).

- Model-based approaches such as stochastic testing using statistical information about failure rates (such as reliability growth models) or usage (such as operational profiles).

- Methodical approaches, such as failure-based (including error guessing and fault attacks), checklist based and quality-characteristic based.

- Standard-compliant approaches, specified by industry-specific standards such as The Railway Signalling standards (which define the levels of testing required) or the MISRA (which defines how to design, build and test reliable software for the motor industry).

- Process-compliant approaches, which adhere to the processes developed for use with the various Agile methodologies or traditional waterfall approaches.

- Dynamic and heuristic approaches, such as exploratory testing (see **Chapter 4**) where testing is more reactive to events than pre-planned, and where execution and evaluation are concurrent tasks.

- Consultative approaches, such as those where test coverage is driven primarily by the advice and guidance of technology and/or business domain experts outside or within the test team.

- Regression-averse approaches, such as those that include reuse of existing test material, extensive automation of functional regression tests, and standard test suites.

Different approaches may be combined if required. The decision as to how and why they will be combined will depend on the circumstances prevalent in a project at the time. For example, an organisation may as a standard use an Agile method, but in a particular situation the structure of the test effort could use a risk-based approach to ensure the testing is correctly focused.

Deciding on which approach to take may be dictated by standards, for example those used in the motor industry that are set by MISRA, or at the discretion of those developing the approach or strategy. Where discretion is allowed, the context or scenario needs to be taken into account. Therefore the following factors should be considered when defining the strategy or approach:

- Risk of failure of the project, hazards to the product and risks of product failure to humans, the environment and the company, for example the cost of failure would be too high (safety-critical environments).

- Skills and experience of the people in the proposed techniques, tools and methods. There is no point in implementing a sophisticated component-level, technique-driven approach or strategy when the only resources available are business users with no technical grounding.

- The objective of the testing endeavour and the mission of the testing team, for example if the objective is to find only the most serious defects.

- Regulatory aspects, such as external and internal regulations for the development process, for example The Railway Signalling standards that enforce a given level of test quality.

- The nature of the product and the business, for example a different approach is required for testing mobile phone coverage than for testing an online banking operation.

CHECK OF UNDERSTANDING

1. Name and explain five approaches to the development of the test approach or test strategy.
2. Name one of the standards referred to that dictate the test approach.
3. Can discretion be used when defining a test approach and if so what can influence the decision as to which way to approach testing?

TEST PLANNING AND ESTIMATION

Test planning

Test planning is the most important activity undertaken by a test leader in any test project. It ensures that there is initially a list of tasks and milestones in a baseline plan to track progress against, as well as defining the shape and size of the test effort. Test planning is used in development and implementation projects (sometimes called 'greenfield') as well as maintenance (change and fix) activities.

The main document produced in test planning is often called a master test plan or a project test plan. This document defines at a high level the test activities being planned. It is normally produced during the early phases of the project (e.g. initiation) and updated as required via change control as the project develops. It will provide sufficient information to enable a test project to be established (bearing in mind that at this point in a project little more than requirements may be available from which to plan).

The details of the test-level activities are documented within test-level plans, for example the system test plan. These documents will contain the detailed activities and estimates for the relevant test level.

Figure 5.2 shows where test-level test plans fit into the V-model. It shows how a test plan exists for each test level and that they will usually refer to the master test plan.

Figure 5.2 Test plans in the V-model

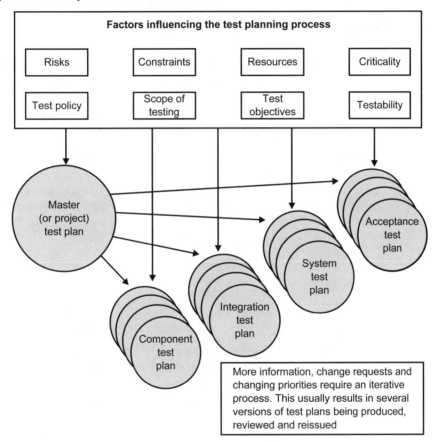

The contents sections of a test plan for either the master test plan or test-level plans are normally identical or very similar. IEEE 829, the *Standard for Software Test Documentation*, contains details of what the content of the plans should be.

The IEEE 829 standard identifies that there should be a minimum of 16 sections present in a test plan, as in Table 5.2.

Test planning is a continual activity that spans the life of the test project; it takes place in all life cycle stages. As risks and changes occur, the plan and planning should be amended to recognise these and reflect the current position. The plans will have been baselined (locked down) after initial sign-off, so these changes would normally be managed by the project change process. Baselining a document effectively secures it from further change unless authorised via a change control process.

Table 5.2 Test plan sections

Section no.	Heading	Details
1	Test plan identifier	A unique identifying reference such as 'Doc ref XYZ v2'
2	Introduction	A brief introduction to the document and the project for which it has been produced
3	Test items	A test item is a software item that is the object of testing
		A software item is one or more items of source code, object code, job control code, or control data
		This section should contain any documentation references, e.g. design documents
4	Features to be tested	A feature is a distinguishing characteristic of a software item (e.g. performance, portability, or functionality)
		Identify all software features and combinations of features and the associated test design specification
5	Features not to be tested	Identify all software features and significant combinations and state the reasons for not including them
6	Approach	Details the overall approach to testing; this could include a detailed process definition, or could refer to other documentation where the detail is documented, i.e. a test strategy
7	Item pass/fail criteria	Used to determine whether a software item has passed or failed its test
8	Suspension and resumption requirements	Suspension requirements define criteria for stopping part or all of the testing activity
		Resumption requirements specify the requirements to resume testing
9	Test deliverables	The documents that testing will deliver, e.g. from IEEE 829 documents such as:
		• test plans (for each test level)

(Continued)

Table 5.2 (Continued)

Section no.	Heading	Details
		• test specifications (design, case and procedure)
		• test summary reports
10	Testing tasks	All tasks for planning and executing the testing, including the intertask dependencies
11	Environmental needs	Definition of all environmental requirements such as hardware, software, PCs, desks, stationery etc.
12	Responsibilities	Identifies the roles and tasks to be used in the test project and who will own them
13	Staffing and training needs	Identifies any actual staffing requirements and any specific skills and training requirements, e.g. automation
14	Schedule	Document delivery dates and key milestones
15	Risks and contingencies	High-level project risks and assumptions and a contingency plan for each risk
16	Approvals	Identifies all approvers of the document, their titles and the date of signature

A useful revision aid to help remember the 16 sections of the IEEE 829 test plan is the acronym 'SPACEDIRT', each letter mapping to one or several sections of the test plan:

S scope (including test items, features to be tested and features not to be tested)

P people (including responsibilities, staff and training and approvals)

A approach

C criteria (including item pass/fail criteria and suspension and resumption requirements)

E environment needs

D deliverables (test)

I identifier and introduction (test plan)

R risks and contingencies

T testing tasks and schedule

Test-planning activities

During test planning various activities for an entire system or a part of a system have to be undertaken by those working on the plan. They include:

- Working with the project manager and subject matter experts to determine the scope and the risks that need to be tested. Also identifying and agreeing the objectives of the testing, be they time, quality or cost focused, or a mixture of all three. The objectives will enable the test project to know when it has finished – has time or money run out, or has the right level of quality been met?

- Understanding what delivery model is to be used (waterfall, iterative, Agile etc.) and putting together the overall approach of testing (sometimes called the test strategy) based on this, ensuring that the test levels and entry and exit criteria are defined.

- Liaising with the project manager and making sure that the testing activities have been included within the software life cycle activities such as:

  - design – the development of the software design;

  - development – the building of the code;

  - implementation – the activities surrounding implementation into a live environment.

- Working with the project to decide what needs to be tested, what roles are involved and who will perform the test activities, planning when and how the test activities should be done, deciding how the test results will be evaluated, and defining when to stop testing (exit criteria).

- Building a plan that identifies when and who will undertake the test analysis and design activities. In addition to the analysis and design activities test planning should also document the schedule for test implementation, execution and evaluation.

- Finding and assigning resources for the different activities that have been defined.

- Deciding what the documentation for the test project will be, for example which plans, how the test cases will be documented etc.

- Defining the management information, including the metrics required and putting in place the processes to monitor and control test preparation and execution, defect resolution and risk issues.

- Ensuring that the test documentation generates repeatable test assets, for example test cases.

Entry criteria

Entry criteria are used to determine when a given test activity can start. This could include the planning, when test design and/or when test execution for each level of testing is ready to start.

Examples of some typical entry criteria to test execution (for example) may include:

- Test environment available and ready for use (it functions).

- Test tools installed in the environment are ready for use.

- Testable code is available.

- All test data is available and correct.
- All test design activity has completed.

Exit criteria

Exit criteria are used to determine when a given test activity has been completed or when it should stop. Exit criteria can be defined for all of the test activities, such as planning, specification and execution as a whole, or to a specific test level for test specification as well as execution.

Exit criteria should be included in the relevant test plans.

Some typical exit criteria might be:

- All tests planned have been run.
- A certain level of requirements coverage has been achieved.
- No high-priority or severe defects are left outstanding.
- All high-risk areas have been fully tested, with only minor residual risks left outstanding.
- Cost – when the budget has been spent.
- The schedule has been achieved, for example the release date has been reached and the product has to go live. This was the case with the millennium testing (it had to be completed before midnight on 31 December 1999), and is often the case with government legislation.

Exit criteria should have been agreed as early as possible in the life cycle; however, they can be and often are subject to controlled change as the detail of the project becomes better understood and therefore the ability to meet the criteria is better understood by those responsible for delivery.

CHECK OF UNDERSTANDING

1. What is the name of the international standard for test documentation?
2. Identify the 16 sections of the test plan.
3. What activities are contained within test planning?
4. Detail four typical exit criteria.

Test estimation

The syllabus details two test estimation approaches, metrics-based and expert-based. The two approaches are quite different, the former being based on data while the latter is a somewhat subjective approach.

The metrics-based approach

This approach relies on data collected from previous or similar projects. This kind of data might include:

- The number of test conditions.
- The number of test cases written.
- The number of test cases executed.
- The time taken to develop test cases.
- The time taken to run test cases.
- The number of defects found.
- The number of environment outages and how long on average each one lasted.

With this approach and the right data it is possible to estimate quite accurately what the cost and time required for a similar project would be.

It is important that the actual costs and time for testing are accurately recorded. These can then be used to revalidate and possibly update the metrics for use on the next similar project.

The expert-based approach

This alternative approach to metrics is to use the experience of owners of the relevant tasks or experts to derive an estimate (this is also known as the Wide Band Delphi approach). In this context 'experts' could be:

- Business experts.
- Test process consultants.
- Developers.
- Technical architects.
- Analysts and designers.
- Anyone with knowledge of the application to be tested or the tasks involved in the process.

There are many ways that this approach could be used. Here are two examples:

- Distribute a requirement specification to the task owners and get them to estimate their task in isolation. Amalgamate the individual estimates when received; build in any required contingency, to arrive at the estimate.
- Distribute to known experts who develop their individual view of the overall estimate and then meet together to agree on and/or debate the estimate that will go forward.

Expert estimating can use either of the above approaches individually or mixing and matching them as required.

Many things affect the level of effort required to fulfil the test requirements of a project. These can be split into three main categories, as shown below.

- Product characteristics:
  - size of the test basis;
  - complexity of the final product;
  - the amount of non-functional requirements;
  - the security requirements (perhaps meeting ISO 27001, the security standard);
  - how much documentation is required (e.g. some legislation-driven changes demand a certain level of documentation that may be more than an organisation would normally produce);
  - the availability and quality of the test basis (e.g. requirements and specifications).
- Development process characteristics:
  - timescales;
  - amount of budget available;
  - skills of those involved in the testing and development activity (the lower the skill level in development, the more defects could be introduced, and the lower the skill level in testing, the more detailed the test documentation needs to be);
  - which tools are being used across the life cycle (i.e. the amount of automated testing will affect the effort required).
- Expected outcomes of testing such as:
  - the amount of errors;
  - test cases to be written.

Taking all of this into account, once the estimate is developed and agreed the test leader can set about identifying the required resources and building the detailed plan.

CHECK OF UNDERSTANDING

1. Compare and contrast the two approaches to developing estimates.
2. Provide three examples of what a metrics approach to estimates would use as a base.
3. Name three areas that affect the level of effort to complete the test activity.

TEST PROGRESS MONITORING AND CONTROL

Test progress monitoring

Having developed the test plan, the activities and timescales determined within it need to be constantly reviewed against what is actually happening. This is test progress monitoring. The purpose of test progress monitoring is to provide feedback and visibility of the progress of test activities.

The data required to monitor progress can be collected manually, for example counting test cases developed at the end of each day, or, with the advent of sophisticated test management tools, it also possible to collect the data as an automatic output from a tool either already formatted into a report, or as a data file that can be manipulated to present a picture of progress.

The progress data is also used to measure exit criteria such as test coverage, for example 50 per cent requirements coverage achieved.

Common test metrics include:

- Percentage of work done in test case preparation (or percentage of planned test cases prepared).
- Percentage of work done in test environment preparation.
- Test case execution (e.g. number of test cases run/not run, and test cases passed/failed).
- Defect information (e.g. defect density, defects found and fixed, failure rate and retest results).
- Test coverage of requirements, risks or code.
- Subjective confidence of testers in the product.
- Dates of test milestones.
- Testing costs, including the cost compared with the benefit of finding the next defect or to run the next test.

Ultimately test metrics are used to track progress towards the completion of testing, which is determined by the exit criteria. So test metrics should relate directly to the exit criteria.

There is a trend towards 'dashboards', which reflect all of the relevant metrics on a single screen or page, ensuring maximum impact. For a dashboard, and generally when delivering metrics, it is best to use a relatively small but impact-worthy subset of the various metric options available. This is because the readers do not want to wade through lots of data for the key item of information they are after, which invariably is 'Are we on target to complete on time?'

These metrics are often displayed in graphical form, examples of which are shown in Figure 5.3. This reflects progress on the running of test cases and reports on defects found. There is also a box at the top left for some written commentary on progress to be documented (this could simply be the issues and/or successes of the previous reporting period).

The graph in Figure 5.4 is the one shown at the bottom left of the dashboard in Figure 5.3. It reports the number of incidents raised, and also shows the planned and actual numbers of incidents.

Figure 5.3 iTesting Executive Dashboard

Figure 5.4 Incidents planned/raised

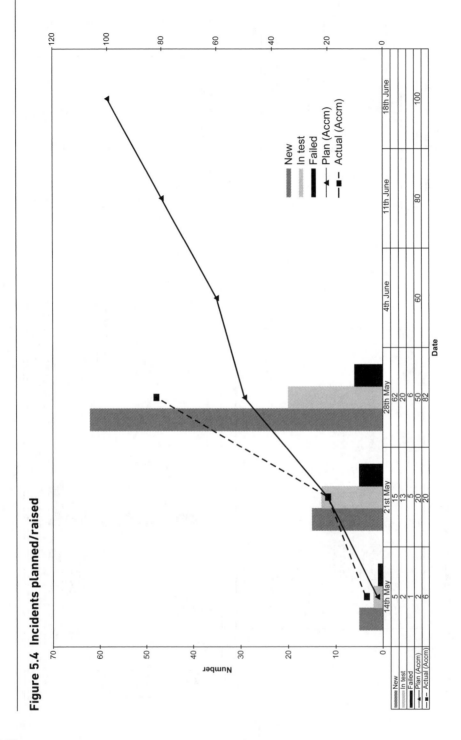

Test reporting

Test reporting is the process where by test metrics are reported in a summarised format to update the reader regarding the testing tasks undertaken. The information reported can include:

- What has happened during a given period of time, for example a week, a test level or the whole test endeavour, or when exit criteria have been met.
- Analysed information and metrics required to support recommendations and decisions about future actions, such as:
  - an assessment of defects remaining;
  - the economic benefit of continued testing, for example additional tests are exponentially more expensive than the benefit of running;
  - outstanding risks;
  - the level of confidence in tested software, for example defects planned versus actual defects found.

The IEEE 829 standard includes an outline of a test summary report that could be used for test reporting. The structure defined in the outline is shown in Table 5.3.

Table 5.3 Test summary report outline

Section no.	Heading	Details
1	Test summary report identifier	The specific identifier allocated to this document, e.g. TSR XYX v1
2	Summary	Identifies the items tested (including any version numbers)
		Documents the environments in which the test activity being reported on took place
		References the testing documentation for each test item, e.g. test plan, test cases, test defect reports
3	Variances	Reports deviations from the test approach or strategy, test plan, test specification or test procedures
4	Comprehensive assessment	Measures the actual progress made against the exit criteria and explains why any differences have arisen

(Continued)

Table 5.3 (Continued)

Section no.	Heading	Details
5	Summary results	Provides an overview of the results from the test activities; it should include details of defects raised and fixed, as well as those that remain unresolved
6	Evaluation	Provides an evaluation of the quality of each test item, including a view of the risks of failure in production of these test items. Based on the test result metrics and test item pass/fail criteria
7	Summary of activities	A summary of the major test activities and events such as test environment unavailability, success or weaknesses of the test specification process etc.
		Should also include resource usage data, e.g. planned spend against actual spend
8	Approvals	Identifies all approvers of the document

The information gathered can also be used to help with any process improvement opportunities. This information could be used to assess whether:

- the goals for testing were correctly set (were they achievable; if not why not?);
- the test approach or strategy was adequate (e.g. did it ensure there was enough coverage?);
- the testing was effective in ensuring that the objectives of testing were met.

Test control

We have referred above to the collection and reporting of progress data. Test control uses this information to decide on a course of action to ensure control of the test activities is maintained and exit criteria are met. This is particularly required when the planned test activities are behind schedule. The actions taken could impact any of the test activities and may also affect other software life cycle activities.

Examples of test-control activities are as follows:

- Make decisions based on information from test monitoring.
- Reprioritise tests when an identified project risk occurs (e.g. software delivered late).

- Change the test schedule due to availability of a test environment.

- Set an entry criterion requiring fixes to be retested (confirmation tested) by a developer before accepting them into a build (this is particularly useful when defect fixes continually fail again when retested).

- Review product risks and perhaps change the risk ratings to meet the target.

- Adjust the scope of the testing (perhaps the amount of tests to be run) to manage the testing of late change requests.

The following test-control activities are likely to be outside the test leader's responsibility. However, this should not stop the test leader making a recommendation to the project manager.

- Descoping of functionality, that is removing some less important planned deliverables from the initial delivered solution to reduce the time and effort required to achieve that solution.

- Delaying release into the production environment until exit criteria have been met.

- Continuing testing after delivery into the production environment so that defects are found before they occur in production.

CHECK OF UNDERSTANDING

1. Name four common test metrics.
2. Name the eight headings in the IEEE 829 summary report.
3. Identify three ways a test leader can control testing if there are more tests than there is time to complete them.

INCIDENT MANAGEMENT

An incident is any unplanned event occurring that requires further investigation. In testing this translates into anything where the actual result is different to the expected result. An incident when investigated may be a defect; however, it may also be a change to a specification or an issue with the test being run. It is important that a process exists to track all incidents through to closure.

Incidents can be raised at any time throughout the software development life cycle, from reviews of the test basis (requirements, specifications etc.) to test specification and test execution.

Incident management, according to IEEE 1044 (*Standard Classification for Software Anomalies*), is 'The process of recognising, investigating, taking action and disposing of incidents.' It involves recording incidents, classifying them and identifying the impact. The process of incident management ensures that incidents are tracked from recognition to correction, and finally through retest and closure. It is important that organisations document their incident management process and ensure they have appointed someone (often called an incident manager/coordinator) to manage/police the process.

Incidents are raised on incident reports, either electronically via an incident management system (from Microsoft Excel to sophisticated incident management tools) or on paper. Incident reports have the following objectives:

- To provide developers and other parties with feedback on the problem to enable identification, isolation and correction as necessary. It must be remembered that most developers and other parties who will correct the defect or clear up any confusion will not be present at the point of identification, so without full and concise information they will be unable to understand the problem, and possibly therefore unable to understand how to go about fixing it. The more information provided, the better.

- To provide test leaders with a means of tracking the quality of the system under test and the progress of the testing. One of the key metrics used to measure progress is a view of how many incidents are raised, their priority and finally that they have been corrected and signed off.

- To provide ideas for test process improvement. For each incident the point of injection should be documented, for example a defect in requirements or code, and subsequent process improvement can focus on that particular area to stop the same defect occurring again.

The details that are normally included on an incident report are:

- Date of issue, issuing organisation, author, approvals and status.
- Scope, severity and priority of the incident.
- References, including the identity of the test case specification that revealed the problem.
- Expected and actual results.
- Date the incident was discovered.
- Identification of the test item (configuration item) and environment.
- Software or system life cycle process in which the incident was observed.
- Description of the incident to enable reproduction and resolution, including logs, database dumps or screenshots.
- Degree of impact on stakeholders' interests.
- Severity of the impact on the system.
- Urgency/priority to fix.
- Status of the incident (e.g. open, deferred, duplicate, waiting to be fixed, fixed awaiting confirmation test or closed).
- Conclusions, recommendations and approvals.

- Global issues, such as other areas that may be affected by a change resulting from the incident.

- Change history, such as the sequence of actions taken by project team members with respect to the incident to isolate, repair and confirm it as fixed.

The syllabus also recognises that IEEE 829 contains the outline of a test incident report. The outline suggests that the report should contain the sections shown in Table 5.4.

Table 5.4 Test incident report outline

Section no.	Heading	Details
1	Test incident report identifier	The unique identifier assigned to this test incident report
2	Summary	A summary of the incident, detailing where expected and actual results differ, identifying at a high level the items that are affected, and the steps leading up to the recognition of the incident,e.g. if in test execution, which test was executed and the actual keystrokes and data loaded
3	Incident description	A detailed description of the incident, which should include: • Inputs • Expected results • Actual results • Anomalies • Date and time • Procedure step • Environment • Attempts to repeat • Testers' comments • Observers' comments Should also include any information regarding possible causes and solutions
4	Impact	If known, document what impact the incident has on progress

CONFIGURATION MANAGEMENT

Configuration management is the process of managing products, facilities and processes by managing the information about them, including changes, and ensuring they are what they are supposed to be in every case.

For testing, configuration management will involve controlling both the versions of code to be tested and the documents used during the development process, for example requirements, design and plans.

In both instances configuration management should ensure traceability throughout the test process, for example a requirement should be traceable through to the test cases that are run to test its levels of quality, and vice versa.

Effective configuration management is important for the test process as the contents of each release of software into a test environment must be understood and at the correct version, otherwise testers could end up wasting time because either they are testing an invalid release of the software or the release does not integrate successfully, leading to the failure of many tests.

In most instances the project will have already established configuration management processes that will define the documents and code to be held under configuration management. If this is not the case then during test planning the process and tools required to establish the right configuration management processes will need to be selected/implemented by the test leader.

The same principle applies to testware. Each item of testware (such as a test procedure) should have its own version number and be linked to the version of the software it was used to test. For example, test procedure TP123a might be used for Release A and TP123b might be used for Release B – even though both have the same purpose and even expected results. However, another test procedure, TP201, may be applicable to all releases.

A good configuration management system will ensure that the testers can identify exactly what code they are testing, as well as have control over the test documentation such as test plans, test specification, defect logs etc.

CHECK OF UNDERSTANDING

1. Define configuration management.
2. What can be stored under configuration management?
3. Why is it important to have effective configuration management?

SUMMARY

In this chapter we have looked at the component parts of test management. We initially explored risk and testing. When developing the test plan, the test leader and tester will look at the product risks (risks that relate directly to the failure of the product in the live environment) to decide what is important to test, as well as ensuring that any project risks (risks relating to the delivery of the project) are mitigated.

The importance of independence in the test organisation and how independence helps to ensure that the right focus is given to the test activity was reviewed. Independence is gained by separating the creative development activity from the test activity and we looked at the different levels of independence that are achievable:

- The developers – low independence.
- Independent testers ceded to the development team.
- Independent permanent test team, centre of excellence within the organisation.
- Independent testers or test team provided by the operational business unit.
- Specialist testers such as security testers or performance testers.
- Outsourced test team or the use of independent contractors – high independence.

We have looked at the test approach and how it shapes the test activity based on many influences, including risks and the objectives of the testing.

We have reviewed two roles that exist within a test project, test leader (also known as a test manager or test coordinator) and tester. Both roles are important to the delivery of testing, but could be vested in one or many people, for example one person could have the role of test manager and tester. A test leader has responsibility for all of the planning activity, while the tester has responsibility for activities that surround the preparation of test cases.

IEEE 829, the test documentation standard, provides outlines of three test planning documents:

- The test plan.
- The test summary report.
- The test incident report.

Test management depends not only on the preparation of the required documents but also on the development of the right entry and exit criteria and estimates, the monitoring of progress through the plan and the control activities implemented to ensure the plan is achieved.

Test estimating can be achieved in one of two ways: using historical metrics or the expert-based approach (involving experts in the subject who agree the estimate between themselves).

After a plan of activity has been developed and time begins to pass the test leader needs to monitor the progress of the activities. If any activity is delayed or there has been a change of any kind in the project itself, the test leader may need to revise the plan or take other actions to ensure the project is delivered on time.

We explored how the incidents found during testing are recorded, and we reviewed the level of detail that needs to be recorded to ensure that any defect is fully understood and that any fix then made is the right one.

Finally we looked at configuration management. When running test cases against the code it is important that the tester is aware of the version of code being tested and the version of the test being run. Controlling the versioning of the software and test assets is called configuration management. Lack of configuration management may lead to issues like loss of already-delivered functionality, reappearance of previously corrected errors and no understanding of which version of the test was run against which version of the code.

Example examination questions with answers

E1. K1 question
When assembling a test team to work on an enhancement to an existing system, which of the following has the highest level of test independence?

    a.   A business analyst who wrote the original requirements for the system.

    b.   A permanent programmer who reviewed some of the new code, but has not written any of it.

    c.   A permanent tester who found most defects in the original system.

    d.   A contract tester who has never worked for the organisation before.

E2. K2 question
What test roles (or parts in the testing process) is a developer *most likely* to perform?

    i.   Executing component integration tests.

    ii.   Static analysis.

    iii.   Setting up the test environment.

    iv.   Deciding how much testing should be automated.

    a.   i and ii.

    b.   i and iv.

    c.   ii and iii.

    d.   iii and iv.

E3. K2 question
Which of the following are valid justifications for developers testing their own code during unit testing?

    i.   Their lack of independence is mitigated by independent testing during system and acceptance testing.

    ii.   A person with a good understanding of the code can find more defects more quickly using white-box techniques.

    iii.   Developers have a better understanding of the requirements than testers.

    iv.   Testers write unnecessary incident reports because they find minor differences between the way in which the system behaves and the way in which it is specified to work.

    a.   i and ii.

    b.   i and iv.

    c.   ii and iii.

    d.   iii and iv.

E4. K1 question
Which of the following terms is used to describe the management of software components comprising an integrated system?

    a.   Configuration management.

    b.   Incident management.

    c.   Test monitoring.

    d.   Risk management.

E5. K1 question
A new system is about to be developed. Which of the following functions has the *highest* level of risk?

    a.   Likelihood of failure = 20%; impact value = £100,000

    b.   Likelihood of failure = 10%; impact value = £150,000

    c.   Likelihood of failure = 1%; impact value = £500,000

    d.   Likelihood of failure = 2%; impact value = £200,000

E6. K2 question
Which of the following statements about risks is most accurate?

    a.   Project risks rarely affect product risk.

    b.   Product risks rarely affect project risk.

    c.   A risk-based approach is more likely to be used to mitigate product rather than project risks.

    d.   A risk-based approach is more likely to be used to mitigate project rather than product risks.

Answers to questions in the chapter

SA1. The correct answer is c.
SA2. The correct answer is d.
SA3. The correct answer is a.

Answers to example questions

E1. The correct answer is d.
In this scenario, the contract tester who has never worked for the organisation before has the highest level of test independence. The three others are less independent because they are likely to make assumptions based on their previous knowledge of the requirements, code and general functionality of the original system.

Note that independence does not necessarily equate to most useful. In practice most test or project managers would recruit a permanent tester who has worked on the original system in preference to a contract tester with no knowledge of the system. However, when assembling a team it would be useful to have staff with varying levels of test independence and system knowledge.

E2. The correct answer is a.

  i.   Executing component integration tests is usually done by developers. Developers are usually responsible for unit and component integration testing. Independent testing usually follows at system and acceptance test levels.

  ii. Static analysis is usually done by developers because: it requires an understanding of the code and therefore the person doing this needs skills in the programming language; and it can be done as soon as the code is written. Therefore it is quick and effective for the developer to do it. The risk of a lack of test independence can be mitigated by performing independent system and acceptance testing.

  iii. Setting up the test environment is an activity typically performed by a tester. It may require support from developers and staff from other departments and on some occasions environments could be set up by developers. However, it is a task that could be done by a tester rather than a developer.

  iv. Deciding how much testing should be automated is typically a decision made by the test leader, who will consult other staff in the decision-making process. Developers may be involved and their skills may be required to automate some tests. However, the decision on how much to automate should not be made by developers.

E3. The correct answer is a.
It is unlikely that developers will have a better understanding of the requirements than testers, partly because testers work closely with the user community (and may be drawn from it) and partly because developers seldom work with the complete set of requirements in a medium to large development.

Testers may raise incidents related to the difference between user expectations and the specification, but these are not unnecessary. Such issues are more likely to arise at the later stages of testing.

Early testing (unit testing) is usually done most effectively by developers with a good understanding of the code and the development environment; they can be more efficient and more effective at this level. Later independent stages of testing offset any disadvantage from the lack of independence at unit testing level.

E4. The correct answer is a.
Incident management is the collection and processing of incidents raised when errors and defects are discovered. Test monitoring identifies the status of the testing activity on a continuous basis. Risk management identifies, analyses and mitigates risks to the project and the product. Configuration management is concerned with the management of changes to software components and their associated documentation and testware.

E5. The correct answer is a.
In b the product of probability × impact has the value £15,000; in c the value is £5,000 and in d it is £4,000. The value of £20,000 in a is therefore the highest.

E6. The correct answer is c.
In general, project risk and product risk can be hard to differentiate. Anything that impacts on the quality of the delivered system is likely to lead to delays or increased costs as the problem is tackled. Anything causing delays to the project is likely to threaten the delivered system's quality. The risk-based approach is an approach to managing product risk through testing, so it impacts most directly on product risk.

6 TOOL SUPPORT FOR TESTING

Peter Williams

INTRODUCTION

As seen in earlier chapters there are many tasks and activities that need to be performed during the testing process. In addition, other tasks need to be performed to support the testing process.

In order to assist in making the testing process easier to perform and manage, many different types of test tools have been developed and used for a wide variety of testing tasks. Some of them have been developed in-house by an organisation's own software development or testing department. Others have been developed by software houses (also known as test-tool vendors) to sell to organisations that perform testing. More recently, open source tools have been developed that can be reused and enhanced. Even within the same type of tool, some will be home-grown while others will be developed as open source tools or by test-tool vendors.

This chapter discusses the potential benefits and pitfalls associated with test tools in general. It then describes the most commonly used types of test tools and concludes with a process for introducing a tool into a test organisation.

Learning objectives

The learning objectives for this chapter are listed below. You can confirm that you have achieved these by using the self-assessment questions at the start of the chapter, the 'Check of understanding' boxes distributed throughout the text, and the example examination questions provided at the end of the chapter. The chapter summary will remind you of the key ideas.

The sections are allocated a K number to represent the level of understanding required for that section; where an individual section has a lower K number than the section as a whole this is indicated for that topic; for an explanation of the K numbers see the **Introduction**.

Types of test tool (K2)

- Classify different types of test tools according to their purpose and to the activities of the fundamental test process and the software life cycle.
- Explain the term test tool and the purpose of tool support for testing.

Effective use of tools: potential benefits and risks (K2)

- Summarise the potential benefits and risks of test automation and tool support for testing.

- Remember special considerations for test execution tools, static analysis and test management tools. (K1)

Introducing a tool into an organisation (K1)

- State the main principles of introducing a tool into an organisation.

- State the goals of a proof-of-concept for tool evaluation and a piloting phase for tool implementation.

- Recognise that factors other than simply acquiring a tool are required for good tool support.

Self-assessment questions

The following questions have been designed to enable you to check your current level of understanding for the topics in this chapter. The answers are at the end of the chapter.

Question SA1 (K2)
Which of the following pairs of test tools are *likely* to be *most useful* during the test analysis and design stage of the fundamental test process?

    i.   Test execution tool.
    ii.   Test data preparation tool.
    iii. Test management tool.
    iv. Requirements management tool.

    a. i and ii.
    b. i and iv.
    c. ii and iii.
    d. iii and iv.

Question SA2 (K2)
Which of the following is *most likely* to cause failure in the implementation of a test tool?

    a. Underestimating the demand for a tool.
    b. The purchase price of the tool.
    c. No agreed requirements for the tool.
    d. The cost of resources to implement and maintain the tool.

Question SA3 (K2)
What benefits do static analysis tools have over test execution tools?

    a. Static analysis tools find defects earlier in the life cycle.
    b. Static analysis tools can be used before code is written.
    c. Static analysis tools test that the delivered code meets business requirements.
    d. Static analysis tools are particularly effective for regression testing.

WHAT IS A TEST TOOL?

Definition of a test tool

The ISTQB Glossary of Testing Terms v2.4 defines a test tool as:

> **A software product that supports one or more test activities, such as planning and control, specification, building initial files and data, test execution and test analysis.**

Therefore a test tool can be thought of as a piece of software that is used to make the testing process more effective or efficient. In other words, anything that makes testing easier, quicker, more accurate etc.

This book will focus on those test tools that are listed in the syllabus. These are, in general, the test tools that are most commonly used in the testing process and designed primarily for the testing process.

Benefits and risks of using any type of tool

Let us consider the building of a new hotel and examine the similarities with the introduction and use of test tools. Test tools need to be thought of as long-term investments that need maintenance to provide long-term benefits. Similarly, building a hotel requires a lot of upfront planning, effort and investment. Even when the hotel is ready for use, there is still a continual long-term requirement for the provision of services such as catering, cleaning, building maintenance, provision of staff to provide ad hoc services to customers etc. and, from time to time, the need for upgrades to infrastructure to keep up with new technology and customer demands. The long-term benefit is that this upfront investment and ongoing maintenance and support can provide substantial income in return.

In addition, there are risks that, over a period of time, the location of the hotel will become less attractive, resulting in lower demand, lower usage and a maintenance cost that is greater than the income received. Therefore the initial investment is wasted because the ongoing need/requirement did not exist.

The graph in Figure 6.1 demonstrates a typical payback model for implementing a test execution tool. The same principle applies to the majority of test tools. Note that there is an ongoing maintenance cost of using the tool, but that this ongoing maintenance cost needs to be less than the cost of performing testing activities without the tool if the investment is to be worthwhile.

The same advantages and disadvantages apply to the use of most types of test tool. However, there are exceptions to this generalisation (and to the same generalisation made in the ISTQB syllabus). Some tools, such as comparators, can be used virtually straight out of the box. A comparator can check whether one large test file is the same as another. If it is different it can identify and report on the differences. This would be very difficult and time-consuming to do manually. In addition, incident management tools are fairly intuitive and easy for both experienced and novice testers to use. They are also likely to provide a 'quick win'.

Figure 6.1 Test tool payback model

Length of time for which tool is used

Other tools can be built by developers in-house as the need arises. For instance, test harnesses, test oracles or test data preparation tools may be relatively easy to produce for developers with a good understanding of the tool requirements and the systems and databases in the test environment. More recently, open source tools have allowed developers and testers to use freeware tools as the building blocks for developing in-house tools to meet specific needs. In addition, test tools have been developed by the UK Financial Conduct Authority for use by banks and building societies that participate in the Faster Payments and Account Switcher schemes.

Benefits

The main benefit of using test tools is similar to the main benefit of automating any process. That is, the amount of time and effort spent performing routine, mundane, repetitive tasks is greatly reduced. For example, consider the time and cost of making consumer goods by hand or in a factory.

This time saved can be used to reduce the costs of testing or it can be used to allow testers to spend more time on the more intellectual tasks of test planning, analysis and design. In turn, this can enable more focused and appropriate testing to be done – rather than having many testers working long hours, running hundreds of tests.

Related to this is the fact that the automation of any process usually results in more predictable and consistent results. Similarly, the use of test tools provides more predictable and consistent results as human failings such as manual-keying errors, misunderstandings, incorrect assumptions, forgetfulness etc., are eliminated. It also means that any reports or findings tend to be objective rather than subjective. For instance, humans often assume that something that seems reasonable is correct, when in fact it may not be what the system is supposed to do.

The widespread use of databases to hold the data input, processed or captured by the test tool, means that it is generally much easier and quicker to obtain and present accurate test management information, such as test progress, incidents found/fixed etc. (see **Chapter 5**). The introduction of web-based tools that have databases stored in the cloud means that such information is available to global organisations 24 hours per day, seven days per week. This facilitates round the clock working and can reduce elapsed times to analyse, fix and retest defects.

Risks

Most of the risks associated with the use of test tools are concerned with over-optimistic expectations of what the tool can do and a lack of appreciation of the effort required to implement and obtain the benefits that the tool can bring.

For example, consider the production environments of most organisations considering using test tools. They are unlikely to have been designed and built with test tools in mind. Therefore, assuming that you want a test environment to be a copy of production (or at least as close to it as possible), you will also have a test environment that is not designed and built with test tools in mind.

Consider the test environments used by vendors to demonstrate their test tools. If you were the vendor would you design the environment to enable you to demonstrate the tool at its best or to demonstrate the shortcomings it may encounter in a typical test environment?

Therefore, unless detailed analysis and evaluation is done, it is likely that test tools will end up as something that seemed a good idea at the time but have been largely a waste of time and money. A process for avoiding such problems when introducing a tool into an organisation is described later in this chapter.

After a test tool has been implemented and measurable benefits are being achieved, it is important to put in sufficient effort to maintain the tool, the processes surrounding it and the test environment in which it is used. Otherwise there is a risk that the benefits being obtained will decrease and the tool will become redundant. Additionally, opportunities for improving the way in which the tool is used could also be missed.

For example, the acquisition of various test tools from multiple vendors will require interfaces to be built or configured to import and export data between tools. Otherwise much time may be spent manually cutting and pasting data from one tool to another. If this is not done, then data inconsistencies and version control problems are likely to arise. Similar problems may arise when testing with third-party suppliers or as a result of mergers and acquisitions. The increase in common standards for interfaces such as Extensible Markup Language (XML) means that the capability for developing successful interfaces is greater, but substantial time and effort are often still required.

Maintenance effort will also be required to upgrade and reconfigure tools so that they remain compliant with new platforms or operating systems.

EXAMPLE – HOTEL CHAIN SCENARIO

An example of a hotel chain with several UK-based hotels will be used throughout this chapter. The systems that comprise the organisation's system architecture are shown in Figure 6.2.

The general public can book rooms at any of the chain's hotels by:

- Contacting staff in the hotel, who then use a Graphical User Interface (GUI) front-end to make the booking.

- Telephoning customer services who then use a GUI front-end to make the booking.

- Using the company's website to make the booking online.

- Using a mobile app that can be downloaded from the hotel chain's website.

Figure 6.2 Hotel system architecture

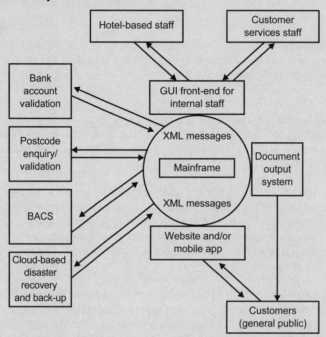

In all cases, communication with the mainframe computer is done via a middleware layer of XML messages.

There is a document production system that produces PDF versions of customer correspondence such as booking confirmations, bills, invoices etc. These are stored securely and can be downloaded by customers from the website.

Direct debit payments are made via Bankers Automated Clearing Services (BACS). Files are transmitted and confirmation and error messages are received back. Credit card payments can be made. An enhancement to the security systems is being made to comply with Payment Card Industry standards. Payments can also be made by leading electronic payment systems (e.g. PayPal).

Validation of bank account details is performed by sending XML messages to and from a third-party system.

Validation and enquiry of address and postcode is also performed by sending XML messages to and from a third-party system.

A new release of the system is planned for six months' time. This will include:

- Code changes to replace the XML middleware layer. Mainframe changes will be performed by an outsourced development team in India.
- Various changes to website screens to improve usability.
- The introduction of a new third-party calendar object from which dates can be selected.
- Removal of the ability for customers to pay by cheque.
- An amended customer bill plus two other amended documents.
- Two new output documents.
- Fixes to various existing low- and medium-severity defects.
- Improvements to disaster recovery by using cloud-based methods.
- Ongoing enhancements to the mobile app using Agile development methods. These will be deployed to production approximately every three weeks.

CHECK OF UNDERSTANDING

1. Would you expect a quick return on your investment in test tools? Why?
2. Describe three potential benefits of using test tools.
3. Describe two risks of using test tools.

TEST TOOLS

Types of tool

There are several ways in which test tools can be classified. They can be classified according to:

- their purpose;
- the activities within the fundamental test process and the software life cycle with which they are primarily associated;
- the type of testing that they support;
- the source of tool (shareware, open source, free or commercial);

- the technology used;

- who uses them.

In this book, test tools will be classified according to the type of activity they support (as in the ISTQB Foundation Level syllabus).

Tool support for management of testing and tests

Test management tools

Test management tools provide support for various activities and tasks throughout the development life cycle. Some of these activities are supported by the provision of interfaces to other more specialist tools (for instance, test execution tools). Other test management tools provide fully integrated modules that provide some or all of the services/functions provided by more specialist tools (such as incident management or requirements management tools).

The diagram in Figure 6.3 shows how a test management tool is the hub or centre of a set of integrated test tools.

Figure 6.3 An integrated set of tools

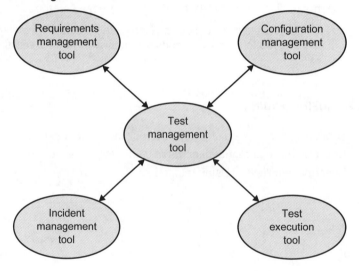

Test management tools provide an architecture for creating, storing and editing test procedures. These may be linked or traced to requirements, test conditions and risks. Such test procedures can then be prioritised or grouped together and scheduled so that they are run in the most effective and efficient order. Some test management tools allow dependencies to be recorded so that tests that will fail owing to a known defect can be highlighted and left unexecuted. This allows testers to be redirected to run the highest priority tests available rather than waste their time and the test data they have prepared on tests that are certain to fail.

Tests can be recorded as passed or failed and usually a test management tool provides an interface to an incident management tool so that an incident can be raised if the actual and expected results differ.

Test management tools can provide management information and reports on test procedures passed or failed. The amount of integration with other specialist tools is significant here. For instance, integration with requirements management tools allows reports to be produced on test progress against one or more requirements. Integration with incident management tools also allows reports to include analysis of defects against requirements.

Test management tools generally hold data in a database. This allows a large amount of reports and metrics to be produced. The metrics produced can be used as inputs to:

- Test and project management to control the current project.
- Estimates for future projects.
- Identifying weaknesses or inefficiencies in the development or test processes that can be subsequently investigated with the aim of improving them.

Test management information reports should be designed to meet the needs of project managers and other key users. It may be necessary to export data to a spreadsheet in order for it to be manipulated into the format required.

A test management tool can enable reuse of existing testware in future test projects.

USE IN HOTEL CHAIN SCENARIO

In the scenario, a test management tool can be used to write down and store requirements for new functionality and subsequently to hold the test conditions necessary to test these requirements.

It can also be used to record whether tests have passed or failed and to produce test management information on progress to date.

Additionally, requirements and test conditions from previous developments will already exist in the test management tool. These can be used as the basis for the regression testing required. Indeed a regression pack may already exist. Clearly the regression pack would have to be reviewed and amended as necessary to make it relevant to this release. However, the benefit is that much of the previous work could be reused, which, in turn, means that much less effort will be involved to create a regression pack.

Incident management tools

Incident management tools (also known as defect management tools) are one of the most widely used types of test tool. At a basic level incident management tools are used to perform two critical activities: creation of an incident report; and maintenance of details about the incident as it progresses through the incident life cycle.

The level of detail to be captured about the incident can be varied depending on the characteristics of the tool itself and the way in which the incident management tool is configured and used by the test organisation.

For example, the incident management tool could be configured so that lots of mandatory information is required in order to comply with industry or generic standards such as IEEE 1044. In addition, workflow rules may also be applied to ensure that the agreed incident life cycle is strictly adhered to, with incidents only able to be assigned to particular teams or users. Alternatively, the tool could be configured to require very limited mandatory information, with most fields being free format.

Incident management tools also use a database to store and manage details of incidents. This allows the incident to be categorised according to the values stored in appropriate fields. Such values will change during the incident life cycle as the incident is analysed, debugged, fixed and retested. It is often possible to view the history of changes made to the incident.

The database structure also enables incidents to be searched and analysed (using either filters or more complex Structured Query Language (SQL)-type queries). This provides the basis for management information about incidents. Note that as the values held against each incident change, the management information will also change. Therefore users need to be aware of the danger of using outdated reports.

This data can also be used in conjunction with data held in test management tools when planning and estimating for future projects. It can also be analysed to provide input to test process improvement projects.

Fields in the database structure normally include:

- Priority (e.g. high, medium, low).
- Severity (e.g. high, medium, low).
- Assignee (the person to whom the incident is currently assigned, e.g. a developer for debugging, a tester to perform retesting).
- Status in the incident life cycle (e.g. New, Open, Fixed, Reopen, Closed).

This would allow management information to be produced from the incident management database about the number of high-priority incidents with a status of Open or Reopen that are assigned to, say, Peter Morgan, compared with the number assigned to Brian Hambling.

Some test management tools include fully integrated incident management tools as part of their core product, while other incident management tools can be integrated with test management, requirements management and/or test execution tools. Such integration enables incidents to be input and traced back to test cases and requirements.

USE IN HOTEL CHAIN SCENARIO

An incident management tool can be used to raise new defects and process them through the defect life cycle until resolved. It can also be used to check whether defects (or similar defects) have been raised before, especially for defects raised during regression testing.

An incident management tool could also be used to prioritise defects so that developers fix the most important ones first. It could also highlight clusters of defects. This may suggest that more detailed testing needs to be done on the areas of functionality where most defects are being found as it is probable that further defects will be found as well.

Requirements management tools

Requirements management tools are used by business analysts to record, manage and prioritise the requirements of a system. They can also be used to manage changes to requirements – something that can be a significant problem for testers as test cases are designed and executed to establish whether the delivered system meets its requirements. Therefore if requirements change after tests have been written then test cases may also need to change. There is also a potential problem of changes not being communicated to all interested parties, thus testers could be using an old set of requirements while new ones are being issued to developers.

The use of a traceability function within a requirements tool (and/or integrated with a test management tool) enables links and references to be made between requirements, functions, test conditions and other testware items. This means that as requirements change, it is easy to identify which other items may need to change.

Some requirements management tools can be integrated with test management tools, while some test management tools enable requirements to be input and related to test cases.

Requirements management tools also enable requirements coverage metrics to be calculated easily as traceability enables test cases to be mapped to requirements.

As can be seen, traceability can create a lot of maintenance work, but it does highlight those areas that are undergoing change.

USE IN HOTEL CHAIN SCENARIO

A change is required to three PDF documents that are stored securely on the website so that customers can log in and download them. The requirements are documented in the requirements management tool. Testers obtain the requirements from the tool and begin to devise test conditions and test cases. A subsequent change means that further changes are made to the requirements. The testers should be made aware of the changes so that they can provide input to the impact analysis. Traceability within a requirements management tool will also highlight the test conditions affected by the changed requirement. The testers can review the change in requirements and then consider what changes need to be made to the test conditions and test cases.

Configuration management tools

Configuration management tools are designed primarily for managing the versions of different software (and hardware) components that comprise a complete build of the system; and various complete builds of systems that exist for various software platforms over a period of time.

A build is a development activity where a complete system is compiled and linked (typically daily) so that a consistent system is available at any time including all the latest changes.

USE IN HOTEL CHAIN SCENARIO

Within the hotel booking system, there will be many versions of subsystems due to the date at which the version was included in a build, or the operating system on which the version works etc. Each version of a subsystem will have a unique version number and will comprise many different components (e.g. web services, program files, data files etc.).

The configuration management tool maps the version number of each subsystem to the build (or release) number of the integrated system. As shown in Table 6.1, Build A (UNIX) and Build B (Microsoft Windows 2003) might use the same version (v1.02) of the Payments In subsystem, but Release C might use version v1.04.

Table 6.1 Configuration traceability

Build for integrated system	Version of Payments In system	Credit card payment test procedure ID	Electronic payment test procedure ID
Build A	v1.02	TP123a	TP201
Build B	v1.02	TP123b	TP201
Build C	v1.04	TP123b	TP201

The same principle applies to testware with a different version number for a test procedure being used, depending on the version number of the build. For instance, test procedure TP123a might be used for Build A and TP123b might be used for Build B – even though both have the same purpose and even expected results. However, another test procedure, TP201, may be applicable to all builds.

The amount of benefit to be obtained from using configuration management tools is largely dependent on:

- the complexity of the system architecture;
- the number and frequency of builds of the integrated system;
- how much choice (options) is available to customers (whether internal or external).

For example, a software house selling different versions of a product to many customers who run on a variety of operating systems is likely to find configuration management tools more useful than an internal development department working on a single operating system for a single customer. In addition, the use of Agile developments with frequent deployments has increased the value of configuration management tools.

The use of configuration management tools allows traceability between testware and builds of an integrated system and versions of subsystems and modules. Traceability is useful for:

- identifying the correct version of test procedures to be used;
- determining which test procedures and other testware can be reused or need to be updated/maintained;
- assisting the debugging process so that a failure found when running a test procedure can be traced back to the appropriate version of a subsystem.

CHECK OF UNDERSTANDING

1. What is traceability?
2. Which tool is likely to be most closely integrated with a requirements management tool?
3. Which tool would you use to identify the version of the software component being tested?

Tool support for static testing

Review tools
Review tools (also known as review process support tools) provide a framework for reviews or inspections. This can include:

- Maintaining information about the review process, such as rules and checklists.
- The ability to record, communicate and retain review comments and defects.
- The ability to amend and reissue the deliverable under review while retaining a history or log of the changes made.
- Traceability functions to enable changes to deliverables under review to highlight other deliverables that may be affected by the change.

- The use of web technology to provide access from any geographical location to this information.

Review tools can interface with configuration management tools to control the version numbers of a document under review.

If reviews and inspections are already performed effectively then a review tool can be implemented fairly quickly and relatively cheaply. However, if such a tool is used as a means for imposing the use of reviews then the training and implementation costs will be fairly high (as would be the case for implementing a review process without such tools). These tools support the review process, but management buy-in to reviews is necessary if benefits from them are to be obtained in the long run.

Review tools tend to be more beneficial for peer (or technical) reviews and inspections rather than walkthroughs and informal reviews.

USE IN HOTEL CHAIN SCENARIO

The hotel company could use a review tool to perform a review of a system specification written in the UK, so that offshore developers can be involved in the review process. In turn, the review of program code, written offshore, could also be performed using such a tool. This means that both the UK and offshore staff could be involved in both reviews, with no excuses for the right people not being available to attend.

Static analysis tools
Static analysis tools (also known as static code analysers) analyse code before it is executed in order to identify defects as early as possible. Therefore they are used mainly by developers prior to unit testing. A static analysis tool generates lots of error and warning messages about the code. Training may be required in order to interpret these messages and it may also be necessary to configure the tool to filter out particular types of warning messages that are not relevant. The use of static analysis tools on existing or amended code is likely to result in lots of messages concerning programming standards. A way of dealing with this situation should be considered during the selection and implementation process. For instance, it may be agreed that small changes to existing code should not use the static analysis tool whereas medium to large changes to existing code should use the static analysis tool. A rewrite should be considered if the existing code is significantly non-compliant.

Static analysis tools can find defects that are hard to find during dynamic testing. They can also be used to enforce programming standards (including secure coding), improve the understanding of the code and to calculate complexity and other metrics (see **Chapter 3**).

Some static analysis tools are integrated with dynamic analysis tools and coverage measurement tools. They are usually language specific, so to test code written in C++ you would need to have a version of a static analysis tool that was specific to C++.

188

Other static analysis tools come as part of programming languages or only work with particular development platforms. Note that debugging tools and compilers provide some basic functions of a static analysis tool, but they are generally not considered to be test tools and are excluded from the ISTQB syllabus.

The types of defect that can be found using a static analysis tool can include:

- Syntax errors (e.g. spelling or missing punctuation).
- Variance from programming standards (e.g. too difficult to maintain).
- Invalid code structures (missing ENDIF statements).
- The structure of the code means that some modules or sections of code may not be executed. Such unreachable code or invalid code dependencies may point to errors in code structure.
- Portability (e.g. code compiles on Windows but not on UNIX).
- Security vulnerabilities.
- Inconsistent interfaces between components (e.g. XML messages produced by component A are not of the correct format to be read by component B).
- References to variables that have a null value or variables declared but never used.

USE IN HOTEL CHAIN SCENARIO

Static analysis tools may be considered worthwhile for code being developed by offshore development teams who are not familiar with in-house coding standards. Such tools may also be considered beneficial for high-risk functions such as BACS and other external interfaces.

Modelling tools

Modelling tools are used primarily by developers during the analysis and design stages of the development life cycle. The reason modelling tools are included here is because they are very cost-effective at finding defects early in the development life cycle.

Their benefits are similar to those obtained from the use of reviews and inspections, in that modelling tools allow omissions and inconsistencies to be identified and fixed early so that detailed design and programming can begin from a consistent and robust model. This in turn prevents fault multiplication that can occur if developers build from the wrong model.

For instance, a visual modelling tool using UML can be used by designers to build a model of the software specification. The tool can map business processes to the system architecture model, which, in turn, enables programmers and testers to have a better and common understanding of what programs should do and what testing is required.

Similarly, the use of database, state or object models can help to identify what testing is required and can assist in checking whether tests cover all necessary transactions. Integration with test design tools may also enable modelling tools to support the generation of test cases.

USE IN HOTEL CHAIN SCENARIO

The modelling tool could help to identify missing scenarios from letter templates or the need to update letters with new paragraphs. Again, the benefits of a clearly defined, consistent model of the software will assist offshore companies to develop software that meets the requirements of the customer.

The use of modelling tools is particularly useful in complex system architectures such as in this scenario.

CHECK OF UNDERSTANDING

1. Which of the tools used for static testing is/are most likely to be used by developers rather than testers?
2. In which part of the fundamental test process are static analysis tools likely to be most useful?
3. What is a significant benefit of using modelling tools from a testing perspective?

Tool support for test specification

Test design tools
Test design tools are used to support the generation and creation of test cases. In order for the tool to generate test cases, a test basis needs to be input and maintained. Therefore many test design tools are integrated with other tools that already contain details of the test basis such as:

- modelling tools;
- requirements management tools;
- static analysis tools;
- test management tools.

The level of automation can vary and depends on the characteristics of the tool itself and the way in which the test basis is recorded in the tool. For example, some tools allow specifications or requirements to be specified in a formal language. This can allow test cases with inputs and expected results to be generated. Other test design tools allow a GUI model of the test basis to be created and then allow tests to be generated from this model.

Some tools (sometimes known as test frames) merely generate a partly filled template from the requirement specification held in narrative form. The tester will then need to add to the template and copy and edit as necessary to create the test cases required.

Tests designed from database, object or state models held in modelling tools can be used to verify that the model has been built correctly and can be used to derive some test cases. Tests derived can be very thorough and give high levels of coverage in certain areas.

Some static analysis tools integrate with tools that generate test cases from an analysis of the code. These can include test input values and expected results.

A test oracle is a type of test design tool that automatically generates expected results. However, these are rarely available because they perform the same function as the software under test. Test oracles tend to be most useful for:

- replacement systems;
- migrations;
- regression testing.

USE IN HOTEL CHAIN SCENARIO

A test oracle could be built using a spreadsheet to support the testing of customers' bills. The tester can then input details for calculating bills such as the total bill based on various transaction types, refunds, VAT etc. The spreadsheet could then calculate the total bill amount and this should match the bill calculated by the system under test.

However, test design tools should be only part of the approach to test design. They need to be supplemented by other test cases designed with the use of other techniques and the application of risk.

Test design tools could be used by the test organisation in the scenario but the overhead to input the necessary data from the test basis may be too great to give any real overall benefit. However, if the test design tool can import requirements or other aspects of the test basis easily then it may become worthwhile.

Test design tools tend to be more useful for safety-critical and other high-risk software where coverage levels are higher and industry, defence or government standards need to be adhered to. Commercial software applications, like the hotel system, do not usually require such high standards and therefore test design tools are of less benefit in such cases.

Test data preparation tools
Test data preparation tools are used by testers and developers to manipulate data so that the environment is in the appropriate state for the test to be run. This can involve making changes to the field values in databases, data files etc., and populating files with a spread of data (including depersonalised dates of birth, names and addresses etc. to support data anonymity).

USE IN HOTEL CHAIN SCENARIO

A set of test data may be created by taking, say, 5 per cent of all records from the live system and scrambling personal details so that data is protected and to ensure that customer letters being tested are not wrongly sent to real customers. Data could be taken from the mainframe system, but it is also very important to retain integrity of data between different systems. Data that is held in other databases would need to remain consistent with records on the mainframe.

The knowledge of the database structure and which fields need to be depersonalised is likely to lie with the development team – so it is important to consider whether to buy a tool or build it within the organisation.

CHECK OF UNDERSTANDING

1. What is the main difference and similarity between a test frame and a test oracle?
2. What types of inputs can a test design tool use to generate test cases?

Tool support for test execution and logging

Test comparators

Test comparators compare the contents of files, databases, XML messages, objects and other electronic data formats. This allows expected results and actual results to be compared. They can also highlight differences and thus provide assistance to developers when localising and debugging code.

They often have functions that allow specified sections of the file, screen or object to be ignored or masked out. This means that a date or time stamp on a screen or field can be masked out because it is expected to be different when a comparison is performed.

Table 6.2 shows an extract from the transaction table in the hotel chain database for data created on 20/10/2014.

Table 6.2 Hotel system extract (20/10/2014)

Transaction ID	Trans_Date	Amount _exc_VAT	VAT	Customer ID
12345	20/10/2014	359.66	71.93	AG0012
12346	20/10/2014	2312.01	462.40	HJ0007

A regression test was run on 5/11/2014. Table 6.3 shows an extract from the transaction table for this data.

Table 6.3 Hotel system extract (5/11/2014)

Transaction ID	Trans_Date	Amount _exc_VAT	VAT	Customer ID
12369	5/11/2014	359.66	71.93	AG0012
12370	5/11/2014	2312.01	462.40	HJ0007

The Transaction ID and Trans_Date fields contain different values. But we know why this is the case and we would expect them to be different. Therefore we can mask out these values. Note that some automated test comparators use test oracles while others provide functions to add on values to take into account known differences (e.g. 15 days later) so that the actual results and expected results can be compared.

Comparators are particularly useful for regression testing since the contents of output or interface files should usually be the same. This is probably the test tool that provides the single greatest benefit. For instance, manually comparing the contents of a database query containing thousands of rows is time-consuming, error prone and demotivating. The same task can be performed accurately and in a fraction of the time using a comparator. Comparators are usually included in test execution tools.

Test execution tools
Test execution tools allow test scripts to be run automatically (or at least semi-automatically). A test script (written in a programming language or scripting language) is used to navigate through the system under test and to compare predefined expected outcomes with actual outcomes. The results of the test run are written to a test log. Test scripts can then be amended and reused to run other or additional scenarios through the same system. Some tools offer GUI-based utilities that enable amendments to be made to scripts more easily than by changing code. These utilities may include:

- configuring the script to identify particular GUI objects;
- customising the script to allow it to take specified actions when encountering particular GUI objects or messages;
- parameterising the script to read data from various sources.

Record (or capture playback) tools: Record (or capture playback) tools can be used to record a test script and then play it back exactly as it was executed. However, a test script usually fails when played back owing to unexpected results or unrecognised objects. This may sound surprising but consider entering a new customer record onto a system:

- When the script was recorded, the customer record did not exist. When the script is played back the system correctly recognises that this customer record already exists and produces a different response, thus causing the test script to fail.

- When a test script is played back and actual and expected results are compared a date or time may be displayed. The comparison facility will spot this difference and report a failure.

- Other problems include the inability of test execution tools to recognise some types of GUI control or object. This might be able to be resolved by coding or reconfiguring the object characteristics (but this can be quite complicated and should be left to experts in the tool).

Also note that expected results are not necessarily captured when recording user actions and therefore may not be compared during playback.

The recording of tests can be useful during exploratory testing for reproducing a defect or for documenting how to execute a test. In addition, such tools can be used to capture user actions so that the navigation through a system can be recorded. In both cases, the script can then be made more robust by a technical expert so that it handles valid system behaviours depending on the inputs and the state of the system under test.

Data-driven testing: Robust test scripts that deal with various inputs can be converted into data-driven tests. This is where hard-coded inputs in the test script are replaced with variables that point to data in a data-table. Data-tables are usually spreadsheets with one test case per row, with each row containing test inputs and expected results. The test script reads the appropriate data value from the data-table and inserts it at the appropriate point in the script (e.g. the value in the Customer Name column is inserted into the Customer Name field on the input screen).

Keyword-driven testing: A further enhancement to data-driven testing is the use of keyword-driven (or action word) testing. Keywords are included as extra columns in the data-table. The script reads the keyword and takes the appropriate actions and subsequent path through the system under test. Conditional programming constructs such as IF ELSE statements or SELECT CASE statements are required in the test script for keyword-driven testing.

Technical skills: Programming skills and programming standards are required to use the tool effectively. It may be that these can be provided by a small team of technical experts within the test organisation or from an external company. In data-driven, and particularly keyword-driven approaches, the bulk of the work can be done by manual testers, with no knowledge of the scripting language, defining their test cases and test data and then running their tests and raising defects as required. However, this relies on robust and well-written test scripts that are easy to maintain. This takes much time and effort before any sort of payback is achieved.

Maintenance: It is essential that time (and subsequent budget) is allowed for test scripts to be maintained. Any change to a system can mean that the test scripts need to be updated. Therefore, the introduction of a new type of object or control could result in a mismatch being found between the previous object type and the new one. The relevant level of technical skills and knowledge is also required to do this.

Effective and efficient use: The efficiency and effectiveness benefits that come from the use of a test execution tool take a long time to come to fruition. First, the selection and implementation process needs to be planned and conducted effectively (a generic process for selecting and implementing any type of test tool is detailed later in this chapter). However, there are certain issues that are particularly relevant to test execution tools and these are described below.

The long-term benefits of test execution tools include:

- Cost savings as a result of the time saved by running automated tests rather than manual tests.
- Accuracy benefits from avoiding manual errors in execution and comparison.
- The ability and flexibility to use skilled testers on more useful and interesting tasks (than running repetitive manual tests).
- The speed with which the results of the regression pack can be obtained.

Note that benefits come primarily from running the same or very similar tests a number of times on a stable platform. Therefore they are generally most useful for regression testing.

USE IN HOTEL CHAIN SCENARIO

Let us assume that a test execution tool is already used for regression testing. Existing automated test scripts could be analysed to identify which ones can be reused and to identify gaps in the coverage for the new enhancement. These gaps could be filled by running cases manually or by writing new automated test scripts. Rather than starting from scratch, it may be possible to produce additional automated scripts by reusing some code or modules already used by existing scripts, or by using parameterisation and customisation utilities. In this enhancement, the automated scripts used to test the unchanged documents could be run without having to be amended.

The automated scripts to produce the amended documents would need to be analysed and updated as required. The navigation part of the script would be largely unchanged but the comparison between actual and expected results would probably be performed manually the first time round. Once the test has passed manually, the comparison could be added to the script for reuse in the future.

Automated scripts for new documents could be added to the regression pack after this release is complete.

The graph in Figure 6.4 shows how the benefits of using test execution tools take some time to pay back. Note how in the early stages the cost of using automated regression testing is greater than the cost of manual regression testing. This is due to the initial investment, implementation, training, initial development of automated scripts etc. However, the cost each additional time the test is run is less for automated regression testing than it is for manual regression testing. Therefore the lines on the graph converge and at a point in time (known as the break-even point) the lines cross. This is the point at which the total cost to date for automated testing is less than the total cost to date for manual regression testing.

Figure 6.4 Test execution tools payback model

This is clearly a simplistic view but it demonstrates how an initial investment in test execution tools can be of financial benefit in the medium to long term. There are other less tangible benefits as well. However, to get this financial benefit you will need to be sure that there is a requirement to run the same (or very similar) regression tests on many occasions.

Test harnesses
Test harnesses (also known as unit test framework tools) are used primarily by developers to simulate a small section of the environment in which the software will operate. They are usually written in-house by developers to perform component or integration testing for a specific purpose. Test harnesses often use 'mock objects' known as 'stubs' (which stub out the need to have other components or systems by returning predefined values) and 'drivers' (which replace the calling component or system and drive transactions, messages and commands through the software under test).

Test harnesses can be used to test various systems or objects ranging from a middleware system (as in Figure 6.5) to a single or small group of components. Test harnesses are frequently used in Agile development so that existing tests can be rerun as regression tests to establish whether existing functionality is adversely impacted by the changes made.

USE IN HOTEL CHAIN SCENARIO

Bookings are entered via the web or GUI front-ends and are loaded onto the mainframe. An overnight batch runs on the mainframe and generates XML messages that are then processed by the middleware system, which makes a further call to the mainframe to read other data. The middleware system then generates further XML messages, which are processed by other systems, resulting in the production of letters to customers.

There are several benefits that can be obtained from using a test harness that generates the XML messages produced by the mainframe:

- It would take a lot of time and effort to design and execute test cases on the mainframe system and run the batch.
- It would be costly to build a full environment.
- The mainframe code needed to generate the XML messages may not yet be available.
- A smaller environment is easier to control and manage. It enables developers (or testers) to perform component and integration testing more quickly because it is easier to localise defects. This allows a quicker turnround time for fixing defects.

The diagram in Figure 6.5 shows that a test harness has been built using a spreadsheet and macros (the driver) to generate XML messages and send them to the middleware. A stub is used to simulate the calls made by the middleware to the mainframe. The contents of the XML messages produced by the middleware can then be compared with the expected results.

Figure 6.5 Test harness for middleware

There are similarities with the principle behind data-driven testing using test execution tools because the harness allows many different test cases to be designed and run without the time-consuming process of keying them manually. This raises the question of how much benefit can be obtained from using a test execution tool when a test harness can be used instead. As usual, it depends on the circumstances, the risk, the purpose and the level of testing being performed.

Coverage measurement tools

Coverage measurement tools measure the percentage of the code structure covered across white-box measurement techniques such as statement coverage and branch or decision coverage. In addition, they can also be used to measure coverage of modules and function calls. Coverage measurement tools are often integrated with static and dynamic analysis tools and are primarily used by developers.

Coverage measurement tools can measure code written in several programming languages, but not all tools can measure code written in all languages. They are useful for reporting coverage measurement and can therefore be used to assess test completion criteria and/or exit criteria.

Coverage measurement of requirements and test cases/scripts run can usually be obtained from test management tools. This function is unlikely to be provided by coverage measurement tools.

Coverage measurement can be carried out using intrusive or non-intrusive methods. Non-intrusive methods typically involve reviewing code and running code. Intrusive methods, such as 'instrumenting the code' involve adding extra statements into the code. The code is then executed and the extra statements write back to a log in order to identify which statements and branches have been executed.

Instrumentation code can then be removed before it goes into production.

Intrusive methods can affect the accuracy of a test because, for example, slightly more processing will be required to cope with the additional code. This is known as the probe effect and testers need to be aware of its consequences and try to keep its impact to a minimum.

USE IN HOTEL CHAIN SCENARIO

Coverage measurement tools are generally used on high-risk and safety-critical systems and therefore would probably not be used in the Hotel Chain Scenario. However, as an example, assume that the exit criteria for a test phase include the criteria shown in Table 6.4.

Table 6.4 Exit criteria

Function	Module risk level	Branch coverage	Statement coverage
BACS	High	100%	100%
Email message to selected customers	Medium	Not specified	100%
Look-up error message/screen navigation	Low	50%	75%

In this case, coverage measurement tools would be the most appropriate method of assessing whether the exit criteria have been met.

Security testing tools
Security testing tools are used to test the functions that detect security threats and to evaluate the security characteristics of software. The security testing tool would typically be used to assess the ability of the software under test to:

- handle computer viruses;
- protect data confidentiality and data integrity;
- prevent unauthorised access;
- carry out authentication checks of users;
- remain available under a denial of service attack;
- check non-repudiation attributes of digital signatures.

Security testing tools are mainly used to test ecommerce, ebusiness and websites. For example, a third-party security application such as a firewall may be integrated into a web-based application.

The skills required to develop and use security testing tools are very specialised and such tools are generally developed and used on a particular technology platform for a particular purpose. Therefore it maybe worth considering the use of specialist consultancies to perform such testing. For example, specialist consultancies are often engaged to carry out penetration testing. This type of testing is to establish whether malicious attackers can penetrate through the organisation's firewall and hack into the organisation's systems.

Security testing tools need to be constantly updated because there are problems solved and new vulnerabilities discovered all the time – consider the number of Windows security releases to see the scale of security problems.

USE IN HOTEL CHAIN SCENARIO

Security testing tools could be used to test that the firewall and other security applications built into the Hotel Chain's systems can:

- resist a denial of service (DOS) attack;
- prevent unauthorised access to data held within the database;
- prevent unauthorised access to encrypted XML messages containing bank account details.

This work could be carried out by a third-party consultancy which specialises in penetration testing and related services.

CHECK OF UNDERSTANDING

1. Why is implementing a comparator likely to be cheaper and quicker than implementing a test execution tool?
2. Why is the use of test execution tools for record and playback not as effective as it may sound?
3. Are test execution tools likely to be more useful for testing new systems or testing changes to existing systems? Explain why.
4. Would both a test execution tool and a test harness be appropriate for acceptance testing?
5. Name three potential benefits from implementing a test execution tool.
6. Give three reasons why a test harness is an efficient way of testing components.
7. Which test execution and logging tools are typically used by developers?
8. Which test execution and logging tools are likely to be used by specialists in the use of that tool?

Tool support for performance and monitoring

Dynamic analysis tools
Dynamic analysis tools are used to detect the type of defects that are difficult to find during static testing. They are typically used by developers, during component testing and component integration testing, to:

- report on the state of software during its execution;
- monitor the allocation, use and deallocation of memory;
- identify memory leaks;
- detect time dependencies;
- identify unassigned pointers;
- check pointer arithmetic.

They are generally used for safety-critical and other high-risk software where reliability is critical.

Dynamic analysis tools are often integrated with static analysis and coverage measurement tools. For example, a developer may want to perform static analysis on code to localise defects so that they can be removed before component test execution. The integrated tool may allow:

- the code to be analysed statically;
- the code to be instrumented;
- the code to be executed (dynamically).

Dynamic analysis tools are usually language specific, so to test code written in C++ you would need to have a version of a dynamic analysis tool that was specific to C++.

The tool could then:

- report static defects;
- report dynamic defects;
- provide coverage measurement figures;
- report on the code being (dynamically) executed at various instrumentation points.

USE IN HOTEL CHAIN SCENARIO

The hotel chain would probably not use dynamic analysis tools as the benefits for a normal commercial software system (such as this) are relatively small compared with the investment and ongoing costs of dynamic testing tools. However, if static analysis and coverage measurement tools are used then the additional cost of using dynamic analysis tools may be reduced because they usually come in the same package. Another contributory factor in the decision is that the work done during static analysis and coverage measurement may mean that little additional effort is required to run dynamic tests.

Performance testing/load testing/stress testing tools

Performance testing is very difficult to do accurately and in a repeatable way without using test tools. Therefore performance testing tools have been developed to carry out both load testing and stress testing.

Load testing reports on the performance of a system under test, under various loads and usage patterns. A load generator (which is a type of test driver) can be used to simulate the load and required usage pattern by creating virtual users that execute predefined scripts across one or more test machines. Alternatively, response times or transaction times can be measured under various levels of usage by running automated repetitive test scripts via the user interface of the system under test. In both cases output will be written to a log. Reports or graphs can be generated from the contents of the log to monitor the level of performance.

Performance testing tools can also be used for stress testing. In this case, the load on the system under test is increased gradually (ramped up) in order to identify the usage pattern or load at which the system under test fails. For example, if an air traffic control system supports 200 concurrent aircraft in the defined air space, the entry of the 201st or 205th aircraft should not cause the whole system to fail.

Performance testing tools can be used against whole systems but they can also be used during system integration test to test an integrated group of systems, one or more servers, one or more databases or a whole environment.

If the risk analysis finds that the likelihood of performance degradation is low then it is likely that no performance testing will be carried out. For instance, a small enhancement to an existing mainframe system would not necessarily require any formal performance testing. Normal manual testing may be considered sufficient (during which poor performance might be noticed).

There are similarities between performance testing tools and test execution tools in that they both use test scripts and data-driven testing. They can both be left to run unattended overnight and both need a heavy upfront investment, which will take some period of time to pay back.

Performance testing tools can find defects such as:

- General performance problems.
- Performance bottlenecks.
- Memory leakage (e.g. if the system is left running under heavy load for some time).
- Record-locking problems.
- Concurrency problems.
- Excess usage of system resources.
- Exhaustion of disk space.

The cost of some performance tools is high and the implementation and training costs are also high. In addition, finding experts in performance testing is not that easy. Therefore it is worth considering using specialist consultancies to come in and carry out performance testing using such tools.

USE IN HOTEL CHAIN SCENARIO

The likelihood of poor website performance and the cost of lost business and reputation are likely to be sufficient to justify the use of performance testing to mitigate this risk. Performance testing can range from using a relatively cheap tool to indicate whether performance has improved or deteriorated as a result of the enhancement, to an extensive assessment of response times under normal or maximum predicted usage and identification of the usage pattern that will cause the system to fail.

It is likely that performance test tools will have been used when the website was first developed. Therefore it may be easy to reuse existing tools to do a regression test of performance. If performance tools were not used when the website was developed it is unlikely to be worthwhile buying and implementing expensive performance testing tools.

An alternative option would be to use tools that already exist on servers or in the test environment to monitor performance. It may also be worth considering using external consultants.

Monitoring tools

Monitoring tools are used to check whether whole systems or specific system resources are available and whether their performance is acceptable. Such tools are mainly used in live rather than test environments and are therefore not really testing tools. They tend to be used for monitoring ecommerce, ebusiness or websites as such systems are more likely to be affected by factors external to the organisation and the consequences can be severe in terms of business lost and bad publicity. Generally, if a website is not available, customers will not report it but will go elsewhere. For example, it was reported in 2003 that a well-known online retailer would lose sales of $660,000 per hour if it were offline during the US trading day. The advent of websites that continually check the status of popular websites means that such information is much more easily available to the general public.

The use of monitoring tools is generally less important for internal systems because failure is more likely to be noticed only within the organisation and contingency plans may also exist. However, the availability of monitoring tools on mainframes, servers and other forms of hardware means that it is relatively easy to monitor the majority of an organisation's infrastructure.

USE IN HOTEL CHAIN SCENARIO

A monitoring tool may be beneficial to monitor the website. A monitoring tool may also exist as part of the mainframe system. However, it is less likely that monitoring tools will be used for the GUI front-end that is used by internal staff.

Data quality assessment tools
Data quality assessment tools allow files and databases to be compared against a format that is specified in advance. They are typically used on large scale data intensive projects such as:

- Conversion of data used on one system into a format suitable for another system.
- Migration of data from one system to another.
- Loading of data into a data warehouse.

Data quality assessment tools are not specifically designed for testing purposes. They are used primarily for the migration of production data, but typically the development and testing of a migration project will also use these tools.

USE IN HOTEL CHAIN SCENARIO

Suppose that the hotel chain buys a smaller group of hotels, 'Small Hotel Group'.

It could use a data quality assessment tool during the development and testing of an enhancement to its existing systems to include the additional hotels.

The data quality assessment tools could be configured to establish whether the customer data being migrated meets particular quality requirements. These requirements may include:

- valid postcodes;
- valid title for gender;
- numeric values in financial fields;
- numeric values in date fields.

The tool could also be used to reconcile file record counts with data held in header and footer records to confirm that the number of records in the file equals the number of records loaded into the database.

Usability test tools
Usability test tools typically record the mouse clicks made by remote usability testers when carrying out a specified task. Some tools also enable other data to be captured

such as screenshots, written comments and voice recordings of verbal comments. This recorded data is generally stored in a database so that it can then be analysed easily by staff at the organisation commissioning the testing.

Note that the usability testing tool market is changing very quickly and new types of usability tools may appear over the next few years.

USE IN HOTEL CHAIN SCENARIO

The changes to the website to improve usability could be tested by a specialist usability testing company who employ, say 50, remote users. The remote users would be given a high-level requirement that would exercise the website changes such as:

- Go to a specified test URL and book three rooms from 3 August to 5 August and two rooms from 7 August. Pay by credit card XYZ.

The mouse clicks, other inputs, and comments recorded by the 50 remote users in carrying out this task would be stored in a database and an analysis report produced by the specialist usability testing company for the hotel chain. This analysis could highlight poor areas of usability in the test website, which could be improved before being deployed to the live website.

CHECK OF UNDERSTANDING

1. Describe two types of defect that can typically be found using dynamic analysis tools.
2. Describe two drawbacks associated with performance testing tools.
3. Which of the tools that provide support for performance and monitoring is most likely to be used by developers?

Other tools

Other tools that are not designed specifically for testers or developers can also be used to support one or more test activities. These include:

- Spreadsheets.
- Word processors.
- Email.
- Back-up and restore utilities.
- SQL and other database query tools.
- Project planning tools.
- Debugging tools (although these are more likely to be used by developers than testers).

For example, in the absence of test management or incident management tools, defects could be recorded on word processors and could be tracked and maintained on spreadsheets. Tests passed or failed could also be recorded on spreadsheets.

USE IN HOTEL CHAIN SCENARIO

Other software tools could also be used:

- A spreadsheet could be used for producing decision tables or working out all the different test scenarios required. It could also be used to manipulate test management information so that it can be presented in the format required in weekly or daily test progress reports.

- Word processors could be used for writing test strategies, test plans, weekly reports and other test deliverables.

- Email could be used for communicating with developers about defects and for distributing test reports and other deliverables.

- Back-up and restore utilities could be used to restore a consistent set of data into the test environment for regression testing.

- SQL could be used for analysing the data held in databases in order to obtain actual or expected results.

- Project planning tools could be used to estimate resources and timescales and monitor progress.

- Debugging tools can be used by developers to localise and fix defects.

CHECK OF UNDERSTANDING

Name four tools that are not specifically designed for testers. Give an example of how each of them could be of use to a tester.

Summary of test tools

Table 6.5 summarises the types of test tools discussed above. It includes the definition given in the ISTQB Glossary of Testing Terms v2.4 and gives a guide to:

- the main ISTQB syllabus classification;

- the activity in the fundamental test process for which the tool is usually most useful;

- the most likely users of the tool.

Table 6.5 Types of test tool

Tool type	ISTQB syllabus classification	Activity in fundamental test process where it is usually most beneficial	ISTQB Glossary of Testing Terms definition	Most likely users
Test management tool	Management of testing and tests	All activities	A tool that provides support to the test management and control part of a test process. It often has several capabilities, such as testware management, scheduling of tests, the logging of results, progress tracking, incident management and test reporting.	Testers
Incident management tool	Management of testing and tests	Implementation and execution	A tool that facilitates the recording and status tracking of incidents. They often have workflow-oriented facilities to track and control the allocation, correction and retesting of incidents and provide reporting facilities. See also **Incident management tools.**	Various, but particularly testers
Requirements management tool	Management of testing and tests	Analysis and design	A tool that supports the recording of requirements, requirements attributes (e.g. priority, knowledge responsible) and annotation, and facilitates traceability through layers of requirements and requirements change management. Some requirements management tools also provide facilities for static analysis, such as consistency checking and violations to predefined requirements rules.	Various, but particularly business analysts

(Continued)

Table 6.5 (Continued)

Tool type	ISTQB syllabus classification	Activity in fundamental test process where it is usually most beneficial	ISTQB Glossary of Testing Terms definition	Most likely users
Configuration management tool	Management of testing and tests	Implementation and execution	A tool that provides support for the identification and control of configuration items, their status over changes and versions, and the release of baselines consisting of configuration items.	Various
Review tool	Static testing	Implementation and execution	A tool that provides support to the review process. Typical features include review planning and tracking support, communication support, collaborative reviews and a repository for collecting and reporting of metrics.	Various
Static analysis tools / Static code analyser	Static testing	Implementation and execution	A tool that carries out static code analysis. The tool checks source code, for certain properties such as conformance to coding standards, quality metrics or data flow anomalies.	Developers
Modelling tools	Static testing	Implementation and execution	A tool that supports the creation, amendment and verification of models of the software or system.	Developers
Test design tools/script generators	Test specification	Analysis and design	A tool that supports the test design activity by generating test inputs from a specification held in the tool repository or in a requirements management tool.	Testers

(Continued)

Table 6.5 (Continued)

Tool type	ISTQB syllabus classification	Activity in fundamental test process where it is usually most beneficial	ISTQB Glossary of Testing Terms definition	Most likely users
Test oracles (considered to be a subset of test design tools)	Test specification	Analysis and design	A source to determine expected results to compare with the actual result of the software under test. An oracle may be the existing system (for a benchmark), other software, a user manual, or an individual's specialised knowledge, but should not be the code. (After Adrion.)	Testers
Test (input) data preparation tools	Test specification	Analysis and design	A type of test tool that enables data to be selected from existing databases or created, generated, manipulated and edited for use in testing.	Various
Test execution/test running tools	Test execution and logging	Implementation and execution	A type of test tool that is able to execute other software using an automated test script, e.g. capture/playback.	Testers
Test harness/unit test framework tools (stubs and drivers)	Test execution and logging	Implementation and execution	A test environment composed of stubs and drivers needed to conduct a test.	Developers
Test comparators	Test execution and logging	Implementation and execution	A test tool to perform automated test comparison of actual results with expected results.	Testers and developers

(Continued)

Table 6.5 (Continued)

Tool type	ISTQB syllabus classification	Activity in fundamental test process where it is usually most beneficial	ISTQB Glossary of Testing Terms definition	Most likely users
Coverage measurement tools	Test execution and logging	Implementation and execution	A tool that provides objective measures of what structural elements, e.g. statements, branches, have been exercised by a test suite.	Developers
Security testing tools	Test execution and logging	Implementation and execution	A tool that provides support for testing security characteristics and vulnerabilities.	Security testing specialists
Dynamic analysis tools	Performance and monitoring	Implementation and execution	A tool that provides run-time information on the state of the software code. These tools are most commonly used to identify unassigned pointers, check pointer arithmetic and to monitor the allocation, use and deallocation of memory and to flag memory leaks.	Developers
Performance testing/load testing/stress testing tools	Performance and monitoring	Implementation and execution	A tool to support performance testing that usually has two main facilities: load generation and test transaction measurement. Load generation can simulate either multiple users or high volumes of input data. During execution, response time measurements are taken from selected transactions and these are logged. Performance testing tools normally provide reports based on test logs and graphs of load against response times.	Performance testing specialists

(Continued)

Table 6.5 (Continued)

Tool type	ISTQB syllabus classification	Activity in fundamental test process where it is usually most beneficial	ISTQB Glossary of Testing Terms definition	Most likely users
Monitoring tools	Performance and monitoring	Implementation and execution	A software tool or hardware device that runs concurrently with the component or system under test and supervises, records and/or analyses the behaviour of the component or system.	Various
Data quality assessment tools	Data quality	Implementation and execution	Not defined.	Various
Usability tools	Usability	Implementation and execution	Not defined. (Usability testing is defined as testing to determine the extent to which the software product is understood, easy to learn, easy to operate and attractive to the users under specified conditions.)	Usability testing specialists
Spreadsheets	Other tools	All activities	Not defined.	Various
SQL	Other tools	Implementation and execution	Not defined.	Various
Project planning/ resource	Other tools	Planning and control	Not defined.	Various
Debugging tools	Other tools	Not used for testing activities	A tool used by programmers to reproduce failures, investigate the state of programs and find the corresponding defect. Debuggers enable programmers to execute programs step by step, to halt a program at any program statement and to set and examine program variables.	Developers

211

INTRODUCING A TOOL INTO AN ORGANISATION

There are many stages in the process that should be considered before implementing a test tool.

Analyse the problem/opportunity

An assessment should be made of the maturity of the test process used within the organisation. If the organisation's test processes are immature and ineffective then the most that the tool can do is to make the repetition of these processes quicker and more accurate – quick and accurate ineffective processes are still ineffective.

It is therefore important to identify the strengths, weaknesses and opportunities that exist within the test organisation before introducing test tools. Tools should only be implemented that will either support an established test process or support required improvements to an immature test process. It may be beneficial to carry out a TPI (Test Process Improvement) or CMMI (Capability Maturity Model Integration) assessment to establish the maturity of the organisation before considering the implementation of any test tool.

Generate alternative solutions

It may be more appropriate and cost-effective to do something different. In some organisations, performance testing, which may only need to be done from time to time, could be outsourced to a specialist testing consultancy. Training or recruiting better staff could provide more benefits than implementing a test tool and improve the effectiveness of a test process more significantly. In addition, it is more effective to maintain a manual regression pack so that it accurately reflects the high-risk areas than to automate an outdated regression pack (that is no longer relevant) using a test execution tool.

An early investigation of what tools are available is likely to form part of this activity.

Constraints and requirements

A thorough analysis of the constraints and requirements of the tool should be performed. Interested parties should attend workshops and/or be interviewed so that a formal description of the requirements can be produced and approved by the budget holder and other key stakeholders.

A failure to specify accurate requirements (as with a failure to specify accurate requirements for a piece of software) can lead to delays, additional costs and the wrong things being delivered. This could lead to a review tool being implemented that does not allow access across the internet, even though there is a need for staff from many countries to participate in reviews. Any financial or technical constraints (e.g. compatibility with particular operating systems or databases) should also be considered.

It is useful to attach some sort of priority or ranking to each requirement or group of requirements.

Training, coaching and mentoring requirements should also be identified. For example, experienced consultants could be used for a few weeks or months to work on overcoming implementation problems with the tool and to help transfer knowledge to permanent staff. Such consultants could be provided by the vendor or could be from the contract market.

Requirements for the tool vendor should also be considered. These could include the quality of training and support offered by the vendor during and after implementation and the ability to enhance and upgrade the tool in the future. In addition, their financial stability should be considered because the vendor could go bankrupt or sell to another vendor. Therefore, using a small niche vendor may be a higher risk than using an established tool supplier.

If non-commercial tools (such as open source and freeware) are being considered then there are likely to be risks around the lack of training and support available. In addition, the ability or desire of the service support supplier (or open-source provider) to continue to develop and support the tool should be taken into account.

Evaluation and shortlist

The tools available in the marketplace should be evaluated to identify a shortlist of the tools that provide the best fit to the requirements and constraints. This may involve:

- searching the internet;
- attending exhibitions of test tools;
- discussions with tool vendors;
- engaging specialist consultants to identify relevant tools.

It may also be useful for the test organisation to send a copy of its list of requirements and constraints to tool vendors so that:

- the vendor is clear about what the test organisations wants;
- the vendor can respond with clarity about what its own tools can do and what workarounds there are to meet the requirements that the tool cannot provide;
- the test organisation does not waste time dealing with vendors that cannot satisfy its key requirements.

The outcome of this initial evaluation should result in a shortlist of perhaps one, two or three tools that appear to meet the requirements.

Detailed evaluation/proof of concept

A more detailed evaluation (proof of concept) should then be performed against this shortlist. This should be held at the test organisation's premises in the test environment in which the tool will be used. This test environment should use the system under test and other software, operating systems and hardware with which the tool will be used. There are several reasons why there is little benefit from evaluating the tool on something different. For example:

- Test execution tools do not necessarily recognise all object types in the system under test, or they may need to be reconfigured to do so.

- Performance measurement tools may need to be reconfigured to provide meaningful performance information.

- Test management tools may need to have workflow redesigned to support established test processes and may need to be integrated with existing tools used within the test process.

- Static analysis tools may not work on the version of programming languages used.

In some cases, it may be worth considering whether changes can be made to the organisation's test environments and infrastructure, but the costs and risks need to be understood and quantified.

(Note that if there is only one tool in the shortlist then it may be appropriate to combine the proof of concept and the pilot project.)

After each proof of concept the performance of the tool should be assessed in relation to each predefined requirement. Any additional features demonstrated should be considered and noted as potential future requirements.

Once all proofs of concept have been carried out it may be necessary to amend the requirements as a result of what was found during the tool selection process. Any amendments should be agreed with stakeholders. Each tool should then be assessed against the finalised set of requirements.

There are three likely outcomes at this stage:

- None of the tools meets the requirements sufficiently well to make it worthwhile purchasing and implementing them.

- One tool meets the requirement much better than the others and is likely to be worthwhile. In this case select this tool.

- The situation is unclear and more information is needed. In this case a competitive trial or another cycle/iteration of the process may be needed. Perhaps the requirements need to be revised or further questions need to be put to vendors. It may also be time to start negotiations with vendors about costs.

Negotiations with vendor of selected tool

Once a tool has been selected discussions will be held with the vendor to establish and negotiate the amount of money to be paid and the timing of payments. This will include some or all of the following:

- purchase price;
- annual licence fee;
- consultancy costs;
- training costs;
- implementation costs.

Discussions should establish the amount to be paid, first, for a pilot project and, secondly (assuming the pilot project is successful), the price to be paid for a larger scale implementation.

The pilot project

The aims of a pilot project include the following:

- It is important to establish what changes need to be made to the high-level processes and practices currently used within the test organisation. This involves assessing whether the tool's standard workflow, processes and configuration need to be amended to fit with the test process or whether the existing processes need to be changed to obtain the optimum benefits that the tool can provide.

- To determine lower level detail such as templates, naming standards and other guidelines for using the tool. This can take the form of a user guidelines document.

- To establish whether the tool provides value for money. This is done by trying to estimate and quantify the financial and other benefits of using the tool and then comparing this with the fees paid to the vendor and the projected internal costs to the organisation (e.g. lost time that could be used for other things, the cost of hiring contractors etc.).

- A more intangible aim is to learn more about what the tool can and cannot do and how these functions (or workarounds) can be applied within the test organisation to obtain maximum benefit.

The pilot project should report back to the group of stakeholders that determined the requirements of the tool.

If a decision is made to implement the tool on a larger scale then a formal project should be created and managed according to established project management principles.

Key factors in successful implementations of test tools

There are certain factors or characteristics that many successful tool implementation projects have in common:

- Implementing findings from the pilot project such as high-level process changes and using functions or workarounds that can add additional benefits.

- Identifying and subsequently writing user guidelines, based on the findings of the pilot project.

- An incremental approach to rolling out the tool into areas where it is likely to be most useful. For example, this can allow 'quick wins' to be made and good publicity obtained, resulting in a generally positive attitude towards the tool.

- Improving the process to fit with the new tool, or amending the use of the tool to fit with existing processes.

- Ensuring that the appropriate level of training, coaching and mentoring is available. Similarly, there may be a need to recruit permanent or contract resources to ensure that sufficient skills exist at the outset of the tool's use within the organisation.

- Using a database (in whatever format) of problems encountered and lessons learnt to overcome them. This is because new users are likely to make similar mistakes.

- Capturing metrics to monitor the amount of use of the tool. Recording the benefits obtained. This can then be used to support arguments about implementing to other areas within the test organisation.

- Agreeing or obtaining a budget to allow the tool to be implemented appropriately.

Summary of test tool implementation process

The diagram in Figure 6.6 outlines the process for selecting and implementing a test tool in an organisation. This shows that there are several points at which a decision could be made **not** to introduce a tool. It also demonstrates that the activities during the evaluation and negotiation stages can follow an iterative process until a decision is made.

CHECK OF UNDERSTANDING

1. Why is an understanding of the test organisation's maturity essential before introducing a test tool?
2. What is the purpose of defining requirements for the tool?
3. Why is it important to evaluate the tool vendor as well as the tool itself?
4. What is meant by a proof of concept?
5. What is the purpose of a pilot project?
6. When is it appropriate to combine a proof of concept and pilot project?
7. Name three factors in the successful implementation of tools.

SUMMARY

We have seen that the main benefits of using test tools are generally the same as the benefits from automating a process in any industry. These are: time saved; and predictable and consistent results.

However, we have also seen that there can be considerable costs in terms of both time and money associated with obtaining such benefits. The point at which the use of tools becomes economically viable depends on the amount of reuse, which is often difficult to predict.

Other risks include over-optimistic expectations of:

- what the tool can do;
- how easy it is to use;
- the amount of maintenance required.

Figure 6.6 Test tool implementation process

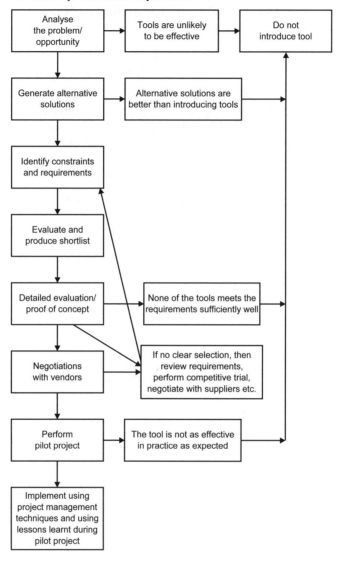

We have seen that there are many types of test tools and that they provide support to a variety of activities within the fundamental test process. We have also seen that tools are used by a variety of staff in the software development process and that some are of greater benefit to developers than testers.

We have looked at the different scripting techniques that can be used with test execution tools. This ranges from the simple record–playback to data-driven and keyword-driven scripts.

We identified a process for selecting and introducing a test tool into an organisation. This involves understanding the interactions between activities within the process and examining the purposes of a proof of concept and of a pilot project. We also examined the problems likely to be encountered when implementing a tool and looked at actions that can be taken in an attempt to overcome or avoid such problems.

We also noted that a decision **not** to introduce a tool could well be a valid decision at several stages within the process.

Example examination questions with answers

E1. K1 question
For which of the following activities in the fundamental test process would an incident management tool be *most useful*?

    a.   Test planning and control.

    b.   Test analysis and design.

    c.   Test implementation and execution.

    d.   Evaluating exit criteria and reporting.

E2. K2 question
Which of the following principles should be followed when introducing a test tool into an organisation?

    i.   Assessing organisational maturity to establish whether a tool will provide expected benefits.

    ii.   Requiring a quick payback on the initial investment.

    iii.   Including a requirement for the tool to be easy to use without having to train unskilled testers.

    iv.   Identifying and agreeing requirements before evaluating test tools.

    a.   i and ii.

    b.   i and iv.

    c.   ii and iii.

    d.   iii and iv.

E3. K1 question
Which of the following defects is *most likely* to be found by a test harness?

    a.   Variance from programming standards.

    b.   A defect in middleware.

    c.   Memory leaks.

    d.   Regression defects.

E4. K2 question
How can test execution tools be of *most benefit* during exploratory testing?

    a.   They can record user actions so that defects are easier to recreate.

    b.   They can be used to perform the regression aspects of exploratory testing.

    c.   They can help to mitigate the risk of low test coverage.

    d.   They can use data-driven tests to increase the amount of exploratory testing performed.

E5. K2 question
Which of the following types of test tool are *most likely* to include traceability functions?

    i.   Performance testing tool.

    ii.   Requirements management tool.

    iii. Configuration management tool.

    iv. Static analysis tool.

    a. i and ii.

    b. i and iv.

    c. ii and iii.

    d. iii and iv.

E6. K1 question
A test management tool is *most likely* to integrate with which of the following tools?

    a. Performance testing tool.

    b. Test data preparation tool.

    c. Static analysis tool.

    d. Requirements management tool.

Answers to questions in the chapter

SA1. The correct answer is d.
SA2. The correct answer is c.
SA3. The correct answer is a.

Answers to example questions

E1. The correct answer is c.
Incident management tools are most useful during test implementation and execution because this is the stage at which the tool is used to raise, manage, retest and close incidents.

The data collected during the defect life cycle can then be manipulated into information that is useful for other activities within the fundamental test process.

Information on numbers of defects outstanding may be useful for evaluating exit criteria (option d). This information could also be used for planning future testing and for taking control (option a).

Incident management tools can also assist in test analysis and design (option b) as information about defects found when testing the previous release of the system could be used when analysing the type of testing required for the next enhancement.

E2. The correct answer is b.
Assessing organisational maturity (i) is very important when deciding whether to introduce a test tool because implementing a tool in an immature test organisation with poor processes is unlikely to produce any benefits.

A quick return on the initial investment (ii) in a test tool is rare. See the graph in Figure 6.1.

Having a requirement that a tool should be easy to use for untrained and unskilled testers (iii) is generally a false hope. This is comparable with expecting someone who has never driven a car to be able to drive safely and effectively.

Agreeing requirements before evaluating tools (iv) is essential. Not to do so would be comparable with building and testing a system without requirements.

In conclusion, (i) and (iv) are good principles to follow when introducing a tool and (ii) and (iii) are not.

E3. The correct answer is b.
Variance from programming standards defects (option a) are found during the review or static testing process. Therefore a test harness is unlikely to find a defect in programming standards.

Memory leak defects (option c) could potentially be found by a test harness designed to run many test cases.

Regression defects (option d) could be found using many types of test tool.

Defects in middleware (option b) are generally more likely to be found by a test harness or a dynamic analysis tool than by any other type of tool (see Figure 6.5).

E4. The correct answer is a.
Exploratory testing is used when it is unclear what the system is supposed to do. Therefore test execution tools are of little use because expected results cannot be predicted.

However, the record feature of a test execution tool can be used to log the actions performed so that defects can be recreated (option a) and rectified more easily.

E5. The correct answer is c.
Requirements management tools (ii) have traceability because they enable test conditions and subsequently test scripts and defects to be traced back to requirements. Configuration management tools (iii) also need to trace the appropriate version of a test script to the release or version of a system or module.

Performance monitoring tools (i) and static analysis tools (iv) are designed for specific objectives. Neither of these tools particularly need traceability functions.

E6. The correct answer is d.
Requirements management tools (option d) often have interfaces with test management tools. In some cases they will be sold as a package or in other cases a test management tool may have its own requirements module. The use of such interfaces or integrated packages aids traceability from requirements through to test scripts and defects.

Performance management tools (option a), test data preparation tools (option b) and static analysis tools (option c) are unlikely to have an interface or be integrated with a test management tool. They serve different purposes and therefore there is little need for such interfaces.

7 THE EXAMINATION

THE EXAMINATION

The examination structure

The Certified Tester Foundation Level (CTFL) examination is a one-hour examination made up of 40 multiple choice questions. There are five main aspects to the examination's structure:

- The questions are all equally weighted.
- Questions are set from learning objectives stated in each section.
- The number of questions associated with each section of the syllabus is in proportion to the amount of time allocated to that section of the syllabus, which roughly translates into:
  - Section 1, seven questions.
  - Section 2, six questions.
  - Section 3, three questions.
  - Section 4, twelve questions.
  - Section 5, eight questions.
  - Section 6, four questions.

These proportions are approximate and the precise breakdown is not mandatory, but examinations will be structured along these lines and as close to these relative proportions as possible.

- The number of questions at each level of understanding will be as follows:
  - K1 50 per cent, that is 20 questions.
  - K2 30 per cent, that is 12 questions.
  - K3 and K4 20 per cent, that is 8 questions.

The breakdown of K3 and K4 questions is not defined in the exam structure, but there is only a single K4 learning objective (LO-4.4.4) and this deals with statement and decision coverage. There will therefore be no more than two K4 questions and more likely only one, and the topic will be assessing statement and/or decision coverage for complete-ness with respect to defined exit criteria.

This is a mandatory requirement and examinations will adhere more strictly to these proportions than to those related to the syllabus section.

Since the majority of K3 questions will be likely to be based on section 4 of the syllabus, it is likely that all or most K3 questions will be about applying test design techniques. All K4 questions will be related to statement and decision coverage.

- The pass mark is 26 correct answers and there are no penalties for incorrect answers.

The question types

All questions will contain a 'stem', which states the question, and four optional answers. One and only one of the optional answers will be correct. The remainder can be expected to be plausibly incorrect, which means that anyone knowing the correct answer will be unlikely to be drawn to any of the incorrect answers, but anyone unsure of the correct answer will be likely to find one or more alternatives equally plausible.

Questions will be stated as clearly as possible, even emphasising keywords by embold-ening or underlining where this will add clarity. There should be very few negative questions (e.g. which of the following is **not** true?) and any negative questions included will be worded so that there is no ambiguity. Questions will be set to test your knowl-edge of the content of the topics covered in the syllabus and not your knowledge of the syllabus itself.

There are no absolute rules for question types as long as they are appropriate to the level of understanding they are testing, but there are some common types of questions that are likely to arise.

As a general rule, K1 questions will be of the straightforward variety shown in the next box.

EXAMPLE OF A K1 QUESTION

(This one is taken from **Chapter 3**.)

What do static analysis tools analyse?

    a. Design.
    b. Test cases.
    c. Requirements.
    d. Program code.

(The correct answer is d.)

K2 questions may be of the same type as the K1 example but with a more searching stem. The more common form of K2 question, however, is known as the Roman type. This is particularly well suited to questions involving comparisons or testing the candidate's ability to identify correct combinations of information. The example in the next box is a K2 question of the Roman type.

EXAMPLE OF A K2 QUESTION

(This one is taken from **Chapter 3**.)

Which of the following statements are correct for walkthroughs?

     i.   Often led by the author.
     ii.   Documented and defined results.
     iii.   All participants have defined roles.
     iv.   Used to aid learning.
     v.   Main purpose is to find defects.

     a.   i and v are correct.
     b.   ii and iii are correct.
     c.   i and iv are correct.
     d.   iii and iv are correct.

(The correct answer is c.)

K3 questions test the candidate's ability to apply a topic, so the most common form of these is related to test design techniques (though this is not the only topic that can be examined at the K3 level). The next box gives a typical example of a techniques question.

EXAMPLE OF A K3 QUESTION

A system is designed to accept values of examination marks as follows:

Fail   0–39 inclusive
Pass   40–59 inclusive
Merit   60–79 inclusive
Distinction   80–100 inclusive

Which of the following sets of values are all in different equivalence partitions?

     a.   25, 40, 60, 75
     b.   0, 45, 79, 87
     c.   35, 40, 59, 69
     d.   25, 39, 60, 81

(The correct answer is b.)

K4 questions test a candidate's ability to analyse information and decide on a course of action. In this examination, K4 questions will be used to test ability to decide whether defined exit criteria have been met.

EXAMPLE OF A K4 QUESTION

A software component has the code shown below:

```
Program Biggest

A, Biggest: Integer
Begin
Read A
Biggest = 10
While A > 0
Do
        If A > Biggest
        Then Biggest = A
        Endif
Read A
Enddo
End
```

The component has exit criteria for component testing that include 100 per cent statement coverage. Which of the following test cases will satisfy this criterion?

    a. 0
    b. 10, 0
    c. 10, 5, 0
    d. 10, 11, 0

(The correct answer is d.)

Remember that K1, K2, K3 and K4 do not equate to easy, moderate or hard. The K level identifies the level of understanding being tested, not the difficulty of the question. It is perfectly possible to find K2 questions that are more difficult (in the sense of being more challenging to answer) than a K3 question. It is, however, true that K1 questions will always be the most straightforward and anyone who knows the material in the syllabus should have no difficulty in answering any K1 question. Every question has the same value; any 26 correct answers will guarantee a pass.

Remember, too, that topics can be examined at any level up to the maximum identified in the syllabus for that topic, so a K3 topic can be examined at the K1 or the K2 level.

Questions in the examination are not labelled by the K level they are testing, but the example questions at the end of each chapter of this book include examples of K1, K2, K3 and K4 questions, and these are labelled by level for your guidance.

The sample examination

A sample examination paper is available from the **ISTQB website**. It is designed to provide guidance on the structure of the paper and the 'rubric' (the rules printed on the front of the paper) of the real examination. The questions in the sample paper are not necessarily typical, though there will be examples of the various types of questions so that candidates are aware of the kinds of questions that can arise. Any topic or type of question in the sample paper can be expected to arise in a real examination at some time. For example, the sample paper may contain an example of a question testing the application of decision testing to a program with a looping structure in it; the existence of this question can be taken to imply that questions involving programs with looping structures may appear in the real examination. Bear in mind that the sample paper may change from time to time to reflect any changes in the syllabus or to reflect any changes in the way questions are set.

Examination technique

In a relatively short examination there is little time to devote to studying the paper in depth. However, it is wise to pause before beginning to answer questions while you assimilate the contents of the question paper. This brief time of inactivity is also a good opportunity to consciously slow down your heart rate and regulate your breathing; nervousness is natural, but it can harm your performance by making you rush. A few minutes spent consciously calming down will be well repaid. There will still be time enough to answer the questions; a strong candidate can answer 40 questions in less than 45 minutes.

When you do start, go through the whole paper answering those questions that are straightforward and for which you know the answer. When you have done this you will have a smaller task to complete and you will probably have taken less than a minute for each question that you have already answered, giving you more time to concentrate on those that you will need more time to answer.

Next, turn to those you feel you understand but that will take you a little time to work out the correct answer, and complete as many of those as you can. The questions you are left with now should be those that you are uncertain about. You now know how long you have to answer each of these and you can take a little more time over each of them.

REVISION TECHNIQUES

There are some golden rules for exam revision:

- Do as many example questions as you can so that you become familiar with the types of questions, the way questions are worded and the levels (K1, K2, K3, K4) of questions that are set in the examination.

- Be active in your reading. This usually means taking notes, but this book has been structured to include regular checks of understanding that will provide you with prompts to ensure you have remembered the key ideas from the section you have just revised. In many cases information you need to remember is already in note form for easy learning.

- One important way to engage with the book is to work through all the examples and exercises. If you convince yourself you can do an exercise, but you do not actually attempt it, you will only discover the weakness in that approach when you are sitting in the examination centre.

- Learning and revision need to be reinforced. There are two related ways to do this:

  - By making structured notes to connect together related ideas. This can be done via lists, but a particularly effective way to make the connections is by using a technique known as mind mapping.

  - By returning to a topic that you have revised to check that you have retained the information. This is best done the day after you first revised the topic and again a week after, if possible. If you begin each revision section by returning to the 'Check of understanding' boxes in some or all of the chapters you worked with in previous revision sessions it will help to ensure that you retain what you are revising.

- Read the syllabus and become familiar with it. Questions are raised directly from the syllabus and often contain wording similar to that used in the syllabus. Familiarity with the syllabus document will more than repay the time you will spend gaining that familiarity.

REVIEW

The layout, structure and style of this book are designed to maximise your learning: by presenting information in a form that is easy to assimilate; by listing things you need to remember; by highlighting key ideas; by providing worked examples; and by providing exercises with solutions. All you need for an intense and effective revision session is in these pages.

The best preparation for any examination is to practise answering as many realistic questions as possible under conditions as close to the real examination as possible. This is one way to use the ISTQB sample paper, or you can construct a sample paper of your own from the questions included in this book. However, the best check of your readiness of tackling the real examination would be to attempt the mock exam that is contained in **Appendix A1**. All the answers are provided in **Appendix A2** so that you can see how well you did, and a full commentary is provided in **Appendix A3** so that you can identify where you went wrong in any questions.

Good luck with your Foundation Certificate examination.

APPENDICES

A1 MOCK CTFL EXAMINATION

Question 1
Which of the following is a valid objective of testing?

    a.   Locating defects in the code.
    b.   Preventing defects.
    c.   Ensuring no defects are present.
    d.   Correcting defects.

Question 2
Which of the following are *most* important in determining the quality of test cases?

    i.   Referencing the current version of the requirements.
    ii.   Traceability to requirements via test conditions.
    iii.   Incorporating well-defined expected results.
    iv.   Referencing the test procedure and test execution schedule.
    v.   Identifying the author of the test case.

    a.   i and ii.
    b.   ii and iii.
    c.   iii and iv.
    d.   ii and v.

Question 3
Which of the following is true of both linear and cyclical development models for software development?

    a.   They both require system requirements to be defined fully upfront.
    b.   They both require that working versions of the system are produced early.
    c.   They both require that each development activity is matched by a testing activity.
    d.   They both require four levels of testing.

Question 4

Candidates for a software developer role must be at least 18 years of age, achieve a pass (at least 60 per cent) in the relevant certification examination and demonstrate at least two years of experience as a developer. Candidates may be declined, accepted as a trainee (if their experience is not yet adequate) or accepted. How many valid input equivalence partitions would be needed to test the acceptance of candidates?

    a. 3

    b. 4

    c. 5

    d. 6

Question 5

What is the main benefit of use case testing?

    a. Use case tests correspond to business rules and check the outputs for multiple input conditions.

    b. Use test cases always contain alternative scenarios to test what happens when a component fails.

    c. Use cases are good for defining user acceptance tests with user participation.

    d. Use case tests can be used to achieve input and output coverage goals.

Question 6

You have been asked to generate a defect report for a test failure in a ticket booking system that maintains a small database containing details of bookings made. You have collected together what you believe is the necessary information, as follows:

- Reference of the test script that failed.
- Expected and actual results.
- Description of the incident.
- Date of the report.
- Your name.
- System under test.
- Identification of the item under test.

Which of the following fields would be *most* important to add to the incident report to provide adequate detail for the developer tasked with investigating the incident report?

    i.   Test level at which the incident was raised.

    ii.   Log of the session during which the test failure occurred.

    iii. Database dump.

    iv. Test tools used.

    v.   Proposed priority.

a. i, ii and iii.
b. ii, iii and v.
c. i, iii and iv.
d. ii, iv and v.

Question 7
Which *two* of the following statements *best* describe the difference between testing and debugging?

i. Testing aims to identify defects.
ii. Testing aims to identify failures caused by defects.
iii. Testing aims to assess the quality of the software.
iv. Debugging aims to find and remove defects.
v. Debugging aims to find, analyse and remove the causes of failures.

a. i and iv.
b. ii and iv.
c. iii and v.
d. i and v.

Question 8
In the following state transition diagram, if the system is initially in the neutral state, what would be the expected value for a test case with the following sequence of inputs: D, +, +, N, – ?

Figure A1.1 State transition diagram for question 8

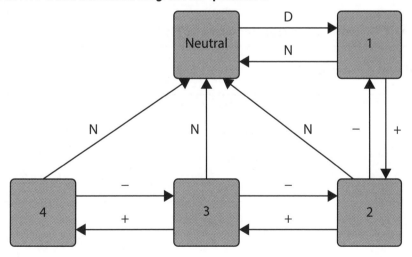

a. 3
b. neutral
c. 1
d. 4

Question 9
In the following state transition diagram and table how many non-valid transitions are there?

Figure A1.2 State transition diagram for question 9

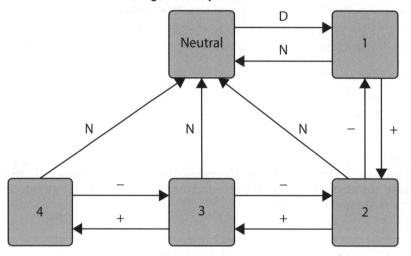

Table A1.1 State transition table for question 9

State/Event	Neutral	1	2	3	4
D	1	X	X	X	X
N	X	Neutral	Neutral	Neutral	Neutral
+	X	2	3	4	X
–	X	X	1	2	3

a. 7
b. 8
c. 9
d. 10

Question 10
Why are both specification-based and structure-based test design techniques needed?

    a.   Because specification-based techniques do not provide coverage measures.

    b.   Because structure-based techniques can only test code.

    c.   Because both are needed to improve the chances of finding defects.

    d.   Because neither can take advantage of users' and testers' experience of the type of system being tested.

Question 11
Which of the following would be the most suitable test basis for system testing when following the V-model?

    a.   A program specification.

    b.   A detailed design document.

    c.   A copy of the coding standards.

    d.   A functional specification.

Question 12
An airline frequent flyer scheme provides rewards based on the mileage flown. Every route or leg of a route attracts loyalty points based on the mileage associated with that route, which is calculated to the nearest 10 miles. Mileage is added to a frequent flyer's account within 10 days of a completed flight. Frequent flyers can hold accounts at the 'blue', 'silver' or 'gold' level. Rewards include ticket upgrades, free tickets and promotion from one colour of card to a higher one. A ticket upgrade requires a minimum of 1000 miles, a free ticket requires 10,000 miles and card upgrades are automatically triggered when the holder has completed 100,000 miles since the previous upgrade.

Which of the following would be suitable for boundary value tests on this system?

    a.   990, 1000, 9990, 10,000, 99,990, 100,000

    b.   999, 1000, 9999, 10,000, 99,999, 100,000

    c.   999, 1001, 9999, 10,001, 99,999, 100,001

    d.   900, 1000, 9900, 10,000, 99,900, 100,000

Question 13
How does software testing contribute to the quality of delivered software?

    a.   By detecting and removing all the defects in the delivered code and ensuring that all tests adhere to the quality standards set for the project.

    b.   By measuring reliability of the software and ensuring that it is always above 99.99 per cent.

    c.   By detecting all deviations from coding good practice and ensuring that these are corrected.

    d.   By identifying root causes of defects from past projects and using lessons learnt to improve processes and thus help to reduce the defect count.

Question 14
Which of the listed roles matches the listed activities?

1. Moderator.
2. Scribe.
3. Reviewer.
4. Manager.

A. Sets timescales for individual preparation.
B. Allows time for reviews in project schedule.
C. Ensures that actions are noted.
D. Notes defects as part of individual preparation.

a. 1–A; 2–B; 3–C; 4–D
b. 1–A; 2–C; 3–D; 4–B
c. 1–B; 2–C; 3–D; 4–A
d. 1–B; 2–C; 3–A; 4–D

Question 15
Which of the following are benefits provided by configuration management to testing?

i. The integrity of work-products can be maintained.
ii. All testware items are uniquely identified.
iii. Defect reports are raised.
iv. Defect fixes are matched to code versions.
v. The test plan is signed off.

a. i, iii and v.
b. i, ii and iv.
c. iii, iv and v.
d. i, ii and iii.

Question 16
Which of the following test case design techniques is structure-based?

a. State transition testing.
b. Decision table testing.
c. Boundary value analysis.
d. Decision testing.

Question 17
Which of the following is a type a defect easier to find in a review than in a dynamic test?

a. The price of a product incorrectly displayed.
b. A system which is running too slowly.
c. A hacker gaining access to customer details.
d. Code which does not meet the required coding standards.

Question 18
Consider the control flow below.

Figure A1.3 Control flow diagram for question 18

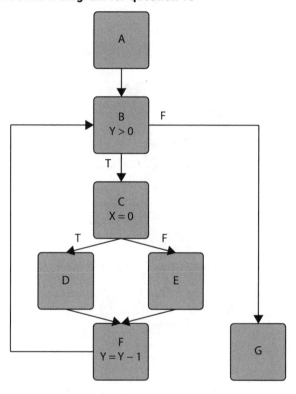

Which of the following sets of test cases would achieve 100 per cent decision coverage?

    a.   X = 0, Y = 1; X = 1, Y = 1
    b.   X = 1, Y = 0; X = 2, Y = 1
    c.   X = 1, Y = 1; X = 2, Y = 1
    d.   X = 0, Y = 0; X = 1, Y = 1

Question 19
Consider the following flow graph.

One of the goals for the project is to achieve 100 per cent statement coverage and 100 per cent decision coverage. The following three tests have been executed:

- Test A covers path ABCEFGI.

- Test B covers path ABCEBDEFGI.

- Test C covers path ABDEFHI.

Figure A1.4 Flow graph for question 19

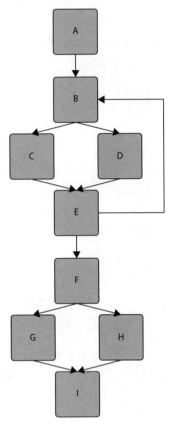

Which of the following statements related to the coverage goal is correct?

a. The statement testing coverage goal has been achieved, but not the decision coverage goal

b. Neither the statement testing coverage goal nor the decision coverage goal has been achieved.

c. Both the statement testing coverage goal and the decision coverage goal have been achieved.

d. The statement testing coverage goal has not been achieved, but the decision coverage goal has been achieved.

Question 20
Which of the following statements correctly describes the defect clustering testing principle?

 a.   Testing should be targeted at the most junior developer's code. This is where most defects will occur.

 b.   If no defects are found in the first 25 per cent of the time available, the code can be deemed safe to deliver to production.

 c.   Testing effort is to be targeted at what is thought to be the riskiest areas, and later those areas where there are more defects found.

 d.   Finding and fixing defects does not help if the system built is unstable and does not match user needs/expectations.

Question 21
Which of the following statements are true?

 i.   Functional testing includes specification-based testing.

 ii.   The purpose of structural testing is to test non-functional requirements.

 iii.   Both functional and structural testing can be carried out at all test levels.

 iv.   Functional testing is the same as regression testing.

 a.   i and ii.

 b.   ii and iii.

 c.   i and iv.

 d.   i and iii.

Question 22
Which of the following provides the best match of activity to resulting document?

 1.   To prepare test cases.

 2.   To determine the order in which test cases should be run.

 3.   To determine the time required to execute tests.

 4.   To highlight outstanding high priority defects.

 A.   Test plan.

 B.   Test design specification.

 C.   Test procedure specification.

 D.   Test summary report.

 a.   1–A, 2–B, 3–C, 4–D

 b.   1–B, 2–C, 3–A, 4–D

 c.   1–C, 2–B, 3–D, 4–A

 d.   1–B, 2–A, 3–C, 4–D

Question 23
Which of the following are benefits of static analysis?

    i.   Improved maintainability of code.

    ii.   Identification of highly complex code.

    iii. Finding defects by executing code.

    iv. Finding defects before test execution.

    v.   Better system design documentation.

a. i, iii and iv.

b. ii, iii and v.

c. i, ii and v.

d. i, ii and iv.

Question 24
Why is it important to have test case design techniques based on the tester's experience?

a. Because experience-based techniques are more effective than specification-based techniques at finding functional defects.

b. Because experience-based techniques are more effective than structure-based techniques at finding defects in code.

c. Because experience-based techniques can be used when no specifications are available or when specifications are not detailed enough.

d. Because users with knowledge of the system under tests are always better at finding defects than testers with no experience of the system under test.

Question 25
Which of the following matches the activity to its most suitable type of tool?

1. Managing test assets.

2. Analysis of code structure.

3. Simulating the interface of a component.

4. Generation of test cases.

A. Test design tool.

B. Test harness.

C. Configuration management.

D. Static analysis tool.

a. 1–D, 2–B, 3–C, 4–A

b. 1–C, 2–A, 3–D, 4–B

c. 1–C, 2–D, 3–B, 4–A

d. 1–A, 2–C, 3–D, 4–B

Question 26
Which of the following test tools are mainly used by developers?

    a.   Monitoring tools.

    b.   Dynamic analysis tools.

    c.   Review tools.

    d.   Incident management tools.

Question 27
Which of the following is a scripting technique used with test execution tools?

    a.   Using a unit test framework.

    b.   Use of data-driven tests.

    c.   Validation of object modules.

    d.   Use of a test oracle.

Question 28
Which of the following gives the *most* independence in testing?

    a.   Test designed by a fellow member of the design team.

    b.   Tests designed by a different organisation.

    c.   Tests designed by a different group within the organisation.

    d.   Tests designed by the code author.

Question 29
Consider the following:

- A test project is underway.
- There are five high priority test cases (TC1–TC5) and two test environments (TE1 and TE2).
  - TC1, TC3 and TC5 require use of TE1.
  - TC2 and TC4 require use of TE2.
  - TC1 requires TC2 to be run first.
  - TC2 must be run after TC4.
  - TC3 must be run after TC5.
- Testing will take place over two days.
  - TE2 will be ready on day 1 and TE1 on day 2.

Which of the following accurately reflects the order in which tests should be run over the two days?

    a.   TC4, TC2, TC1, TC5, TC3

    b.   TC2, TC4, TC1, TC5, TC3

    c.   TC4, TC2, TC1, TC3, TC5

    d.   TC1, TC3, TC5, TC2, TC4

Question 30
Which of the following is the *best* description of maintenance testing?

    a.   It is a form of non-functional testing and focuses on maintainability of the code.

    b.   It is carried out on an operational system after changes have been made.

    c.   It is a form of regression testing and checks the impact of code changes.

    d.   It uses impact analysis to decide how much regression to do at acceptance testing after a fix has been implemented.

Question 31
Which of the following correctly identifies a reason for writing test cases based on knowledge about common defects?

    a.   Testers can use their knowledge of how the system is specified to construct systematic test cases.

    b.   Users can make use of their experience of using other software to help them decide how the software should work.

    c.   Testers can anticipate where defects are most likely to be found and direct tests at those areas.

    d.   Users can create specification-based tests from their knowledge of how the software performs.

Question 32
Which of the following is a product risk?

    a.   The product may not be ready on time.

    b.   A calculation may not be performed correctly.

    c.   The team may not be properly trained.

    d.   The agreed contract may increase our costs.

Question 33
Which of the following statements *best* describes the role of testing?

    a.   Testing ensures that the right version of code is delivered.

    b.   Testing can be used to assess quality.

    c.   Testing improves quality in itself.

    d.   Testing shows that the software is error free.

Question 34
Which of the following would improve how a tool is deployed within an organisation?

    i.   Ensure the test process is not changed as a result of the tool's implementation.

    ii.   Define best practice guidelines for users.

    iii.   Roll out the tool across the organisation as quickly as possible to all users.

    iv.   Introduce a system to monitor tool usage and user feedback.

    v.   Provide technical support to the test team for each type of tool.

    a. i, ii and iv.
    b. i, iii and v.
    c. ii, iv and v.
    d. iii, iv and v.

Question 35
Which of the following are potential drawbacks of independent testing?

    i.   Testers can offer an unbiased view.

    ii.   Testers may become isolated from development.

    iii.   Testing processes may be seen as bottlenecks.

    iv.   Developers may assume less responsibility for software quality.

    v.   Testers may be able to verify assumptions made.

    a. ii, iii and iv.
    b. i, ii and v.
    c. ii, iv and v.
    d. i, iii and iv.

Question 36
Which of the following would be best carried out as part of operational acceptance testing?

    a. Testing that the business considers the system fit for purpose.
    b. Testing that the system meets the required regulatory standards.
    c. Testing that potential customers would buy the system.
    d. Testing that system can be recovered after a disaster.

Question 37
Which of the following *best* describes metrics-based and expert-based approaches to test estimation?

a. Metrics-based estimation requires test points to be counted; expert-based uses the judgement of the tester.

b. Metrics-based estimation requires use of data from previous similar projects; expert-based uses the judgement of the senior developer.

c. Metrics-based estimation requires use of a work-breakdown structure; expert-based uses the judgement of the tester.

d. Metrics-based estimation requires use of data from previous similar projects; expert-based uses the judgement of the tester.

Question 38
Which of the following statement pairs correctly describes testing and debugging?

a. Testing is the process of fixing defects; debugging is undertaken by developers.

b. Debugging identifies and fixes the cause of failures; testing identifies failures.

c. Formal testing is usually undertaken by the development team; debugging is performed before any testing has taken place.

d. Testing aims to assess the quality of the software; debugging assesses whether fixes have been correctly applied.

Question 39
Which of the following is a characteristic of good testing in any life cycle model?

a. Testers should be involved in reviewing relevant documents early.

b. Testing should begin when the requirements have been captured fully.

c. When buying a commercial-off-the-shelf product, all levels of testing must always be carried out by the buyer.

d. Test analysis and design should be carried out once the system has been built.

Question 40
Which of the following would be a suitable metric for monitoring test execution?

a. Percentage of planned test cases prepared.

b. Percentage of work done in test environment preparation.

c. Percentage of tests cases passed.

d. Test coverage of requirements.

A2 MOCK CTFL EXAMINATION ANSWERS

Q1	b	Q11	d	Q21	d	Q31	c
Q2	b	Q12	a	Q22	b	Q32	b
Q3	c	Q13	d	Q23	d	Q33	b
Q4	a	Q14	b	Q24	c	Q34	c
Q5	c	Q15	b	Q25	c	Q35	a
Q6	b	Q16	d	Q26	b	Q36	d
Q7	d	Q17	d	Q27	b	Q37	d
Q8	b	Q18	a	Q28	b	Q38	b
Q9	c	Q19	c	Q29	a	Q39	a
Q10	c	Q20	c	Q30	b	Q40	c

A3 MOCK CTFL EXAMINATION COMMENTARY

Question 1
This is a K1 question relating to Learning Objective CTFL-1.2.1 – Recall the common objectives of testing.

Testing identifies defects, but it neither locates them in the code (which rules out option a) nor debugs or corrects them (which rules out option d). Both of these activities are the responsibility of developers, once any defects have been identified. Testing cannot ensure that no defects are present (which rules out option c) – in fact this is one of the seven testing principles identified in the syllabus. This leaves option b as the correct response. As a quick cross-check, preventing defects is given as a testing objective in section 1.2 of the syllabus.

Question 2
This is a K2 question relating to Learning Objective CTFL-4.1.3 – Evaluate the quality of test cases in terms of clear traceability to the requirements and expected results.

A good test case must incorporate the expected results (iii) and should be traceable back to the requirements (i) (which is option b). Referencing the current version of the requirements is important but does not, in itself, provide traceability (i). Test cases are generated before test procedures and test execution schedules, so (iv) is incorrect. Identifying the author of a test case does not, in itself, affect quality (v).

Question 3
This is a K2 question relating to Learning Objective CTFL-2.1.1 – Explain the relationship between development, test activities and work-products in the development life cycle by giving examples using project and product types.

Option a is a requirement of a linear model such as the V-model only, not iterative models, which allow for requirements to be changed throughout development.

Option b is a requirement of iterative models to allow the user representatives to try the system out early. Linear models expect the system to be delivered at the end of the process.

Option c is the correct answer.

Option d is incorrect because neither model stipulates the required levels of testing. The V-model representations often show four design activities on the left matched by four testing activities on the right, but this is not mandatory.

Question 4
This is a K3 question relating to Learning Objective CTFL-4.3.1 – Write test cases from given software models using equivalence partitioning, boundary value analysis, decision tables and state transition diagrams/tables.

The valid input partitions would be >=18 years of age, score >=60 in the certification exam, >=2 years of experience as a developer. These three valid input partitions can generate all valid outputs and any other input partitions would be invalid partitions, so option a is the correct answer.

Question 5
This is a K2 question relating to Learning Objective CTFL-4.3.2 – Explain the main purpose of each of the four testing techniques, what level and type of testing could use the technique, and how coverage may be measured.

Option a is incorrect because use cases model process flow, but do not model the detail of business rules, which would be decision table testing.

Option b is incorrect because alternative scenarios are not always included and they test alternative paths through the process flow not what happens when a component fails.

Option d is incorrect because use cases do not model all inputs and outputs, which would be equivalence partitioning.

This leaves option c, which correctly states that 'Use cases are good for defining user acceptance tests with user participation'. This is a common way of tackling user acceptance testing.

Question 6
This is a K3 question relating to Learning Objective CTFL-5.6.2 – Write an incident report covering the observation of a failure during testing.

The information provided covers most of the key areas of an incident report, but more detail would help the initial investigation. All of the five additional items suggested would add some value, with the possible exception of item (i), which will be valuable for later analysis, but is not really needed for initial investigation. Item (iv), test tools used, is also not essential for an initial investigation. The other three items are important because they provide more detail about the failure and provide a guide to the urgency of the investigation. Option b is the only one that lists all these three key pieces of information.

Question 7
This is a K2 question relating to Learning Objective CTFL-1.2.3 – Differentiate testing from debugging.

Of the statements about testing, (i) is better than (ii) because it relates to removing defects before failures are detected. Of the statements about debugging, (v) is better than (iv) because it relates to removing causes of failure rather than simply removing defects as they are found. Item (iii) relates to another aspect of testing, so is not directly relevant to the question. The **best** combination is therefore (i) and (v) – option d – because it combines the best descriptions of testing and debugging in the list.

Question 8
This is a K3 question relating to Learning Objective CTFL-4.3.1 – Write test cases from given software models using equivalence partitioning, boundary value analysis, decision tables and state transition diagrams/tables.

The sequence of inputs would take the system through the following sequence of states. From Neutral, 'D' would transition to state 1, then '+' would transition to state 2, another '+' would transition to state 3, the 'N' would return the system to the Neutral state and the final '–' would have no effect. This sequence is provided by option b.

The main distracter is option c, which assumes, incorrectly, that a '–' from state 'Neutral' would transition to state 1.

Question 9
This is a K3 question relating to Learning Objective CTFL-4.3.1 – Write test cases from given software models using equivalence partitioning, boundary value analysis, decision tables and state transition diagrams/tables.

From the state transition table the nine entries with a X indicate non-valid transitions and the answer is therefore 9 (option c). The same information can be gleaned from the diagram by applying every possible event to every possible state and counting those that do not achieve a state transition.

Question 10
This is a K1 question relating to Learning Objective CTFL-4.2.1 – Recall reasons that both specification-based (black-box) and structure-based (white-box) test design techniques are useful and list the common techniques for each.

Option a is incorrect because specification-based techniques do have associated coverage measures, as do structure-based techniques.

Option b is incorrect because structure-based techniques can be used to test any programmatic aspects of software, such as menus.

Option d is incorrect because, while it is true that neither provides opportunities for using experience in deriving tests, this is a reason for a third class of test design techniques based on experience rather than a reason to use both specification-based and structure-based techniques.

Option c is correct because each technique is effective for certain classes of defect so that they complement each other.

Question 11
This is a K2 question relating to Learning Objective CTFL-2.2.1 – Compare the different levels of testing: major objectives typical objects of testing, typical targets of testing (e.g. functional or structural), and related work-products, people who test, types of defects and failures to be identified.

Option a would be a test basis for unit testing.

Option b would also be a test basis for unit testing.

Option c is incorrect because coding standards are used by the developers when programming and would not form a test basis for any testing.

Option d is the correct answer because it defines the system functionality.

Question 12
This is a K3 question relating to Learning Objective CTFL-4.3.1 – Write test cases from given software models using equivalence partitioning, boundary value analysis, decision tables and state transition diagrams/tables.

The system has a precision of ±10 miles, so boundary values need to be 10 miles above or below the boundary.

Option a takes the lower boundary value to be 10 miles below the actual boundary in each case, which is correct.

Option b takes the lower boundary values to be 1 mile below the boundary, but this is a higher precision value than the system can generate.

Option c also adds 1 to the boundary values, so is still incorrect.

Option d takes the precision to be ±100 instead of 10.

Question 13
This is a K2 question relating to Learning Objective CTFL-1.1.4 – Describe why testing is part of quality assurance and give examples of how testing contributes to higher quality.

All of the options have some element of truth about them, but correct statements are combined with falsehood except in the correct response.

Option a states that testing is about 'detecting and removing all the defects', but testing cannot necessarily find all defects, and is not about correcting defects that are found. In any event, the risk may be considered so small that correction is considered unnecessary in some cases.

Option b suggests that testing can contribute to quality by measuring reliability, which is correct, but it also asserts that reliability should be always over 99.99 per cent, which is not correct and is not mentioned in the syllabus.

Coding standards (option c) are also not mentioned in syllabus section 1.1.4 but, even if they were, some deviations from coding standards may not be deemed necessary to correct and testing is about discovery, not correction.

This leaves option d. Testing enables root causes of defects to be found, which makes it possible to reduce defect counts by applying lessons learned. So option d is the only response that makes a correct assertion and does not also contain a false statement about testing.

Question 14
This is a K2 question relating to Learning Objective CTFL-3.2.2 – Explain the differences between different types of review: informal review, technical review, walkthrough and inspection.

The roles of moderator and manager are similar in that they are both coordinating roles. A moderator manages the review activity, including the setting of timescales for individual preparation – so role 1 relates to activity A. Role 2 is the note taker, which relates to activity C. Role 3 carries out the review of the document and will note defects found, so it relates to activity D. Role 4 is the role which decides that formal reviews will be conducted, so it relates to activity B. Option b is therefore the correct answer.

Question 15
This is a K2 question relating to Learning Objective CTFL-5.4.1 – Summarise how configuration management supports testing.

Item (iii) is part of incident management and item (v) is part of test planning, so options a, c and d are incorrect because they contain either item (iii) or item (v) or both.

Option b contains items (i), (ii) and (iv), all of which are correct, so it is the correct answer.

Question 16
This is a K1 question related to Learning Objective CTFL-4.2.1 – Recall reasons that both specification-based (black-box) and structure-based (white-box) test design techniques are useful and list the common techniques for each.

Options a, b and c are all specification-based test case design techniques.

Options a and c can both distract a candidate who is not certain which techniques are structure-based because they sound 'technical'.

Option b can distract because its name is similar to decision testing even though the technique is very different.

Question 17
This is a K2 question relating to Learning Objective CTFL-3.1.3 – Explain the difference between static and dynamic techniques.

Option a will be detected during functional testing.

Option b will be detected during non-functional testing.

Option c is related to security testing.

Option d can be found during a review because the code can be checked against the coding standards.

Question 18
This is a K3 question relating to Learning Objective CTFL-4.4.3 – Write test cases from given control flows using statement and decision test design techniques.

Option a would take path ABCEFBG and then ABCDFBG to achieve 100 per cent decision coverage, and is the correct answer.

Option b would take ABG and then ABCDFBG to achieve 75 per cent decision coverage.

Option c would take ABCDFBG and then ABCDFBG again to achieve 75 per cent decision coverage.

Option d would take ABG and then ABCDFBG to achieve 75 per cent decision coverage.

Question 19
This is a K3 question relating to Learning Objective CTFL-4.4.3 – Write test cases from given control flows using statement and decision test design techniques.

Test A covers one exit from B, one exit from E and one exit from F.

Test B covers both exits from B and E, but only one exit from F (the same as covered by Test A).

Test C covers one exit from B, one exit from E and the second exit from F.

So the three tests cover both exits from each of the three decisions in the control flow graph and therefore 100 per cent decision coverage is achieved. One hundred per cent decision coverage guarantees 100 per cent statement coverage, so option c is correct.

Question 20
This is a K2 question relating to Learning Objective CTFL-1.3.1 – Explain the seven principles in testing.

Option c is the best statement of the defect clustering principle – defects are often found in the same places, so testing should focus first on areas where defects are expected or where defect density is high.

Option a appears to reflect the defect clustering principle, but there no reason to assume that defect clustering will be associated with the work of the most junior developer.

Option b is an example of the 'absence of errors' fallacy – the fact that no errors have been found does not mean that code can be released into production.

Option d is a direct statement of the 'absence of errors' fallacy.

Question 21
This is a K1 question relating to Learning Objective CTFL-2.3.2 – Recognise that functional and structural tests occur at any test level.

Item (i) is correct – specification-based testing is one technique appropriate to functional testing.

Item (ii) is incorrect – the purpose of structural testing is not to test non-functional requirements but to test structural aspects of software, such as program code and menu structures.

Item (iii) is correct as stated in the syllabus.

Item (iv) is incorrect – regression testing may be functional in nature, but its purpose is to test that changes to software have not introduced new defects, so the terms functional testing and regression testing do not have the same meaning.

Items (i) and (iii) are correct, which leads to option d being the correct answer.

Question 22
This is a K2 question relating to Learning Objective CTFL-5.2.2 – Summarise the purpose and content of the test plan, test design specification, test procedure and test report documents according to IEEE Std. 829 – 1998.

Item 1 is an activity leading to a test design specification (B).

Item 2 is an activity leading to a test procedure specification (C).

Item 3 is an activity leading to a test plan (A).

Item 4 is an activity leading to a test summary report (D).

Option b is the required combination.

Question 23
This is a K2 question relating to Learning Objective CTFL-3.3.2 – Describe, using examples, the typical benefits of static analysis.

The purpose of static analysis is to analyse code prior to execution. This applies to items (i), (ii) and (iv). Option d is therefore the correct answer.

Item (iii) is a benefit of test execution, while item (v) is a benefit of reviews rather than static analysis (note that reviews are also a static technique, but distinct from static analysis).

Note also that items (ii) and (iv) apply to reviews as well as to static analysis.

Question 24
This is a K1 question relating to Learning Objective CTFL-4.5.1 – Recall reasons for writing test cases based on intuition, experience and knowledge about common defects.

Option a suggests that experience-based techniques are more effective than specification-based techniques at finding functional defects, which is not true; experience-based techniques are good at complementing the systematic tests derived from specifications.

Option b suggests that experience-based techniques are more effective than structure-based techniques at finding defects in code. This is not true, though experience can usefully supplement structure-based tests.

Option d suggests that users are better at finding defects than testers with no experience of the system under test. This is not always true, though it may sometimes be true.

This leaves option c, which correctly states that experience-based tests are needed 'Because experience-based techniques can be used when no specifications are available or when specifications are not detailed enough'.

Question 25
This is a K2 question relating to Learning Objective CTFL-6.1.1 – Classify different types of test tools according to the activities of the fundamental test process and the software life cycle.

A configuration management tool (C) enables assets to be managed (whether code, documents or test plans) (1).

A test design tool (A) enables tests to be created, from the information provided (4).

Static analysis tools (D) look at software code, and examine ('test') it without executing it; the purpose is to identify any aspect of the code that will cause the program to malfunction when executed (2).

A test harness (B) provides an interface that is identical to that of a software program (which might not have been written yet) to allow programs that will interface with that program to be tested (3).

The only option that contains this set of relationships is option c.

Question 26
This is a K1 question relating to Learning Objective CTFL-6.1.1 – Classify different types of test tools according to the activities of the fundamental test process and the software life cycle.

Tools mainly used by developers are marked by a 'D' in the syllabus, and the only one so indicated is option b. This type of tool is used to search for memory lost, for example, and is used by staff during the development stages.

Option a, monitoring tools used to monitor system resources and network traffic, are mainly used when the whole system comes together and basic functionality is present, so they are used widely by testers.

Option d, incident management tools, are used to record and monitor defects and incidents and are used extensively by testers.

Option c, review tools are used during the review process by anyone undertaking a review and are not limited to software developers.

Question 27
This is a K1 question relating to Learning Objective CTFL-6.2.2 – Remember special considerations for test execution tools, static analysis and test management tools.

A unit test framework (option a) may or may not be used to facilitate unit testing, but this is not a scripting technique.

Option c is useful to ensure that the correct modules and the correct versions of modules are available for testing. This is not a scripting technique.

A test oracle (option d) would be used to identify expected results, but this is not a scripting technique.

Option b is the only scripting technique.

Question 28
This is a K1 question relating to Learning Objective CTFL-1.5.1 – Recall the psychological factors that influence the success of testing.

The options are taken directly from the syllabus, section 1.5, where the answers are listed in ascending order of independence. The order is, from low to high:

- Code author (option d).
- A fellow member of the design team (option a).
- A different group in the **same** company (option c).
- Someone from a different organisation (option b).

Question 29
This is a K3 question relating to Learning Objective CTFL-5.2.5 – Write a test execution schedule for a given set of test cases, considering prioritisation, technical and logical dependencies.

- TE2 will be available on day 1.
- Test cases requiring TE2 are TC2 and TC4.
- TC2 must be run after TC4.

Thus our first two test cases in order are TC4 and TC2.

- On day 2 TC1, 3 and 5 can be executed.
- TC3 must be run after TC5.

The question does not make clear when TC1 should be run. However, the only option with an order of TC4, TC2, TC5 and TC3 is option a, so this is the correct answer.

Question 30
This is a K1 question relating to Learning Objective CTFL-2.4.2 – Recognise indicators for maintenance testing (modification, migration and retirement).

Option a is incorrect because non-functional testing can include tests for maintainability of the code, but this is not the focus of maintenance testing.

Option b is the correct answer as defined in the syllabus.

Option c is incorrect because regression testing forms a key part of maintenance testing to check for unintended changes after modifications have been performed, but maintenance testing is not just a form of regression testing.

Option d is incorrect because maintenance testing does indeed use impact analysis to decide how much regression to do, but after the system has gone live, not during user acceptance testing (i.e. before the system has gone live).

Question 31
This is a K1 question relating to Learning Objective CTFL-4.5.1 – Recall reasons for writing test cases based on intuition, experience and knowledge about common defects.

Option a is a definition of specification-based testing, which is a formal approach.

Option b is not true in that knowledge of how other software works does not translate into a new system.

Option d is invalid in that knowledge of how software performs does not enable users (or anyone else) to create specification-based tests; this would need access to a specification.

This leaves option c, which correctly states that 'Testers can anticipate where defects are most likely to be found and direct tests at those areas'. The tests are prioritised using the testers' intuition, knowledge and experience.

Question 32
This is a K1 question relating to Learning Objective CTFL-5.5.3 – Distinguish between the project and product risks.

Options a, c and d are project risks: option a is a risk to project schedule; option c is a risk to project completion; option d is a risk to project cost.

Option b is the correct answer; an incorrect calculation would cause the product to fail.

Question 33
This is a K2 question relating to Learning Objective CTFL-1.1.3 – Give reasons why testing is necessary by giving examples.

The testing process can state that using a particular version of software, there are no residual risks, but that is not ensuring the correct version is actually implemented. Testing is not responsible for the right version of software being delivered – that is configuration management – so option a is incorrect.

Testing can be used to assess quality, for example by measuring defect density or reliability, so option b is correct.

Testing in itself does not improve quality (option c). Testing can identify defects, but it is in the fixing of defects that quality actually improves.

Testing cannot show that software is error free – it can only shows the presence of defects (this is one of the seven testing principles), which rules out option d.

Question 34
This is a K1 question relating to Learning Objective CTFL-6.3.3 – Recognise that factors other than simply acquiring a tool are required for good tool support. In fact this question is arguably at K2 because it requires selection of multiple correct options, but each of these is based on recall rather than comparison or any other K2 level behaviour. The syllabus content does not support the Learning Objective very effectively.

Two of the five stated answers are explicitly excluded from the list of success factors listed in the syllabus. The syllabus specifically states that process should be adapted to fit with the use of the tool (against answer (i)) and that the tool is rolled out incrementally (against answer (iii)), so any option containing either of these items must be incorrect. As a check, the remaining three items ((ii), (iv) and (v)) are included in the same list in section 6.3 of the syllabus. Option c has the three required answers, and excludes the other two, and is therefore the correct option.

Question 35
This is a K1 question relating to Learning Objective CTFL-5.1.2 – Explain the benefits and drawbacks of independent testing within an organisation.

Items (i) and (v) are benefits of independent testing.

Items (ii), (iii) and (iv) are identified in the syllabus as potential drawbacks of independent testing, so option a is the correct answer.

Question 36
This is a K2 question relating to Learning Objective CTFL-2.2.1 – Compare the different levels of testing: related work-products.

Option a is incorrect because it describes user acceptance testing.

Option b is incorrect because it describes regulatory acceptance testing.

Option c is incorrect because it describes beta testing.

Option d is the correct answer – recovery testing is part of operational acceptance testing.

Question 37
This is a K2 question relating to Learning Objective CTFL-5.2.3 – Differentiate between two conceptually different estimation approaches: the metrics-based approach and the expert-based approach.

In option a, the first statement on metrics-based is incorrect; metrics-based estimation is not based on counting test points, so option a is incorrect.

In option b, the second statement is incorrect because test estimation is not reliant on the opinion of the developer, so option b is incorrect.

In option c, the first statement on metrics-based is incorrect because metrics-based estimation is not based on work-breakdown structures, so option c is incorrect.

Option d is correct because both statements are correct.

Question 38
This is a K2 question relating to Learning Objective CTFL-1.2.3 – Differentiate testing from debugging.

Each option has two parts, and the correct answer will be the option in which both parts are true.

In option a, the first part states that 'Testing is the process of fixing defects', which is false; testing is about identifying defects, but not fixing them. Option a is therefore incorrect.

The first part of option b first part states that 'Debugging identifies and fixes the cause of failures', which is correct. The second part states that 'testing identifies failures', which is also correct. So option b appears to be the correct answer.

As a cross check, we look at options c and d to ensure these are incorrect.

Option c states that 'Formal testing is usually undertaken by the development team; debugging is performed before any testing has taken place.' Both of these statements are incorrect, so option c is incorrect.

Option d states that 'Testing aims to assess the quality of the software; debugging assesses whether fixes have been correctly applied.' The first part of this is correct, but the second part is incorrect, so option d is incorrect.

This confirms that option b is the correct answer.

Question 39
This is a K1 question relating to Learning Objective CTFL-2.1.3 – Recall characteristics of good testing that are applicable in any life cycle model.

Option a is the correct answer.

Option b is incorrect because testing in an iterative model does not require requirements to be captured fully before development or testing begin.

Option c is incorrect because, when buying commercial-off-the-shelf products, the buyer may only need to conduct integration and acceptance testing. The vendor would usually be responsible for the other levels of testing.

Option d is incorrect because test analysis and design should begin during the corresponding development activity.

Question 40
This is a K1 question relating to Learning Objective CTFL-5.3.1 – Recall common metrics used for monitoring test preparation and execution.

Option a is a suitable metric for test case preparation.

Option b is a suitable metric for preparation for test execution.

Option d is a suitable metric for test design.

Option c is the most appropriate metric for test execution.

INDEX

259